THE
BREAKDOWN
OF
NATIONS

THE BREAKDOWN OF NATIONS

LEOPOLD KOHR

FOREWORD BY
IVAN ILLICH

ROUTLEDGE & KEGAN PAUL
LONDON AND NEW YORK

To
Colin Lodge

First published in 1957
This paperback edition first published in 1986 by
Routledge & Kegan Paul plc
11 New Fetter Lane, London EC4P 4EE

Published in the USA by
Routledge & Kegan Paul Inc.
in association with Methuen Inc.
29 West 35th Street, New York, NY 10001

Printed and bound in Great Britain
by Billing and Sons Ltd,
Worcester.

ISBN 0-7102-0889-8

CONTENTS

FOREWORD BY IVAN ILLICH

Translated by I. V. Porsolt

An introductory address to the 'SYMPOSIUM ON THE HUMAN SCALE' held in honour of Leopold Kohr April 28–30, 1982, in Salzburg

---

Leopold Kohr, Initiator of Social Morphology

Dear, honoured Leopold Kohr,
Here we are, about to have a Salzburg Festival in your honour. I am deeply moved and want to give you thanks at this festive opening for what you have given to many of us, and for having become our teacher. You have always been an unobtrusive teacher.You have always behaved as one who knew that whoever has ears to hear you would sooner or later of necessity stumble upon you. And so, many guests at this festivity have, like myself, stumbled one time or another, and taken away a memento. What was written in these mementoes, and what we have made of them, will be what we shall report here. But you have also always been a witty teacher. Though entirely a son of Oberndorf, in the Salzburg country town of 'Silent Night', your way of teaching was that of a Semite. Like a Rabbi or a Mullah, you avoided putting forward theories and told stories instead. All your life you have spoken and written like one who knows that arguments can end merely in conclusions and only stories make sense. When I read the Gospels, I only know that I have grasped the point when the parable makes me smile, and it is the same with your writings. Your stories form the thread which you have woven, with scientific thoughts, into the fabric of your teaching. In this manner, you have broken open the prosaic framework of the science of latterday. In this way, you wove together the two strands of what is scientifically measured and aesthetically assured, and made this weave the foundation of social morphology. You made us dare still to teach with parables, even in the late twentieth century, and to make modern science play the role of commentary. And there is a third

vii

thing I want to thank you for: your courageous readiness to be surprised. In the discipline of which I think you are the founder, you have always been one or two decades ahead of us—John Seymour made this beautifully clear. But whenever one of us has caught up with you with some elegant deduction, such as 'that small is beautiful'—or the thesis 'that acceleration paralyses society'—you were always, more than others, modest enough to be surprised by our seemingly brand-new discoveries, that had been so obvious to you for so long. We honour you for this exemplary humility. It alone made it possible for you to make modesty itself the central object of your researches. I speak, that is, of social modesty as your central research object. In this year of 1982, I purposely avoid the term 'self-limitation' because, during the last ten years, self-limitation has become the *thème-célèbre* of science. 'Autopoiesis' of living or even social systems is the great new land of cybernetics, of theoretical biology, and of the generalized 'shortageologies' which go under the name of economics. For quite a long time now, some scientists have taken seriously your insight of forty years standing that, whatever is wrong today, it is because it is too big. A compulsion to trivial smallness, scientifically underpinned and permeated by technology, threatens today to become the new ideology, and tries to appropriate your teachings. I call your research project social modesty in order to present this misappropriation. Modesty is not a utilitarian but an ethical-aesthetic motivation for action. The modesty of this Salzburg dreamland of yours is neither genetic—like the self-limitation of a mussel to five turns and not six—nor is it predetermined by a cybernetic programme. It stems from the consciousness of a society that an ambit of say 22 km is best because such people as live in these mountains can fill it with life and enjoy it. It is simply impossible to reduce the feeling for ethical and aesthetic proportion to an objectively calculated span of variations. The common living space of Oberndorf corresponds with a human dimension given by you in your hymn to Salzburg as a radius of 22 km. It is a human environment. Its *reach* cannot be reduced to the *territory* of an animal, nor that of the *radius* of an automobile with shoes on. The measure of this environment is correct because it is capable of being built upon with taste, settled in style, conceived with brain and heart, and celebrated in a local dialect. Not only are field and meadow thus made beautiful, but also the town itself. Your style has the lively simplicity which makes it difficult for socio-biologists or cyberneticians to claim you.

The first thing I learned from you was the importance of quite a simple little word: 'gewiss'. You probably no longer remember the occasion. It was Everett Reimer, at that time my mentor, who introduced me to you. You asked me to your patio in Rio Piedras, and our conversation (with lemonade), drove us from statistical diagrams to the platonic meaning of the just measure. All three of us knew Plato's distinction between the 'ell', which one would use to measure out a size, and the 'logos' through which one comprehends a relationship. This is when you said that such relatednesses (or proportions) can exist only, and be beautiful only to a 'certain' extent. Ever since, and more and more compactly, this little word 'certain' permeates my teaching, as it does yours too, and angers many of my colleagues.

Dictionaries do not disguise the ambiguity of this unassuming word. On the one hand, 'gewiss' means sure, firm, certain, indubitable, determined once for all, 'this way and no other way'. Science seeks certainty in this sense—a test anyone can make afterwards. The second sense of 'gewiss' runs right across the first. *Duden's Dictionary* gives it as 'not exactly expressible, difficult to establish or describe, not closely defined, or for decency reasons better left unsaid'. It is in this sense one speaks of a certain share, of certain people, of a certain self-evidence, without which no one can live. Certainty in the first sense comes from a clarified discrimination between 'correct' and 'false', the inquest to be carried on with new means. Certain in the second sense appeals to good taste—'et de gustibus non est disputandum'.

You speak often indeed of a 'certain' magnitude of society: it is one which can be encompassed as a whole. It is not only you, honoured *magister*, who calls this encompassability 'certain'—all wise people call it that. Encompassable is the meaning of the root from which the little word 'certain' stems. And so, social morphology is the quest for that 'certain' order of magnitude within which 'certain' social relationships are beautiful.

To be more precise: may I denote social morphology as research seeking out the subjective limits within which the use of objective-scientific yardsticks can result in sensible insights, proper decisions, and beautiful form? 'Si placet haec definitio', a research neither reducible to science nor without reference to science. For social morphology thus conceived represents a search for the applicability of scientific yardsticks, and thus quite essentially refers to forms of cognition which are objective and universally scientific. On the other hand, this definition lifts social morphology out of the whole array of natural and social sciences, since its job is precisely the tradition-bound, aesthetic, and often even perhaps religious, search for how far science is applicable to a community encompassed subjectively by an historic 'us', a concrete community. The morphology I learned from you is the exploration of the limits within which the subjective social senses for proportion and beauty makes it desirable for *us* to put up with, or even to make use of, scientific-technological procedures. And in order to be encompassable, a society has to be not only small but also beautiful. Ugliness revolts us, even if small. One refuses to consider it. Smallness and beauty are necessities of life. A small democracy is impossible if it is not beautiful. Forced smallness is always ugly, never encompassable, violates the feeling for life, and simply cries out for more and more police. For a society to 'content itself' with the best is only possible where ethical-ideological sharing of responsibility rests on aesthetic sharing, on a celebration of beauty. The Scholastics of the thirteenth century spoke of beauty as the splendour of goodness; you, Leopold Kohr, speak again and again of beauty as of that which is, *in a certain measure*, the best, because it can be encompassed with pleasure by people imbued by this beauty.

Up to this point, dear honoured friend, I have spoken as a pupil to you. I have tried to profess *how I* understand *you*. From here onwards, I would like to report *to where I* am led now by the research into social modesty. Just as you have built upon Darcy Thompson and John Haldane, and made their biological morphology the starting point of a social morphology, so would I too like to answer the questions raised by your representation.

Ever since *Breakdown of Nations* was published, that is for 40 years, you have been working on the mutual conditioning of social measure and social form. I am driven by curiosity to discover the fundamental formal principle which enables a surviving traditional society,—nay, all of them—to restrain itself in modesty with regard to the order of magnitude of its spaces, rhythms, goals, and means. This is to say, that if I do not succeed in finding such an independent, characteristic principle of social morphology, the theory and practice of modesty will remain open to the danger of being interpreted either cybernetically, i.e. in the last resort mechanistic, or utilitarian, i.e. as economically optimized, or even voluntaristically, ultimately professionally, as architecture. Neither the binary code of atomic physics, nor the thermodynamics of theoretical biology, nor even the duality of spirit and matter in which architects wallow, can give me that *certain complementariness* which is the weft and warp of live social patterns.

For this reason, I begin my reflections with the study of the 'Kohr'. A Kohr—you will surely forgive my usurping your family name in the service of social morphology—is not an area but a reach, not a size but a dimension and reflects that feeling of life you point to by your 22 km, that is the four walking or one-and-a half cycling hours between Oberndorf and Salzburg. Thus I confront metric units diametrically, but also only 'to a certain extent', with the Kohr.

Schumacher has implicitly formulated the thesis that only a world made up of Kohrs can be beautiful. You gave richer content to the definition of beauty. You said that things humanly just are also *sybaritic*. You refer here to the cookery book of Athenaeus which explains the legendary opulence of the city of Sybaris by the fact that its coast, in contrast to those of Athens or Corinth, does not suit harbour installations or commerce and that therefore the Sybarites have to enjoy everything they produce themselves. And so, life in a humanly just reach is—characteristically—a joy. But all forms of experience which I, and people like myself, would call enjoyment, contain of necessity a duality. Not the sum of one plus one, but a certain duality, never expressible with exactitude, difficult to identify, not to be closely characterized, and for fateful reasons better wrapped in silence—this is at the root of our enjoyment of modesty, of social frugality. Consequently, the Kohr is not a term for a measure but for the reach of a quite certain duality. And what is the substance, in the final count, of this specifically social duality? I seek and find it the same as any other reasonable human surely would too: enjoyment.

You see, the question I put to myself is this: what is it that makes one Kohr distinguishable from another, and every Kohr homogeneous in itself? And I believe it is to be found in the principle expressible in the English word 'gender', in German 'genus'. Nowhere can one find a homogeneously formed ensemble of men and women to extend beyond a whole Kohr. A Kohr is the morphological term for a unique, vernacular correlation of the sexes. Men and women work out their system of who uses which implement in the most harmonious manner within the confines of one Kohr. In one particular Kohr, only men use the scythe and women the sickle, and the local patron saint will see to it that it should stay so. In the next Kohr, women too will take up the scythe, but only when making hay, and only in the second mowing. The reach of the Kohr is fixed by this quite certain and definite yet not quite comprehensible, asymmetrical complementarity between what is socially stamped as masculine and as feminine spheres. I owe it in part to my Salzburg studies, this understanding of the vernacular Kohr as the term for a self-restraint to a characteristic correlation of the sexes, a singular gender-formation. What helped me were the comments of my doctoral patron Auer to the epistle of Augustinus to Paulina, the seminar on the womb and the umbilical cord in the religious ethnography course of Professor Rudolf Kriss, and the many years with two colleagues from Salzburg times, Lenz and Ruth Kriss–Rettenbeck. But for the thorn of curiosity which goaded me to find in the duality of social gender a this-worldly reflection of the *relatio subsistens*—for this, *LAUS TIBI DOMINE.*

PREFACE TO
THE 1986 PAPERBACK EDITION

'Some of you perhaps will think that I am jesting;'
—SOCRATES AT HIS TRIAL

'There was a time when "Small is Beautiful" was a catchprase for cranks,'
wrote *The Guardian* in an editorial of March 3, 1977. 'With remarkable
speed it has become a key-note of policy in a whole range of areas, from
education to industrial organization. The belief that bigness is best that
dominated the 1950s and 1960s has faded.'

Having urged smallness as a solution to the problems of bigness for
four and a half decades, I was considered a crank as far back as the early
1940s. Not that I was ever disturbed by this. As E. F. Schumacher said
of his similar experience in the 1970s before public opinion became a
little bit more favourably disposed towards the idea: 'Some people call
me a crank. I don't mind at all. A crank is a low-cost, low-capital tool. It
can be used on a moderate small scale. It is non-violent. And it makes
revolutions.'

Moreover, being considered a crank by the rationalizers of bigness
hardly did me any professional damage. It did not interfere with my
academic career at a time when it was thought that the best way to
advancement for an economist was to subscribe to one of the two
varieties of received doctrine, which meant being a controlled marketeer
with the younger generation or a free marketeer with the receding older
one. Nor did it interfere with my pleasures, which have generally been
directly proportionate to the opposition I encountered. Indeed, had my
ideas been embraced in the 1940s, I might have felt like William
Buckley, who, when asked during his mayoral campaign in New York
what he would do if he won the election, answered: 'Demand a recount.'

The pleasure of finding myself in opposition sometimes conveyed that
I never took the idea of smallness seriously myself and that because of
this lack of seriousness, and despite my numerous articles, lectures, and

books on the subject, the idea did not take root until the mid-1970s, when it was presented by E. F. Schumacher with greater religious fervour in a best-selling book bearing the fetching title, *Small is Beautiful.*

However, there has never been a question of my not taking seriously the idea that smallness offers the only solution to the problems of bigness. What I often did was to present my serious proposal in a not-so-serious manner, with the result that on more than one occasion a speaker would express an audience's appreciation by thanking me, not for having enlightened them but for having 'greatly entertained' them. They did not always realize that, by starting to laugh, not about what *I* took seriously but what *they* took seriously, they often admitted a first doubt as to whether they did not view bigness from the wrong angle themselves.

I still remember a talk I gave at Queen's University in Kingston, Canada, soon after the end of World War II, years before *The Breakdown of Nations* was written. Having held forth for fifty minutes on the need for breaking up the great powers rather than uniting them in a world state with the rest of mankind, I was told by a member of the audience that he found my thesis rather convincing. 'But,' he asked, 'do you yourself seriously believe that it will ever be accepted?' When I answered with a resounding 'No,' another gentleman took up the point after the lecture. Identifying himself as Colonel Rothchild, Commanding Officer of Kingston's Imperial Staff college, he informed me that I was scheduled to address more than a hundred highly realistic staff officers from all corners of the British Empire the following day. 'Give exactly the same talk you gave tonight,' he said. 'But, please, don't say at the end that you yourself don't believe in it.'

I gladly promised, deciding to end, instead of my lecture, my as yet unwritten book with this one-word declaration of lack of faith in what a subsequent reviewer called 'the shortest chapter ever penned.' But I urged Colonel Rothchild to be under no illusion: Whatever the entertainment value of my manner of presentation, I myself believed in every word I had said in my talk at Queen's. If the world was to enjoy a measure of peace, the big powers not only *must* be dismembered, but, as I had taken some pains to show, they also *could* be dismembered. The only thing I had my doubts about was that what *had* to be done, and *could* be done, also *would* be done.

I complied with Colonel Rothchild's request, and the lecture before the assembled imperial staff officers produced some amused comments of disbelief, but no offense, as was indeed my normal experience. When

I once showed my patchwork map of a nicely dismembered Europe to an audience at Los Angeles soon after the outbreak of World War II, all a British journalist objected to was that I had not carried the process of division far enough. 'There must be two Irelands,' he demanded. Taking my pencil, I promptly fulfilled his request.[1] A year later, a Frenchman voiced a slightly different objection at the end of a lecture in Washington. 'Dividing Great Britain, Germany, Italy, Russia, the United States—what a wonderful idea. But,' he added with his melodious Gallic accent, 'you cannot split up France.' While his amiable English wartime ally accepted the division of everything, including his own country, as long as Ireland was divided too, the patriotic Frenchman accepted it with even greater enthusiasm as long as France was not affected.

One of the few ever to embrace the idea of division without reservations was an Italian lady from Siena. As a wartime refugee from Mussolini who had fled to London, she understood perhaps better than most that the vast unity of states imparted vastness also to the reach of terrorism and persecution. She alone seemed genuinely delighted at the prospect of a return to an Augustan world of small states. Clapping her hands, she exclaimed: 'What a blessing! Imagine, you would have to flee a distance of only fifteen or twenty miles to reach the safety of exile.'[2]

Thus, although few had taken exception to the idea of smallness ever since the New York left-wing Catholic weekly *The Commonweal* had published my first version of it in its September 26, 1941, issue under the title 'Disunion Now'[3] (in answer to the then widely acclaimed peace plan that Clarence Streit had submitted in his best-selling book *Union*

[1]From the perspective of 1978, the problem caused by the Catholics of Northern Ireland seems to stem precisely from the fact that Ireland is divided rather than united. Yet, like the problems of the Turks in Cyprus, the Palestinians in Israel, or, until recently, the French speakers of the Jura region of the otherwise German-speaking canton of Berne in Switzerland, it is due not to the fact that the country is *divided*, but that it is *badly* divided. And the alternative to bad division is, of course, not unification but good division—unless one resorts to the radical solution proposed by Northcote Parkinson during a conference on devolution in Aberystwyth in 1974, when he answered a question about what he would do with Northern Ireland by stating categorically: 'Submerge it in the ocean, and keep it there for twenty minutes.' (For Swiss-type solutions, see p.60.)

[2]I was reminded of this many years later when sitting in the tropical breeze of a terrace restaurant high up on El Yunque with Mrs and Dr Rómulo Betancourt, the then-exiled president of Venezuela, and his biographer, Robert J. Alexander of Rutgers University. Surrounded by the green jungle of Puerto Rico's rain forest, and with the blue waters of the Atlantic shimmering through the leaves from deep below, I asked Mrs. Betancourt what she had enjoyed most in her life. Was it her husband's presidency? 'No,' she answered wistfully and without hesitation. 'Exile.'

[3]Actually I submitted this article under my brother's name, Hans Kohr. I hoped the editors would pay attention to it in the belief that the article had been sent in by the

Now); practically no one in those years considered smallness as the obvious horse-sense solution to the problems of bigness. At best it was considered romantic, and at worst, as *The Guardian* suggests, an exercise in crackpottery. When I proposed ten years later at the Boston convention of the American Economics Association that the question was no longer how to expand but how to contract; not how to grow but how to put *limits to growth*,[4] I still drew nothing but blank stares from fellow economists, who dismissed my ideas by referring to me as a poet. And they might have dismissed me along with my ideas had I not benefited from an academic policy that was well expressed by a Jesuit friend from Ottawa when he said: 'I always felt that every great university must have some crackpots on its faculty. And if it has not, I consider it the sacred duty of every dean to see to it that some are appointed.'

But much has changed since then. Smallness has ceased to be a 'catchphrase for cranks,' and many who thought it made no sense to step back in this age of vast-scale integration, have come to realize that, as the late Welsh anthropologist Alwyn Rees used to put it: 'When you have reached the edge of the abyss, the *only* thing that makes sense is to step back.' Concepts such as the limits to growth have become academically respectable through books and discussions in scholarly fraternities such as the Club of Rome. And under the impact of my late friend E. F. Schumacher's *Small Is Beautiful*, they have even caught the imagination of the younger generation from campus students all the way up to the Prince of Wales, Governor Brown of California, and Presidents Carter and Reagan of the United States.

In addition, smallness seems to have borne fruit also in practical terms. Large business now tends to expand by splitting rather than fusion. Underdeveloped countries are turning to intermediate technology that works efficiently only on a small scale, in preference to advanced technology that depends on giant markets. Young people are taking refuge in organic farming and the small enclosures of self-

---

well-known authority on nationality questions, Hans Kohn, and, finding that smallness had many good arguments on its side, might publish it anyway even after discovering that the seeming misspelling of the name was no misspelling after all.

[4]My talk at the Boston convention was neither listed nor recorded in the proceedings, as I gave it extemporaneously at shortest notice on the invitation of Professor Harold Innis, an old friend from Toronto who was well acquainted with my theories. As chairman of one of the convention meetings, he asked me to substitute for a speaker who had been taken ill. The phrase 'limits to growth' figures as subtitle in 'The Aspirin Standard,' one of two articles in which I elaborated on my Boston talk for the summer issues 1956 and 1957 of the *Canadian Business Quarterly*.

sufficient communes, under the guidance of missionaries such as John Seymour, rather than in the empty sterility of worldwide ideological embrace. And, politically, centralized states such as Spain or Great Britain will have to come to terms with small-state nationalism and regional devolution under the pressure of inspired leaders such as Gwynfor Evans of Wales, whose programs offer their electorates survival in a fleet of confederated regional lifeboats as an alternative to drowning in brotherly unison on the sinking *Titanics* of great powers.

Now in view of all this, the question arises: Am I still as pessimistic in 1986, when *The Breakdown of Nations* is being republished, about the prospect of a small-state arrangement replacing the current big-power setup, as I was in 1941 when the idea was conceived? As in 1951 when the book was written? Or as in 1957 when I found at last a publisher in the kindred soul of Sir Herbert Read, the gentle anarchist of Routledge & Kegan Paul, just as I had made up my mind to transcribe my manuscript on parchment in illuminated medieval script rather than submit it anywhere ever again? Is my answer still an emphatic 'No' to the question whether I believe that the big powers will ever agree to their dismantlement merely because this would be the only way of saving the world from the atomic war into which their critical mass is inexorably pushing it?

Yes! My answer is still: 'No.' Were it otherwise, I would have written a new book, not a new Preface to an old one. True, smallness has now reached such acclaim that editorialists, economists, and politicians rarely miss a day without paying tribute to its beauty. Yet all this means is what a daily sprinkle of holy water means to the sinner: an attempt to gain benediction for going on sinning. In fact, when an idea becomes universally accepted and its apostles become campus gurus or make the front cover of *Time*, it usually means that the idea has reached the end of its career. As John XXIII said in reply to a reporter's question about how it felt starting as a farmer's boy and ending as pope: 'On top of the heap and at the end of the road'. Or as Maynard Keynes told a doubting Thomas in the early 1930s: in twenty-five years, his theories would be accepted by every treasury in the world; but by then they would not only be obsolete but dangerous.

Well, I don't think the idea of the viability and superior value of the small social unit is either obsolete or dangerous. Nor that it ever will be. If I believe, nonetheless, that nothing will ever come of the idea, it is because, in spite of current acclaim, there is not a shred of evidence that the idea is any nearer being understood than it ever was. The Rt. Hon. Mrs. Margaret Thatcher, Prime Minister of Britain, may be all in favour of smallness in government. But tell her that the only way to reduce the size of government is by reducing the size of the unit to be governed, as is demanded by the regional devolutionists, and she will consider the very thought as an attack on the sacred unity of Great Britain, which is about the last thing the United Kingdom can afford any longer. And so it is with all other leaders of great powers. Be they prime ministers, presidents, or opposition leaders being photographed with *Small is Beautiful* in their hands: Once they have reached the top, they will all react in the same manner as Winston Churchill when he said that he had not become the Queen's First Minister in order to preside over the dissolution of her realm.

So there is no reason to expect a Billy Graham style conversion to smallness from any of the current crop of national leaders. Measuring, like all their predecessors, their stature by the size of the countries over which they rule, they have a vested interest not only in the preservation but in the increase of social bigness; and if they express on occasion a willingness to reexamine their assumptions, it usually amounts to no more than one of those good intentions that Oscar Wilde defined as cheques drawn on a bank where one has no account.

But what about the younger generation? Well, the trouble is that when the younger person gets older, he usually views historic action not from a new, but from exactly the same, perspective as everyone else who has made the transition before him. To judge by the direction of protest movements and campus demonstrations, there has been a turnover of students, but no rejuvenation of outlook. The young people of today have yet to grasp that the unprecedented change that has overtaken our time concerns not the *nature* of our social difficulties, but their *scale*. Like their elders, they have yet to become aware that what matters is no longer war, but *big* war; not unemployment, but *massive* unemployment; not oppression, but the *magnitude* of oppression; not the poor, who Jesus said will always be with us, but the scandalous size of their multitudes.

Nor have they as yet shown any understanding for the real conflict of this age, which is no longer between races, sexes, classes, left and right, youth and age, rich and poor, socialism and capitalism—all hangover confrontations from the past. The real conflict of today is between Man and Mass, the Individual and Society, the Citizen and the State, the Big and Small Community, between David and Goliath. But as long as our youth and campus leaders have the same tendency as their national leaders whom they want to succeed to measure their grandeur by the size of the organization they command, there is little reason to assume that they will do more for smallness than provide it with an Ark and salute it in tribute to its poetry and beauty as it drifts away on the rising waters of the Deluge.

After four decades of developing an interpretation of history out of my theories of size, I come to the same conclusion as Charles de Gaulle, who confided to André Malraux shortly before his death that in all his years of highly successful leadership he knew of not a single problem that had ever been solved—or ever would be. And the same applies to the problem of excessive size. Not that it could not be solved. Of course, it could. But it never will. 'Men,' as Hesiod wrote twenty-eight centuries ago, 'will go on destroying the towns of other men'; and looking around me 2,800 years later gives me little reason for hope that it will ever be otherwise. After all, as Hesiod also tells us, Hope was the only gift from Zeus that stayed trapped in the lid of the box of lovely Pandora, while 'all the others flew, thousands of troubles wandering the Earth' ever since.

This means *The Breakdown of Nations* ends for the second time on a note of pessimism. But pessimism is not despair. Should we be depressed because we all must die? Or should we not rather use this as the very reason for enjoying life? It is the optimist who is usually condemned to a life of misery, disappointment, and gloom by working his head off in the belief that hard labour will get him back into paradise. Like a Sunday preacher, he shows us the way to heaven by talking about nothing but the torments of hell. My interpretation may be pessimistic. But once we accept our imperfections, the wisest thing is to come to terms with them and follow the advice of my father, an Austrian country doctor who, when asked by a distressed farmer what he should do about his belated case of measles, answered: 'Enjoy yourself. Because if you don't, you still have measles.'

So, even though I still do not believe that peace will be assured through the division of the troublemakers—the big powers—I hope my readers will go on enjoying their lives. For if they don't, they will still have to live with the evils released from Pandora's box in punishment for the blessings Prometheus—that archreformer of the human race—wanted to bestow upon them when he brought them the fire of progress.

London   LEOPOLD KOHR
1986

ACKNOWLEDGEMENTS

Most of my inspiration I owe to friends whose love of challenge and debate was invaluable in the formulation of my ideas. This book would therefore never have been written without a long string of animated discussions with Diana Lodge, Anatol and Orlene Murad, Max and Isabel Gideonse, Sir Robert and Lady Fraser, my venerable late friend Professor George M. Wrong and Mrs. Wrong, Noel and Donovan Bartley Finn, my brother John R. Kohr and, above all, Joan and Bob Alexander who for five long years had to bear with my constructions of pleasurable gloom at breakfast, lunch and dinner.

Nor would the book ever have been published without the advice and encouragement of Sir Herbert Read, or without my friends and colleagues from the University of Puerto Rico—Severo Colberg, Adolfo Fortier, Hector Estades, Dean Hiram Cancio, and Chancellor Jaime Benítez—whose interest led to a gratefully acknowledged grant from the Carnegie Foundation.

L.K.

The University of Puerto Rico
January 1957

INTRODUCTION

1

As the physicists of our time have tried to elaborate an integrated single theory, capable of explaining not only some but all phenomena of the *physical* universe, so I have tried on a different plane to develop a single theory through which not only some but all phenomena of the *social* universe can be reduced to a common denominator. The result is a new and unified political philosophy centering in the *theory of size*. It suggests that there seems only one cause behind all forms of social misery: *bigness*.

Oversimplified as this may seem, we shall find the idea more easily acceptable if we consider that bigness, or oversize, is really much more than just a social problem. It appears to be the one and only problem permeating all creation. Wherever something is wrong, something is too big. If the stars in the sky or the atoms of uranium disintegrate in spontaneous explosion, it is not because their substance has lost its balance. It is because matter has attempted to expand beyond the impassable barriers set to every accumulation. Their mass has become too big. If the human body becomes diseased, it is, as in cancer, because a cell, or a group of cells, has begun to outgrow its allotted narrow limits. And if the body of a people becomes diseased with the fever of aggression, brutality, collectivism, or massive idiocy, it is not because it has fallen victim to bad leadership or mental derangement. It is because human beings, so charming as individuals or in small aggregations, have been welded into overconcentrated social units such as mobs, unions, cartels, or great powers. That is when they begin to slide into uncontrollable catastrophe. For social problems, to paraphrase the population doctrine of Thomas Malthus, have the unfortunate tendency to grow at a geometric ratio with the growth of the organism of which they are part, while the ability of man to cope with them, if it can be extended at all, grows only at an arithmetic ratio. Which means

xxiii

that, if a society grows beyond its optimum size, its problems must eventually outrun the growth of those human faculties which are necessary for dealing with them.

Hence it is always bigness, and only bigness, which is the problem of existence, social as well as physical, and all I have done in fusing apparently disjointed and unrelated bits of evidence into an integrated theory of size is to demonstrate first that what applies everywhere applies also in the field of social relations; and secondly that, if moral, physical, or political misery is nothing but a function of size, if the only problem is one of bigness, the only solution must lie in the cutting down of the substances and organisms which have outgrown their natural limits. The problem is not to grow but to stop growing; the answer: not union but division.

This would seem platitudinous if it were submitted to a surgeon, a mason, an engineer, or an editor. Their entire lifework consists of nothing but the cutting of what is too big, and the reassembling of the smaller units into new forms and healthier structures. But it is different with social technicians. Though quite sensible at lower levels, at the more exalted levels of politics and economics they seem for ever out to create still bigger entities. To them, the suggestion of cutting what has become too large is not platitude but sacrilege. Viewing the problem of size upside-down, they think it is one of smallness, not of bigness. So they demand union where every law of logic seems to demand division. Only on rare occasions do they see right side up, as when after years of trouble in the overcrowded Korean prison camps it began to dawn on them that the cause of difficulty was not the incorrigible nature of the communists but the size of the compounds containing them. Once this was recognized, they were quickly able to restore bearable conditions not by appealing to the good will of the prisoners but by cutting their groups into smaller and more manageable units.

However, what is true of men living in overcrowded prison camps is also true of men living in the overgrown compounds of those modern nations whose unmanageable size has become the principal cause of our present difficulties. Hence, just as in the case of Korean camps, the solution of the problems confronting the world as a whole does not seem to lie in the creation of still bigger social units and still vaster governments whose formation is now attempted with such unimaginative fanaticism by our statesmen. It seems to lie in the elimination of those overgrown organisms that go by the name of great powers, and in the restoration of a healthy system of small and easily manageable states such as characterized earlier ages.

This is the proposal advanced in this book, and I have no doubt that many will call it contrary to all our concepts of progress. Which is quite true, of course. All I can do is to answer with Professor Frank Tannenbaum of Columbia University: 'Let them, let the other people have the slogans. Let them progress themselves off the face of the earth and then they'll have *infinite* progress.'

2

In referring to the ideas developed in this book I have used the term *new*. This is only partially correct in so far as I have tried to make the theory of size the basis of an *integrated* system of philosophy, applicable to *all* problems of creation with equal facility. But as a *special* theory applying to special fields, it has been proposed many times before, though even as a special theory it has never been given the central position which it deserves. This is particularly true of its use in the explanation of *social* phenomena. But even here, the concept of the small cell as the foundation of every healthy structure is neither original nor new. It has been beautifully expressed many centuries ago by men such as Aristotle or St. Augustine. It has been advanced by Henry IV of France in one of history's more famous peace plans, the *Great Design*. And in our own time, with the road of bigness approaching its atomic terminus, it has become so pressing that it seems to condense out of a pregnant air almost by itself. Whenever a new attempt is made to bring about international union, we are filled less with hope than with despair. A creeping presentiment seems to tell us that we are pushing into the wrong direction; that, the more united we become, the closer we get to the critical mass and density at which, as in a uranium bomb, our very compactness will lead to the explosion we try to avert.

This is why in the past few years an increasing number of authors have begun to reverse the direction of their search and to look for solutions to our social problems in small rather than large organizations, and in harmony rather than unity. *Arnold Toynbee*, linking the downfall of civilizations not to the fight amongst nations but the rise of universal states, suggests in the place of macropolitical solutions a return to a form of Homonoia, the Greek ideal of a self-regulatory balance of small units. *Kathleen Freeman* has shown in a study of Greek city-states that nearly all Western culture is the product of the disunited small states of ancient Greece, and that the same states produced almost nothing after they had become united under the wings of Rome. In the field of economics, *Justice Brandeis* devoted a lifetime to exposing the 'curse of bigness' by showing that, beyond relatively narrow limits, additional growth of plant or organizational size no longer adds to, but detracts from, the efficiency and productivity of firms. In Sociology, *Frank Tannenbaum,* who challengingly calls himself a parochialist, has come out in defence of small labour unions rather than their giant off-spring. For only small unions seem still able to give the worker what modern vast-scale development has taken away from him: a sense of belonging and individuality. In the political field, *Henry Simons* has pursued the idea that the obstacles to world peace do not lie in the alleged anachronism of little states but in the great powers, those 'monsters of nationalism and mercantilism', in whose dismantlement he sees the only chance of survival. Finally, *André Gide,* to end this sketchy list with a poet, has expressed a similar thought when he wrote as possibly his last words: 'I believe in the virtue of small nations. I believe in the virtue of small numbers. The world will be saved by the few.'

All this indicates that the idea and ideal of littleness as the only anti-dote to the cancerous disease of oversize—in which the bulk of con-temporary theorists still insist in seeing not a deadly malady but a per-verse hope of salvation—seems at last ripe for new recognition and comprehensive formulation. If my own speculations do not carry weight in this respect, perhaps Aristotle's or St. Augustine's will. Though I have used neither them nor the other authors just quoted in developing my theories, I find it naturally highly pleasing to find my-self in so respectable a company. But I shall not hide behind their testi-mony or the authority of their names in an effort to obtain immunity from criticism on the part of those who think that all our time needs in order to solve its problems is to submerge itself in an all-embracing world community. The analysis as well as the conclusions are strictly my own.

Chapter One

THE PHILOSOPHIES OF MISERY

'There is no error so monstrous that it fails to
find defenders among the ablest of men.'
                                    LORD ACTON

*Imaginary cause theories. The witch theory. Cosmic theories.
Secondary cause theories. Economic and psychological explanations. The cultural theory. Military exploits and monstrosities
in folklore and literature. The essence of Western civilization.
Past and present atrocities in the history of civilized peoples.
Man's inherent love of aggressiveness. Relative splendour of
monuments honouring poets and generals. Why our heraldic
animals are beasts of prey. Attlee, Goethe, and Bacon on the
virtue of war. The war record of Germans and Allies, of
aggressors and lovers of peace.*

I N a period of widespread tyranny, brutality, almost perpetual warfare, and other related miseries, it seems legitimate to ask by what
means a more peaceful and socially satisfactory existence might be
secured.

As with every question concerning conditions of misery and their
abolition, a fruitful answer depends on the discernment of their primary
cause. But while modern scientific methods have shed light on the
primary causes of many technical and personal complexities with the
resultant improvement in our private conditions, in the realm of social
problems they have contributed little more than theories involving
either purely imaginary or at best secondary causes. Speaking in the
middle of the twentieth century, Julian Huxley could therefore justly
say that 'the human sciences today are somewhat in the position occupied by the biological sciences in the early 1800s'. They have hardly
penetrated the surface.

The trouble with imaginary and secondary cause theories of social

I

misery is that they are frequently able to furnish highly seductive momentary explanations. As a result, supplying seemingly satisfactory interpretations, they not only discourage further search; they also fail to bring forth useful proposals for solutions, the ones because time sequences are not causal, the others because secondary causes are themselves nothing but consequences of primary forces. The chance of providing the world with a socially more satisfying existence seems therefore to depend on the question whether we are able to pierce the shell of imaginary and secondary phenomena and discover the hidden *primary* cause disturbing the social happiness of man. But before offering a theory which presumes to penetrate to fundamentals, let us analyse the merits of the most popular imaginary and secondary cause theories of past and present, and appraise the solutions they proposed on the basis of their interpretations.

1. *Imaginary Cause Theories*

The Ancients, attributing the cause of most difficulties to the wrath of the gods, thought that the simplest way of improving their condition was to resort to prayer or, if this should prove insufficient, to the sacrificial slaughter of the persons who had antagonized the gods. Sometimes, the results were stunning. Hardly had the prayers been said, than rain would pour down on their thirsty fields, the lava stream of a volcano would come to a sudden stop, or news would reach them of the defeat of a fearful invader. Occasionally, nothing would happen. However, as in the case of most bad guesses, no significance was attached to this, and no reason was seen why their theory, which might be called the *divine theory of social misery*, should be considered invalid on this ground alone, since it had proved so satisfactory in the explanation of so many other misfortunes.

In the Middle Ages, the divine theory was supplemented by a *witch theory of social misery* which attributed the cause of afflictions less to the wrath of God than to the malevolence of an evil spirit. Quite logically, the principal cure was now thought to lie in the elimination of the objects which seemed possessed by the devil. So up in flames went a behexed barn, a cross-eyed hunchback, a very ugly woman, or a very beautiful one. Again, the results were considered highly satisfactory except in a few cases when, instead of suspecting their theory, people suspected they had burned the wrong witch, and so began the merry chase anew.

Later, with man's growing interest in the mechanism of the universe, a bundle of *cosmic theories of misery* began to enjoy wide currency. Disease and wars were now attributed to the occasional appearance of a comet, the more frequent appearance of a red corona around the moon or, when it was discovered that sunspots had an irritating effect on our nervous system, to the cyclical intensification of sunspot activities. Like all earlier theories, these too were considered eminently satisfactory, as there was rarely a misfortune that did not coincide with one or more of these celestial phenomena. Since nothing could be done about the latter, the cosmic theories had, in addition, the advantage of relieving mankind of the difficult task of seeking solutions and cures.

Passive submission to the forces of nature was, however, contrary to the spirit of the gradually rising age of reason. With the advent of modern times we find, therefore, a new string of theories of social misery. In rapid succession there developed an *economic theory*, attributing war and other forms of social evil to the expansive urge of profit-seeking capitalism; a *psychological theory*, attributing them to frustration; a *personal, ideological, cultural,* and a *national* theory, attributing them in turn to the design of evil men such as Hitler, Mussolini, or Stalin; to evil ideologies such as nazism or communism; to evil cultural traditions such as Prussian militarism or British colonialism; and finally, because a majority of these features seemed occasionally to coincide in the history of a particular people, to an evil inheritance, an evil nation such as the Germans as they appeared to the eyes of the Western Allies in the past, or the Americans as they appear to the eyes of the Eastern Allies now.

Like their predecessors, these newer theories proved again highly satisfactory in the explanation of those social miseries during whose occurrence they were developed. But also like their predecessors, they turned out to be singularly incapable of explaining exceptions. Confusing secondary causes with primary causes or, to use the terms of Lucretius, the *property* of things with their mere *accident*, they could explain the brutality of the Moslems but not of the Christians. They could explain the poverty of American but not of Russian slums. And as to wars, they could explain those of the nazis, but not the crusades; the wars of Germany, but not those of France; the wars of Hitler, but not those of Nehru; the wars of capitalists, but not those of socialists. In spite of their subtler reasoning, they seem thus to have shed no more light on the problems they presumed to analyse than the witch or sunspot theories of earlier periods. All they accomplished was to shift attention from imaginary to secondary causes—and sometimes not even that.

3

2. Secondary Cause Theories

However, because of their more recent development and the seeming logic of their analysis, some of these newer theories as well as the solutions they offer merit closer attention. One of the most powerfully argued is the *economic theory*. According to its premises, most forms of social misery, and in particular poverty, war, and imperialism, are inevitable consequences of the working of the capitalist free-enterprise system. Simply stated, its reasoning is as follows: at first the search of profit on the part of the businessman causes the working class to receive less for its contribution to production than is its due. Next comes the unavoidable inability of the latter to buy back from the manufacturers the goods it has helped to produce. As a result, one of two evils must follow. Either production must be cut back to the level at which it can be absorbed in the domestic market; or, with internal consumption and, hence, investment opportunities at an end, new markets must be acquired elsewhere. The first alternative leads to unemployment and its score of attendant miseries; the second to imperialism and war.

The latter consequence provides actually a double incentive for capitalist manufacturers and businessmen to stir up social trouble. For, both war production and war destruction furnish outlets for goods and new sources of profit which the secular stagnation, seemingly developing in every fully matured private enterprise economy, no longer makes available elsewhere. Hence, the absolute need for imperialist expansion and periodic warfare to satisfy the life requirements of a system whose principal driving force is the profit motive.

A socialist system, on the other hand, producing not for profit but for consumption, has the least interest on earth to engage in the enormous waste of military expenditures or in the conquest of foreign markets for goods which could so much better be used in raising living standards at home. By its very character it is as dedicated to the maintenance of peace as capitalism is dedicated to the pursuit of war. As a result the world's principal problems could be solved quite simply. All that is needed is the elimination of capitalism and the establishment of a socialist society.

This may be so. But the theory fails to explain two things. One is: why are the workers of socialist countries apparently no better off than those of capitalist states? And secondly: why are at least two of the world's present chief aggressors communist states, Russia and China, while such capitalist countries as Canada, Belgium, Luxembourg,

4

Monaco, and particularly that last and still shiny citadel of a nearly perfect free-enterprise system, Switzerland, rank amongst the most peace-minded? This seems to indicate that, contrary to the tenets of the economic theory, a society's system of production has in itself very little to do with its social welfare, and still less with the misery of aggressive warfare which it may inflict on its own as well as on other peoples. A switch in systems could therefore contribute little to a solution of problems of which they are not the cause.

The *ideological* and *personal* theories attribute the various forms of social misery either to an evil power philosophy or to the leadership of evil men. Their solution, quite logically, is the substitution of a better for the worse philosophy or the dispatch into eternity of the evil men. Both are interrelated and may be treated as two phases of a single theory. According to them, power would be harmless in the hands of good men animated by a philosophy of good will. This clears up some of the contradictions of the economic theory. It explains Russian and Chinese internal exploitation and external aggressiveness which the economic theory could not, on the ground that communism by aspiring to world rule of the proletariat, represents an uncompromising ideology of power and domination. By the same token it explains German and Italian tyranny, brutality, and aggression as the result of the power philosophies of nazism and fascism, and of a leadership devoid of all moral restraint. By contrast, it explains satisfactorily the present non-aggressiveness of peoples such as the Swiss, French, or Belgians, ascribing it to their virtuous leadership and to the dedication of the democratic form of government to the cause of human happiness and peace.

So far, so good. But it fails to explain why, if fascism is a brutalizing and aggressive power philosophy, as it undoubtedly seems to be, fascist Spain or near-fascist Portugal are, at least in their external relations, as peaceful as democratic Switzerland or Denmark. It fails to explain why Nepal, a most absolutist country, which moreover prides itself on having produced one of the world's fiercest races of fighters, the Gurkhas, seems never even so much as to dream waging a foreign war. It fails to explain why communism, which looks so fearful and tyrannical in Russia, is considered non-aggressive in Yugoslavia, and looks so charming in the tiny mountain republic of San Marino that it exhilarates instead of frightening us. And, by contrast, it fails to explain why such a non-aggressive philosophy of peace as Gandhiism had no restraining effect on so peace-loving a man as Nehru who, in his first year of power, waged two wars, against Hyderabad and Kashmir, has threatened a third, against Pakistan, on numerous occasions ever since, and enforced aggressively his will on the independent neighbouring state of Nepal. It fails to explain the aggressive campaigns and accompanying brutalities of democratic France and Great Britain in their former colonial adventures. And lastly, it fails to explain why even the most perfect of peace philosophies, the teachings of Christ, could not prevent the successors of Saint Peter in the holy city and state of Rome from indulging at times as lustily in aggressions and policies of brutal design as history's worst offenders in this respect.

One would have assumed that at least in their case power was in the hands of men of good will and exalted principles. Which it was, of course. If this made nevertheless hardly any difference, it can only be due to the fact that good ideologies and personal principles have apparently as few causal relationships to social misery as we have found in the case of economic systems. This seems the reason why, though we hanged the war criminals and changed the philosophy of their former supporters, war is still with us as ever.

3. The Cultural Theory of Social Misery

The *cultural theory* goes somewhat deeper. It ascribes our unhappy conditions not to ideologies, which come and change and go in relatively fast succession, but to the long-range pattern and stage of development of a country's civilization. It maintains that savagery, tyranny, mass brutality, aggressive warfare, are nothing but offsprings of intellectual primitivism. Since this is perpetuated by a nation's literary creations and its system of education, the solution of the world's problems would once more seem quite simple. It lies in the purging of folklore and literature, and in the re-education of the retarded by the advanced. In this way social misery would disappear almost automatically. For the more advanced a civilization becomes, the more it is characterized by love of peace and the urge to help, rather than love of war and the urge to destroy.

This theory seemed again for a while to furnish satisfactory explanations for aggressive wars and atrocities such as those perpetrated by the Germans, the Japanese, or the Russians. Compared to the advanced stage reached by the civilization of the West, for example, theirs seemed to have lagged behind in the development of principles of humanism. Hence the attempt to instil into them Western concepts either by direct intervention as was done in Germany and Japan at the end of World War II, or by propagandistic enlightenment as is being done

6

in the case of the as yet undefeated communist half of the world now.

The chief shortcoming of the cultural theory appears to be two-fold. First, it does not seem to understand its own premises. Secondly, for every phenomenon it explains, there are a dozen phenomena in the face of which it seems to collapse.

a. The Meaning of Western Civilization

To begin with the weakness of its premises: if Western civilization is indeed an effective antidote to conditions leading to atrocities and war, it must, above all, be different from the civilization of those peoples whose codes we are wont to consider as basically hostile to peaceful pursuits. In contrast to the latter's glorification of military exploits, its literature must emphasize the blessings of peace. In contrast to the latter's preoccupation with cruelty and witchery, it must dwell primarily on stories describing the virtues of saintly living. Otherwise nothing could be gained by substituting the cultural productions of the West for those of the less peace-loving peoples.

As things stand, Western or not, peace-loving or not, the cultural productions of most creative peoples seem to follow almost identical channels. Their differences are but differences of language, not of substance. If the Germans have the *Nibelungenlied* which glorifies physical prowess and military exploit, the French have the *Song of Roland*, the English *Beowulf*, the Romans the *Aeneid*, the Greeks the matchless *Iliad* and *Odyssey*, all praising the same qualities with equal fervour. If Goethe's *Faust* is full of the devil and hell,[1] so is Marlowe's *Dr. Faustus*, to say nothing of Dante's *Divine Comedy*, which deals not with one but seven hells, and whose poetic presentation of horror exceeds even the imaginative splendour of American funnies. And one wonders what the re-educators of non-Western atrocity lovers would do with a play such as Shakespeare's *King Richard III*, of which it has been written that it is 'certainly tragic enough to satisfy the most voracious appetite for horrors: murder follows murder with breathless rapidity; the jocose

---

[1] The cultural theorists seem to have ascribed great significance to this in explaining nazi monstrosities. To give a typical example: Sterling North, a well-known book reviewer, saw even in the poetry of the Grimms and Goethe typical evidence 'that (a) there is nothing even approaching a moral or ethical code in the German folk mind and (b) that few other tribes on the planet can touch the Germans for bestial, sadistic joy in bloodletting'. And he continues that 'naturally the devil plays an important role not only in Grimm and in Goethe, but throughout German literature. Faust—the man who sold his soul to the devil—is the great German hero.' (*Washington Post*, 3 December 1944.)

7

royal assassin, who in a former play had dismissed Henry the Sixth and the Prince of Wales to their account, begins this tragedy by the slaughter of his brother Clarence, and then goes on with the coolness of a butcher, killing one convenient friend or relative after another, till our memory becomes perplexed by the attempt to recall the names of the victims'.[1]

A similar lack of difference in poetic preoccupation prevails in the culturally perhaps even more significant gems of our various folklores. Matching the Germans' fearful giant *Rübezahl*, who stalks through dense forests with his enormous club, is the Greeks' highway robber *Procrustes*. To adjust the size of his guests to that of their bed, this hospitable robber has the habit of stretching the short until they are long enough and cutting the limbs off the tall until they are short enough for a precise fit. And in the highly Westernized United States we have such neo-classical heroes as Al Capp's *Stubborn J. Tolliver*, President of Dogpatch–West Po'kchop Railroad, who after letting a train full of merrymakers run over a mined section of track, calls out to his employees: 'Pile th' bodies up neatly! Repair th' locomotive! Fill it with more passengers! And we'll try again!! I'm not afraid.' Our radio, television, and film folklore is even better. At one time it seemed to get so out of hand that a British board of censors felt moved to advise Hollywood 'to mop up the gore'.

Thus it seems that the cultural creations of those we consider advanced are hardly less preoccupied with violence and bellicosity than the creations of those whom many of us have come to consider as retarded. However, there is no need for undue apprehension. For, as the poetic description of violence has never been a sign of backwardness, the display of gentle attitudes has never been a sign of either an advanced or a Western concept of civilization. Contrary to the tenets of the cultural theory, the hallmark of *advance* is not love of peace but the discernment of truth, which, as it may be beautiful, may also be ugly, and as it may be good, may also be wicked. And the hallmark of *Western* civilization is not that it is the civilization of the West, as is frequently believed, but that it is based on the philosophy of individualism which, again, does not concern itself with love of peace or *social* happiness, but with love of *personal* freedom and *personal* accomplishment. It would therefore have been less confusing if scholars, instead of using the term *West*, had talked of the civilization of the *Occident*, the Spenglerian *Abendland*, whose common denominator has always been individualism, in contrast to that of the *Orient*, the *Morgenland*,

[1] Shakespeare, *Richard III*. New York: Grosset and Dunlap, 1909, p. xlviii.

8

whose basis has always been collectivism. Though these designations have likewise a faintly geographic origin, they refer more clearly than the others to cultures, not to regions; to ideas, not to nations.

While it is thus true that Germany, Italy, and Russia, whose recent aggressions have furnished the chief argument for the cultural theory, removed themselves from the Western orbit when they adopted racialist *nazism*, statist *fascism*, and collectivist *communism*, their *civilization* continued to remain an integral part of the great cultural family whose link was not geographic location but the individualistic spirit of ancient Greece. As a result, as Western civilization could not be conceived without the personal genius of Shakespeare, Voltaire, Rembrandt, Dante, or Socrates—men from the South and West of Europe—so it could no longer be conceived without the personal contributions of such Easterners as Tolstoy, Dostoyevsky, Tschaikovsky, or of such Germans as Beethoven, Kant, Goethe, Heine, or Dürer. Theirs was not a retarded civilization. Nor was it a civilization different from that of France or England, which could have given a satisfactory cultural explanation for the rise of Hitler, Stalin, or Mussolini. Like that of the other members of the Western family, theirs was a civilization created by persons fulfilling the purpose of their *individual* existence, not by communities or peoples joining in *collective* effort to reach a collectivized end.[1]

Little could therefore be gained by expurgating anybody's literature and instilling into war lovers the creations and concepts of Western civilization. The productions of the various cultural realms are not only too alike in what they praise and what they condemn; most of the recent aggressors in war and perpetrators of atrocities such as the Italians, Germans, and Russians were, moreover, not alien to Western civilization but ranked, like those we consider virtuous lovers of peace, amongst its most outstanding members and contributors.

b. Culture and Atrocity

This leads to the second and principal weakness of the cultural theory—its seemingly total disregard of historic evidence, leaving more phenomena unexplained than it is able to explain. For not only has an

---

[1] It is the face of Michelangelo we see in Saint Peter's Basilica, not that of the Italian people which put the marble in its place. This is the main difference from the massive accumulations of stone built in Egypt not by men but a disindividualized society which, characteristically, poured most of its creative energy into the construction of tombs.

advancing civilization never been known to act as a deterrent to social excess; the most monstrous periods of brutality and aggressiveness in the various countries have usually coincided with the periods of their *greatest* cultural advance. Assuming thus that the theory might indeed explain communist or nazi misdeeds, how could it account for such misdeeds as those of the thirteenth-century tyrant Ezzelino da Romano? Considering himself the divinely appointed scourge of humanity, this famous leader found pleasure in causing, for example, upon the conquest of Friola 'the population of all ages, sexes, occupations to be deprived of their eyes, noses, and legs, and to be cast forth to the mercy of the elements'. He built dungeons designed for torture, and on one occasion entrapped 11,000 Paduan soldiers, 'only 200 of whom escaped the miseries of his prisons'.[1] But, far from being a barbarian age, the thirteenth century was one of the great eras of Italian and Western civilization, culminating in such figures as Saint Francis of Assisi, Thomas Aquinas, Marsilius of Padua, Giotto, Cimabue, Dante. And far from being a solitary phenomenon disgracing an otherwise advancing age, Ezzelino was 'only the first of a long and horrible procession', followed by 'how many Visconti, Sforzeschi, Malatesti, Borgias, Farnesi, and princes of the houses Anjou and Aragon?' If he was the most terror-striking, it was merely because he was 'the earliest, prefiguring all the rest'.[2]

By the end of the fifteenth century not only princes of the world but princes of the Church began to share in responsibility for social misery, whose scale, instead of declining seemed to increase with every advance registered by civilization. A typical example was the sack of the town of Prato near Florence. After taking it by assault on 29 August 1512, the papal army, under the command of Raimondo da Cardona, Viceroy of Naples, was given licence to pillage, rape, and murder for twenty-one days. In a slaughter 'without a parallel in history ... neither youth, age, nor sex, neither the sanctity of place nor office, were respected ... Mothers threw their daughters into wells and jumped in after them, men cut their own throats, and girls flung themselves from balconies on to the paving-stones below to escape from violence and dishonour. It is said that 5,600 Pratans perished.'[1] This during the papacy of Julius II, not a savage but one of the great art patrons of history. He

---

[1] John A. Symonds, *Renaissance in Italy*. New York: The Modern Library, 1935, vol. 1, p. 55.
[2] Ibid., p. 56.
[3] F. A. Hyett, quoted in G. F. Young, *The Medicis*. New York: The Modern Library, 1933, p. 278.

ruled at the very pinnacle of Italian culture, counting amongst his contemporaries such unrivalled masters as Botticelli, Leonardo da Vinci, Michelangelo, Cellini, Raphael, Filippino Lippi, Giorgione, Titian, Perugino, Lorenzo di Credi, besides a host of others who are considered minor only because the age was so sublime.

The same pattern of cultural achievement accompanied by manifestations of social terror prevails in France. Her sixteenth century was so productive in great works of literature, philosophy, theology, and art, that it has justly been called the *grand siècle*. It was the age of Saint Francis de Sales, Montaigne, Bodin, Pasquier, Rabelais, Marot, Ronsard, Regnier, Gringoire. But it was also an age of persecution, murder, rape, and mass extermination. Protestants hounded Catholics and, when at last they stopped, Catholics began to hound Protestants until almost none were left, bequeathing to the world a drama of blood and gore that has been equalled in many other periods and by many other peoples, but surpassed by none. There is nothing the nazis did to the Jews in the twentieth century which the French did not do to their fellow Frenchmen in the sixteenth. They filled wells with corpses until they overflowed. When after a night of massacre a bishop was dragged to one of these mass graves, the busy assassins 'drew attention to the fact that it was already full. "Pooh!" replied another, "they won't mind a little crowding for a bishop." '[1] In Paris 'women approaching maternity were selected for more excruciating torments, and savage delight was exhibited in destroying the unborn fruit of the womb'.[2] In Lyons, an apothecary initiated the murderers of Huguenots into the 'valuable properties of human fat as a medicinal substance', with the result that their 'miserable remains were put to new use before being consigned to the river'.[3] And in Orleans, where more than fourteen hundred men, women, and children were slaughtered within three days, the general degradation was such that even professors at the university were not beneath profiting from the occasion, plundering the libraries of their own students and colleagues who had been executed.[4]

[1] Alexandre Dumas, *Celebrated Crimes*. New York: P. F. Collier and Son, 1910, vol. 2, pp. 425–9.

[2] Henry M. Baird, *History of the Rise of the Huguenots*. London: Hodder and Stoughton, vol. 2, p. 501.

[3] Ibid., p. 517.

[4] This incident is related by Johann Wilhelm von Botzheim, a German student who attended the University of Orleans and, after deploring this sorry behaviour, traces with engaging sincerity his own books 'to the shelves of Laurent Godefroid, Professor of the Pandects, and the entire library of his brother Bernhard to those of his neighbour, Dr. Beaupied, Professor of Canon Law'. (Ibid., p. 570.)

Only slightly less glamorous than the sixteenth century was the age of Louis XIV, *le roi soleil*. During his reign and the following years lived Montesquieu, Voltaire, Chénier, the Abbé Prévost, Diderot, Beaumarchais, and Rousseau. But alongside we find such celebrities as Marshal de Montreval who became so enraged at being interrupted at dinner by a report of one hundred and fifty Huguenots peacefully singing psalms in a mill at Carmes, outside Nîmes, that he went forth with his soldiers and massacred them, though the group was composed only of old people and children. 'A certain number of dragoons entered the mill, sword in hand, stabbing all whom they could reach, whilst the rest of the force stationed outside before the windows received those who jumped on the points of their swords. But soon the butchery tired the butchers, and to get over the business more quickly, the marshal, who was anxious to return to his dinner, gave orders that the mill should be set on fire.'[1] A few weeks later, the same Montreval, in execution of the king's orders[2] 'to root out the heresy', retaliated in a manner subsequently made famous by the destruction of the Czech village of Lidice at the hands of the nazis, by erasing not one but 466 market towns, hamlets, and villages with a total population of 19,500. And Louis XIV himself, the centre and symbol of that polished age, provided orders of the day which would have delighted the shocked prosecutors of Nuremberg. To him we owe that elegant phrase 'Ravage the Palatinate', which the Western advocates of the cultural theory might do well to remember occasionally when talking of barbarians as if they were aliens.

Under Napoleon, culture and brutality continued to follow the now familiar pattern. New instruments of extermination were developed such as the famous *étouffoirs*, wooden cages in which captured Negroes, fighting for the liberation of Saint Dominique, were shut up with burning sulphur. Cast into the sea, the victims succumbed from either asphyxiation or drowning. Since the bodies were washed back to the shore, dogs were imported to devour the remains in the interest of public hygiene.[3] And as late as 1945, the French, proud as ever of the glories of their civilization, retaliated against the killing of a number of

[1] Alexandre Dumas, op. cit., vol. 2, p. 496.

[2] Occasionally it is said that the particular depravity of German atrocities under the nazis lies in the fact that the Germans were the first to elevate mass extermination to the level of an officially sanctioned state policy. That they did so is beyond doubt. But they were preceded in this by every government responsible for directives of the kind of the orders of the French king 'to root out the heresy', or others mentioned in this chapter.

[3] Stephen Alexis, *Black Liberator*. New York: Macmillan, 1949, p. 211.

isolated French families in Algeria at the hands of their Arab compatriots by blasting 'whole communities out of existence', killing 'thousands of men, women and children who had nothing to do with the attacks'.[1]

This seemingly strange parallelism between advancing civilization and intensification of savagery is naturally not confined to Italy and France. It is a feature characteristic of the history of all peoples. During the culminating era of Anglo-Latin literature in the thirteenth century, for example, we find Geoffrey, the father of Henry II of England, performing what Edward Gibbon called a singular act of cruelty on the clergy of Séez after the latter had proceeded with the election of a bishop without first securing his consent. In punishment, the then master of Normandy had all members of the Cathedral Chapter, including the bishop elect, castrated, 'and made all their testicles be brought him in a platter'. Gibbon comments on this: 'Of the pain and danger they might justly complain; yet, since they had vowed chastity, he deprived them of a superfluous treasure.'[2] A few centuries later, when, during the golden age of Queen Elizabeth, English civilization reached its zenith with such poets as Marlowe, Lodge, Ben Jonson, and Shakespeare, it produced at the same time, in the terms of the *Encyclopedia Britannica*, such 'hotheads of war' as Hawkins, Drake, Raleigh, and 'scores of others who recognized no peace beyond the line'. While some of the world's most exalted poetry was being written, the country producing it abounded with executions at home, with piracy on the seven seas, and with aggressions on the five continents such as were rarely witnessed in its less civilized periods. Another century later, the epoch is once more graced by men such as Milton, Herrick, Dryden, Locke, Newton. But along with masterworks of culture, we find again savageries such as the incidents known to the Scots as *Killing Time*, the invention of devices of terror such as the torture of the thumbscrew, mass exterminations such as the massacre of Glencoe in 1691, or a textbook example of genocide such as the expulsion of the entire people of Acadia from their native land. During the last phase of their deportation in 1755, Governor Lawrence of Nova Scotia not only gave his soldiers licence to do with them as they pleased, 'but positive orders to distress them as much as possible'.[3]

In this vein, history goes on right up to our time. There is no need

---

[1] Richmond (Virginia) *Times-Dispatch*, 8 June 1945.

[2] Edward Gibbon, *The History of the Decline and Fall of the Roman Empire.* London: Methuen, 1900, vol. 7, p. 216 n.

[3] George P. Bible, *The Acadians*. Philadelphia: Ferris and Leach, 1906, p. 95.

to quote the well-known atrocities of fascists, nazis, and communists, their police methods, their concentration camps, their crematoria. Having been ascribed to lack of civilization, they might be understood. The more significant items concern contemporary atrocities perpetrated by admittedly advanced peoples, for which the cultural theory provides little understanding and which, therefore, have only rarely been cited except for purposes of hostile propaganda. Here might be mentioned the order of Brigadier-General Jacob H. Smith of the United States Army, issued during the American pacification campaign of the Philippines as a directive for a punitive expedition against the island of Samar. 'I want no prisoners,' it said. 'I wish you to kill and burn: the more you kill and burn, the better you will please me . . . The interior of Samar must be made a howling wilderness.' Being asked how young 'a child must be to escape the massacre', General Smith replied 'Ten years of age'. He was subsequently sentenced 'to be admonished by his superiors'.[1] This was in 1901. In 1919, General Dyer of the British army, retaliating against some local disturbances in the Punjab, took a small body of troops to a meeting of five thousand Indians near the town of Amritsar, opened fire without warning, killed some five hundred people, wounded, according to his own estimate 'about 1,000 more, left the dead and the dying where they fell, without any further concern, and departed quite satisfied with what he had done'.[2] A barbarian age? It was the time when luminaries of literature such as Bernard Shaw, Max Beerbohm, and Yeats wrote in London, when the gentle Fabians began to dominate much of English thought, and the universities of Oxford and Cambridge experienced one of their most brilliant periods.

Compared with the barbaric exploits of the civilized, the savageries of the barbarians seem to lose all significance. And as to wars, almost the only peoples refraining from this primitive form of social activity at the present time are not the most advanced but the most backward ones. In view of all this, it may safely be stated that the cultural theory of social misery, which to this day enjoys illustrious support, which served as the basis of many expurgation and re-education policies, and has led to such hopeful creations as UNESCO, sheds little light on the

[1] A. Frank Reel, *The Case of General Yamashita*. Chicago: The University of Chicago Press, 1949, p. 109.
[2] *The Nation* (New York), 24 January 1920, p. 121.

complex problems it set out to solve; and that the spread of civilization, be it of East or West, of Greeks or Anglo-Saxons, may contribute
to poetry and knowledge, but hardly to social happiness and peace.

4. The National Theory of Social Misery

The last of the theories requiring a more detailed analysis may be
called the *national theory of social misery*. It is a typical by-product of
prolonged warfare. The atmosphere of perpetual frustration resulting
from the inactive drag and the inconclusiveness of interminable fighting seems at a given point to lead to the spontaneous creation of the
idea that the principal cause of mankind's misery is not just the leadership, the philosophy, or the culture of the enemy. It is his very race.
A closer look now reveals quite distinctly that he is *born* to mischief.
From his very childhood he is observed to display a degree of ferocity
and love of aggressiveness unmatched elsewhere. A re-reading of history seems suddenly to make it clear that the current enemy is actually
the historic enemy. And the longer the war lasts, the worse he begins
to look. In the end, not only propagandists but even scholars begin to
furnish evidence of his *collective* perfidy, lawyers to establish his *collective* guilt, and statesmen to think that, in the interests of a peace-loving
humanity, his continued survival can no longer be tolerated. When this
stage is reached, the solution of most problems afflicting society appears
quite simple. It would be useless to re-educate the vanquished. He must
be eliminated. Carthage must be destroyed.

Like the other theories, the national theory seems highly satisfactory
in the explanation of the occurrences it is meant to elucidate. However,
it leaves again more questions unanswered than it answers. In the em-
battled midst of World War II, it furnished a creditable account of the
reasons behind the behaviour of the Axis partners, in particular the
Germans. But when the question is raised why a similar behaviour
seems to characterize most other peoples as well, including those pleased
to consider themselves inherent lovers of peace, it begins to run into
difficulties. And its answers become altogether confusing when in the
enthusiasm of executing the Carthaginian provisions prepared during
the mental idleness and emotional strain of a long war, it is suddenly
realized that the historic enemy may not be the vanquished but the ally
who cunningly helped to defeat him. But up till then, its assumptions
appear to defy challenge.

What are the premises on which the national theory rests? There are
two. One is biological, the other historic. As already indicated, the first

conceives that virtues such as love of peace are inherent in the character of some peoples and absent from that of others. The second is the confirmation of the first, based on the evidence of history.

a. Biology of Aggression

To discuss the biological premise first, and to confine the illustration to the best documented example of the national theory: great significance was, for instance, attached to the fact that the Germans had always been notorious for their admiration of brute force and their militarism. Could this account for their excesses? Maybe. But the more important question is: did this make them different from others? Or did the Germans show these *inborn* qualities not so much because they were *peculiarly* theirs but because they were inherent in the nature of man *generally*? If the latter should turn out to be correct, the national theory with its far-reaching conclusions and solutions must lose at least half of its foundation. And the latter appears to be correct, as already Cicero suggested when he wrote in his *Laws* (I, 10) that 'no single thing is so like one another, so exactly its counterpart, as all of us are to one another', and that 'however we may define man, a single definition will apply to all. This is sufficient proof that there is no difference in kind between man and man; for if there were, one definition could not be applicable to all men.'

But let us not rely on Cicero in appraising the universality of those seemingly strange biologically conditioned attitudes which under duress appear to us as inborn only to the enemy's corrupted race. Let us look at ourselves. What about our own attitude towards aggressiveness for example? Irrespective of whether we are Americans, English, French, or Germans, we have only rarely expressed a genuinely felt aversion to it. On the contrary, collectively as well as individually, most of us are usually full of praise for it. What we actually reject as slightly contemptible is not aggressiveness but peace-loving gentleness. No business man has ever been known to have advertised an opening for a peace-loving, humble, unassuming salesman or executive. The prime qualifying virtue for these jobs is considered to be aggressiveness, and most of us say so quite bluntly. No true woman, even in war-hating societies, has ever been known to have expressed a desire for a peace-loving slipper addict as a husband who might surround her in a cloud of gentleness and verses. What she most likely wants of him is force and aggressiveness, and if he clicks his heels in addition, all the better. And the masses of people, being for ever feminine, will for ever admire the same things. 'When they treat of their love affairs,' writes the French philosopher Julien Benda, 'the most civilized people speak of conquest, attack, assault, siege and of defence, defeat, capitulation, thus clearly tracing the idea of love to that of war.'[1]

Were this not so, it would be a strange paradox to see that most peoples, while commemorating the creators of their civilization in obscure plaques and minor statues, should glorify the heroes of their aggressive achievements in gigantic Arches of Triumph, in monumental mausoleums, in pyramids that pierce the clouds, and in columns which challenge the magnificence of God. Shakespeare, Dante, Voltaire, Goethe, or Poe may have their undisturbed little corners in their respective countries. But what are these compared with the spine-thrilling columns the English have erected in honour of *Admiral* Nelson, the French in honour of *General* Napoleon, the Germans in honour of *General* Arminius, or the Americans in honour of *General* Washington? This is why British monarchs, who are kept so busy with state visits to military institutions or the laying of wreaths on the tombs of soldiers known and unknown, did not get around to visiting the birthplace of Shakespeare, their greatest dramatic poet, until 1950.[2]

But more symbolic of the disturbing similarity of our innermost aspirations than our monuments are our heraldic animals. Here we really seem to show of what substance we ourselves believe we are made. Whether peace-loving or aggressive, in one feature nearly all nations appear alike. Nearly all have chosen as the animal most representative of their soul a *beast of prey*, indicating that they consider it more appropriate to be symbolized by barbaric ferociousness than by civilized beatitude. Italy prefers the voracious wolf to the loyal dog. England and Prussia the growling lion to the sweetly purring cat. Russia the plump, tactless, but powerful bear to the swift and elegant prairie horse. The Habsburg Monarchy, one of the more civilized institutions of history, not satisfied with a one-headed eagle, chose one with two heads to make it wilder still. Others cherish panthers, hawks, snakes, or even dragons. The United States could have been symbolized by the lark, that enchanting bird, ever singing and ever in pursuit of happiness. But it chose the bald eagle of which an inscription in the

[1] Quoted in an article by Simone de Beauvoir on the 'Sexual Initiation of Women', in *Anvil*, New York, Winter 1950, p. 24, from the *Uriel Report*.

[2] The *New York Times* of 21 April 1950 reports: 'It was the first visit a British king made to Shakespeare's home town in the 386 years since the birth of the bard.'

Buffalo Zoo has the following to say: 'This eagle never fishes for himself as long as he can rob the more skillful and industrious fish hawk. The Bald Eagle is our national emblem'—a statement on which the *New Yorker* commented: 'Well, it's impolite to point.'[1] The only exception, or nearly so, is represented by France which, also not quite without significance, chose the ever-amorous cock. But even here the choice may have been due to the fact that the cock's amorous pursuits force him to be a perpetual fighter on the side.

However, there is nothing peculiar about these choices, for though the national theorists may be troubled by this, nothing seems to be more natural to man than aggressiveness and his delight in it. One of our first loves are the funnies, an invention of the seemingly peace-loving Americans. They are so full of lusty warriors of both sexes that their heroes, having conquered all earth, have long begun to conquer the planets and the stars as well. Our first toys are soldiers and, if a little boy fails to show interest in them, we do not hold him up as an example to the war-loving children of the enemy but rush him to a psychiatrist to find out what is wrong with him. A charming little friend of mine, aged seven, after trying for days to get sense out of my typewriter, produced as his first letter ever written the following monument to our inborn human aggressiveness: 'dear Bill when are you going to give me my 5 cent. if you don,t I will bet you up. love tommy.' His father was the most gentle of English poets who would have sworn the British were never capable of anything like this. A little American from Washington, D.C., addressed the following letter to Santa Claus: 'please send me two atom bombs, a couple of pistols and a good sharp knife'.[2] And Edmund Gosse, the famous English critic, tells us how an obscure but highly belligerent poem 'greatly fired' him as a little boy, and how the following stanza, in particular, reached his 'ideal of the Sublime:

'The muskets were flashing, the blue swords were gleaming,
The helmets were cleft, and the red blood was streaming,
The heavens grew dark, and the thunder was rolling,
When in Wellwood's dark muirlands the mighty were falling.'[3]

Even in their more mature periods, people of all countries and walks of life seem to retain these bellicose enthusiasms. Clement Attlee, the amiable socialist leader of Great Britain, confesses that as a student at Oxford, he had 'fallen under the spell of the Renaissance. I admired

[1] *New Yorker*, 8 February 1947.   [2] *Time*, 25 December 1950.
[3] Edmund Gosse, *Father and Son*. London: Penguin Books, 1949, p. 54. .

strong and ruthless rulers.'[1] Goethe, the great *German* humanist and poet, 'commended war'.[2] Sir Francis Bacon, the great *English* philosopher and one-time Chancellor of the Realm, thought that 'the principal point of greatness in any state is to have a race of military men', and that 'nobody can be healthful without exercise, neither natural body nor politic, and certainly to a kingdom or estate, a just and honourable war is the true exercise'.[3] And in the United States, while perhaps not commending war through the mouths of such eminent individuals, we commend the men of war. In spite of our pride in civilian leadership, we have in our short history elected no fewer than eleven generals to our presidency—Washington, Jackson, W. H. Harrison, Taylor, Pierce, Johnson, Grant, Hayes, Garfield, Arthur, and Eisenhower. Only the ancient Romans have surpassed us in this. Indeed, so high a value do we attach to a glamorous martial career, that military excellence has come to be looked upon as a special asset even in the most unmilitaristic fields. Only churches and labour unions are not yet influenced by it. But in our universities, the trend seems unmistakable. Some have already chosen as their heads generals rather than scholars. And as concerns honorary doctorates in philosophy, of all things, an increasing number is being conferred on persons whose sole distinction is that they have proved loyal and successful military leaders. A study of such degrees granted since the end of World War II by seven major American universities—Harvard, Smith, Columbia, Wisconsin, California, Nebraska, and North Carolina—revealed that generals and admirals experienced 'the biggest post-war boom'. They received 10 per cent of the total, while clergymen, the propagators of the gospel of love and peace, were found gravely 'slipping; a century ago they made up 45 per cent of the *honoris causa* list, after World War II, 5 per cent'.[4] A record in harmony with what we believe is the character of Prussians rather than of ourselves.

.   .   .

[1] *Time*, 6 February 1950, p. 19.

[2] *The Listener*, the official organ of the British Broadcasting Corporation, thought this highly indicative of the inherent war-mindedness of Germans. In an editorial commemorating Goethe's two-hundredth anniversary, it pointed out that Goethe 'served at one time as Minister of War' to the Duke of Weimar and was essentially a German and possessed most of the qualities and nearly all the defects of the German character . . . The grandson of an innkeeper, he praised aristocracy; servant of a defenceless principality, he commended war.' (*The Listener*, 25 August 1949, p. 300.) This statement exemplifies well the national theory in its World War II formulation.

[3] Francis Bacon, *Essays and New Atlantis*. New York: Walter Black, 1942, p. 121.   [4] *Time*, 22 January 1951.

b. History of Aggression

Thus, when it comes to man's less flattering inborn characteristics, lovers of peace seem once more hardly distinguishable from lovers of war. Their 'natural body' is as stimulated by the implications of militarism as is the body of the most renowned aggressors. And their 'body politic' does not seem to be much different either. For if we analyse the second premise of the national theory, we find indeed that history confirms the evidence of biology. But contrary to the original assumption, instead of revealing that some nations have a worse aggressive record than others, it merely shows we are all alike once more.

This seems strange in the face of data and figures collected during World War II, and establishing to all appearances that Germany, the then current chief enemy, had the worst war-making record of all. In fact, we proved her so bad that, in spite of the changed circumstances of today, few things keep terrorizing us more than our own figures of then. As the French still point out with a concern undiminished by the passage of years, the same Germans whom we now seek as allies have invaded France three times in less than a century. And, as others add, they have been responsible for five wars during the last seventy-five years, not to speak of three near-misses which, had they had their way, would have given them a record of one war every eight years for the last three-quarters of a century alone. Can one disregard figures?

One cannot disregard figures. But one can complement them. While it is true that the Germans have made five wars during the last three-quarters of a century, the French, during the same period, have made nineteen wars and the English twenty-one. Even if we subtract the wars the two latter fought with the Germans, the French still come out with fifteen and the English with nineteen.[1] Thus, while Germany, had she had her way with her three near-misses as well, would have made a war every eight years, the fact that France and England apparently did have their way provided the world with a war every three and a half years if we take the two countries separately, and every one and a half

---

[1] See compilation prepared by the Carnegie Endowment for International Peace: Memoranda Series No. 1, Washington, D.C., 1 February 1940. To give one example: between 1861 and 1945, aside from the Franco-Prussian and the two world wars, France was involved in the following wars: 1861–7 with Mexico, 1873–4 with Tongking, 1867 against Garibaldi in Rome, 1881–2 with Tunis, 1883–5 with Tongking, 1884–5 with China, 1883–5 with Madagascar, 1890–4 with Sudan, 1893 with Siam, 1893–4 with Morocco, 1894 with Tongking, 1895–7 with Madagascar, 1900 Boxer Insurrection, 1897–1912 with Morocco, 1925–6 Riffian War. It may be said that none of these aggressions involved great powers, which is neither a sign of peaceful intentions nor a compliment.

years if we take them together. And if the Germans have invaded France three times in less than a century, France, between 1792 and 1813, that is in less than a quarter of a century, invaded German territory twelve times. Indeed, had it not been for this veritable mania of French invasions, the movement of German unification, which began in 1815 and ultimately led to the much deplored and long remembered three German invasions of France, might never have found the stimulus to accomplish itself in the first place. As things stand, at the rate of three invasions 'in less than a century', Germany would need another two hundred and fifty years only to break even with France.

Not to confine the figures to a possibly misleading seventy-five to one hundred and fifty years, let us go back a bit further in our search for history's chief aggressor. Professor P. A. Sorokin of Harvard has assembled a table showing the relative strength of armies of the various members of Western civilization during the last nine centuries, from the twelfth to the twentieth. Though the strength of a country's army is not necessarily an absolute indicator of its aggressive urge, an aggressor would have difficulty launching campaigns of conquest without an army of major size. As a result, Professor Sorokin's table is of considerable significance in a study of aggressive militarism. Instead of showing a single chief aggressor, it indicates that 'the comparative position of the countries is changing in the course of time, now one country occupying the first position, now some other'.[1] Germany, whom we might suspect of holding the first position more frequently than others, appeared as a major military power only during the last three centuries and, of the last three, she was outranked by France in two. A similar pattern emerges if we view the problem from still another angle, and include in the analysis, besides the last 150 years and the Middle Ages, also antiquity. Comparing this time the 'per cent' of years with war of the total number of years studied, Professor Sorokin

[1] P. A. Sorokin, *Social and Cultural Dynamics*. 1937, vol. 3, p. 348. The table lists for each century studied the country with the largest army first and with the smallest last:

    XII. Russia, England, France, Austria.
    XIII. Russia, England, France, Austria.
    XIV. England, France, Russia, Austria.
    XV. England, Poland, France, Russia, Austria, Spain.
    XVI. Spain, France, Austria, Poland, England, Russia, Holland, Italy.
    XVII. Austria, France, Spain, Poland, Holland, Russia, England, Italy.
    XVIII. Austria, France, Russia, England, Germany, Poland, Spain, Holland, Italy.
    XIX. France, Russia, Germany, Spain, Austria, England, Italy, Holland.
    XX. Russia, Germany, France, England, Austria, Italy, Spain, Holland.

found that 'Germany has had the smallest (28) and Spain the largest (67) per cent of years with war, the other countries occupying various positions between the two'.[1] Though the world's principal aggressor need not necessarily show the largest percentage of war years, again he could not possibly show the smallest.

Thus, in each of the three sets of figures covering first the past seventy-five to hundred and fifty years, then the last nine centuries, and finally all of Western history, the Germans, in spite of their fearful reputation as lovers of war, emerge with a record that seems not only better than expected but better even than that of some of the best. However, the purpose of these figures is not to prove that the Germans are better than others. They are not. Nor is it to show that we can have trust in the reformed intentions of our former enemies. We cannot. What the figures are meant to prove is merely that the second premise of the national theory is as unsupported as the first. For sketchy as this brief historic survey may be, it is sufficiently representative to establish that the role of chief aggressor is a relative one. Instead of being held by a single people, it has rotated with great fluidity amongst the various nations. Sometimes it was held by the Athenians, Spartans, or Macedonians; sometimes by the Dutch, Danes, or Portuguese; sometimes by the French and English; sometimes, and more recently, by the Germans and Russians; and, unless a different definition applies to us than to other men, at some time it will in all likelihood be held by the Americans. In the eyes of our former Russian comrades in arms, who now call us anything from *Anglo-American cannibals* to *atomshiks*, we may, in fact, hold it already.

Though the historic data could not possibly have produced a different picture, I have dwelled longer on the assumptions of the national theory than might, under the circumstances, seem justified. The reason

[1] Ibid., p. 352. Sorokin's full list is as follows: Spain 67%, Poland and Lithuania 58%, Greece 57%, England 56%, France 50%, Russia 46%, Holland 44%, Rome 41%, Austria 40%, Italy 36%, Germany 28%. Regarding the almost constant involvement in war of France, the Duke of Sully, one of her most eminent statesmen, writes the following: 'The slightest knowledge of our history is sufficient to convince anyone that there is no real tranquillity in the kingdom from Henry III to the peace of Vervins; and, in short, all this long period may be called a war of near four hundred years' duration. After this examination, from whence it incontestably appears that our kings have seldom thought of anything but how to carry on their wars, we cannot be but scrupulous in bestowing on them the title of truly great kings.' (*Memoirs of the Duke of Sully*. London: Henry G. Bohn, 1856, vol. 4, p. 223.)

for this is that, in the first place, in spite of the sobering effect of post-war realities, the theory is bound to regain its full persuasiveness when-ever a war exceeds a certain length. And secondly, its premises have been taken so seriously by so many persons in authority for so long that they represent far more than speculations indulged in by over-wrought minds or mere propagandists. They have furnished the basis on which the most eminent statesmen of our time, supported by some of the most eminent political thinkers, tried to build nothing less than perpetual peace. They provided the philosophy for Yalta and Potsdam. They have led to policy measures such as the contemplated pastoraliza-tion of Germany and the prohibition of German atomic research, or to legal concepts such as collective guilt. These are focal points of action and thought which can be defended only on the assumption that there are indeed peoples whose inborn characteristics make them less acces-sible to virtue than others. They are responsible for arrangements such as the perpetual disarmament provision forced into the constitution of Japan by the Allies of World War II, with the embarrassing effect that the same Allies, now suddenly anxious to have Japanese military sup-port, are unable to obtain it because of the consequences of their own consistency. If Allied reasoning proved slightly less embarrassing in the German case, it was due not to a lingering of statesmanship but to the good fortune that the prospective measures of destruction were in this instance so vast that they never had a chance of being formalized by the signing of an undenounceable treaty. But even in the German case, the implications of the national theory proved so contradictory that many of its foremost protagonists have long come to wish they could hide in the cosy recesses of the Fifth Amendment.

The events have thus demonstrated that the national theory proved no more helpful in the search for the primary cause of social misery than any of the others discussed so far. All it revealed was that biologi-cally as well as historically one people is just as good or bad as the other. Instead of uncovering meaningful differences amongst nations, it merely confirmed Cicero's concept of the similarity of human nature. And not only Cicero's but even God's who, contemplating His creation, came to the sorrowful conclusion that, irrespective of up-bringing or nationality, 'the wickedness of man was great in the earth, and that every imagination of the thoughts of his heart was only evil continually' (Genesis, vi, 5). Which means, that the proposal of the national theory to cure the world's misery by eliminating the evil-doing nation would lead us nowhere. For the moment one evildoer disappears, the vacancy, as post-World-War-II developments have amply shown, will promptly be filled from the unsuspected but ever willing ranks of the previous defenders of better causes.

This being the case, we are back where we started, with our question as to the primary cause of social misery still unanswered. For if we are really all alike in our disposition to mischief we have yet to explain why many of us under apparently similar circumstances nevertheless do react differently. Why should some of us write poetry under the impact of civilization while others in the same cultural orbit should delight in skinning their fellow men? Why should the leaders of communist Yugoslavia and fascist Spain oppress freedom at home while externally allying themselves with the defenders of democracy? Why should the peace-loving Prime Minister of India keep peace with Moscow or Peking but fall aggressively upon Hyderabad? Is it because of lack of civilization? Manifestly not. As we have seen, the greatest aggressions and the most monstrous crimes have been committed by nations at the peak periods of their civilization. Lack of education? Hardly. The most devilish designs of barbarism have not been conceived by illiterates, but by the most educated brains. Ideology? Economic system? Nationality? The phenomenon is too universal. The cause explaining it all must clearly still lie hidden.

Chapter Two

THE POWER THEORY OF AGGRESSION

'Human creatures are observed to be more savage
and cruel in proportion to their bulk.'
Gulliver's Travels

*The spontaneity of social misery at critical magnitudes. Cruelty
of man proportionate to his bulk. Social size, density, integration, and velocity as crime-breeding elements. Criminal mentality not the cause but the result of mass perpetration of
atrocities. The law of diminishing sensitivity. The meaning of
critical magnitudes. Critical power and size as the cause of
war. How Nehru came to be as aggressive as Hitler. Do not
lead us into temptation. The joys of window smashing. Why
Russia's leaders are beyond the reach of reason. The power and
size theory—a materialistic but not atheistic theory. Its significance as a new interpretation of history. The causal role of
power philosophies. Is America the exception to the rule?*

───────────────────────────────

HAVING accomplished nothing in our search for the primary cause
of social misery on the basis of the various prevailing theories,
let us see what might be achieved by a reappraisal of the data of
the preceding chapter from a new angle. And to simplify matters, let
us continue for the time being to concentrate our attention on the most
representative internal and external manifestation of the problem we
set out to solve—the large-scale perpetration of atrocities within
societies and the waging of aggressive wars between societies.

1. *The Cause of Social Brutality*

As regards the scale of socially committed or condoned atrocities,
we have so far discovered one fact. Most nations, irrespective of their
racial background, the stage of their civilization, their ideology, or their

economic system, have managed to roll up an impressively similar record. Mass executions and related monstrosities were perpetrated in Germany under the nazis, in India under the British, in France under the Catholics, in Russia under some of the most savage, and in Italy under some of the most enlightened, princes. There could not have been a vaster difference of conditions. Yet, if similar excesses occurred everywhere and in all phases and periods of historic development, there must apparently be a common element transcending these differences. This common denominator, as we shall see, seems to be the simple ability, the power, to commit monstrosities. As a result, we arrive at what we might call a *power theory of social misery*.

In part, the proposition seems self-evident. For no one could perpetrate atrocities without the power to do so. But this is not the point. The point is that the proposition operates also in the reverse. Everyone having the power will in the end commit the appropriate atrocities.

This sounds somewhat extreme. Clearly, not everybody holding power must necessarily make evil use of it. Which is quite true, but it does not alter the proposition. It merely means that we must sharpen the statement. For just as not any mass of fissionable material will produce an atomic explosion, but only the critical mass, so not just any quantity of power will lead to brutal abuse, but only the critical quantity. Hence we might call our theory also an *atomic theory of social misery*, the more so since, once the critical power is reached, abuse will result *spontaneously*. Lastly, because the vital element is not so much power but the *size* of power which, as will soon become obvious, depends in turn on the *size* of the social group by which it is generated, we might call the theory also the *size theory of social misery*.

But what is the critical magnitude leading to abuse? The answer is not too difficult. It is the volume of power that ensures immunity from retaliation. This it does whenever it induces in its possessor the belief that he cannot be checked by any existing larger accumulation of power. Depending on the nature of different individuals or groups, the critical volume represents a different magnitude in each different case, giving rise to the idea that there are really other elements than mere physical magnitudes responsible for criminal outbursts. However, as the boiling point is low for some substances and high for others, so the volume of power leading to abuse is low for some individuals or groups and high for others. And similarly, as rising temperatures will in the end bring even the most resistant metals to the boiling point, so the rising mass of power will, in the end, brutalize even the best, not necessarily in a subjective sense, but certainly in its effects.

This means that, whether we are individuals or groups, once the critical point is reached, we become brutes almost in spite of ourselves. If prison guards and police officials have such a universal record of brutality, it is not because they are worse than other men but because in their relationship with their captives they are nearly always equipped with the critical quantity of power. The moment this is missing, they are as considerate, humble, and complying as the rest of us. Similarly soldiers, who may have committed their souls to God in the morning, may pillage, rape, and rob by nightfall not because they have suddenly changed, but because the confusion following the conquest of a town often provides them with that dangerous cloak of immunity that goes with the acquisition of a momentarily uncheckable power.

While some professions are thus inherently productive of brutality because they are by their very nature repositories of critical quantities of power, the most dangerous source of brutality is not professional or institutional, but physical. It is bulk—sheer physical bulk. For bulk, size, mass, not only *leads* to power; like energy it *is* power—power congealed into the dimension of matter. This is why Gulliver, after being cast ashore at Brobdingnag, the land of the giants, was not unreasonable in his apprehensions when he remembered that 'human creatures are observed to be more savage and cruel in proportion to their bulk'.[1] It also explains why small children, without losing either charm or innocence, do to little creatures what they would never do to larger ones. Thanks to their almost infinite superiority in size, they do not even *feel* that they are cruel when they tear out the wings of a fly or the legs of a frog, just as the giants of our fairy tales are quite appropriately pictured as no more sensitive and conscious of their monstrosity when they feast on humans, than humans are when they feast on live oysters.

Yet *individual* bulk is only a minor power-breeding magnitude and, hence, only a minor social problem, since even the biggest amongst us cannot grow much bigger than most others. As a result, they will normally need such additional power-creating assets as a hypnotic personality, a gang, or the possession of guns—all bulk-extending devices and all reducible to physical terms—before they can gratify their evil instincts. And then their available power will hover too close to the margin where the critical volume becomes sub-critical to ensure them a wide enough range of immunity for long enough a time. Consequently the relative infrequency of crime as well as the relatively infrequent intervals at which even the most hardened offenders will engage in criminal activities.

[1] Jonathan Swift, *Gulliver's Travels*. New York: Crown Publishers, 1947, p. 88.

But there is one element capable of accumulating its physical substance so far and so unequivocally beyond the critical limit that no force on earth can check it. This is the immense *collective* bulk of the most courted organism of our time, the human mass, the people which, at a given size and density, not only generates the ideal condition of anonymity at which a greater number of individuals can, without danger of detection, sweep up critical quantity of power than would be possible at the more translucent lesser densities; at a given point the mass becomes itself so spontaneously vile that, in addition to the increased quantum of individual misdeeds, performed under the cloak of its darkening multitudes, it begins to produce a quantum of its own, and wholly detached, badness that bears a relationship to its size, but not to the nature of the human molecules composing it.

When this social volume is reached, everything becomes predictable, and nothing preventable. The question is then no longer: how many crimes will be committed, but who will choose in the freedom of his will to be the criminal tool of the law of averages whose provisions are so predetermining that any statistician, after correlating a community's size with its density and the pace of its population,[1] can predict everything from the number of its deaths, fatal accidents, and false fire alarms to the fact that, for instance, in Chicago, within the next thirty days, 'just under 1000 burglaries will be committed. About 500 citizens will be held up and robbed at the point of a gun, or with some dangerous weapon. Some 15 people ... will be murdered. Thirty or more women will be waylaid and attacked.'[2]

A crowded society is thus full of inherent dangers even in a state of relative repose. But this is nothing compared with the danger it creates when it becomes collectively agitated and, besides contracting to still greater density, as frequently happens on occasions such as feast days, it also begins to increase its velocity. Then its misdeeds will not only increase. They will increase at a geometric rate, beginning with pickpocketing, followed by altercations, brawls, knifings and, depending on its rate of further contraction and increasing velocity, by massacres that will explode with the violence of a cosmic occurrence, receding only when enough cohesive energy has been spent to allow the crowds to thin back and slow down to their original density and pace.

[1] As is shown later, the velocity of a population is a conditioning factor of its density, and both are determinants of a community's size. As a faster circulating currency has the effect of increasing the quantity of currency, so a faster moving community has the effect of increasing its social mass.

[2] *The Field Glass*, House Organ of the Marshall Field Co., Chicago, 6 October 1952, p. 4.

This is why the police force of communities, to cope with the ever present danger of sudden social fusion, must increase at a more than proportionate rate as the population increases, not because larger cities harbour proportionately more bad men than smaller ones, but because, after a certain point, social size becomes itself the chief criminal.[1] There is no crowd on earth that could not in an instant turn into a wolf pack, however saintly its original dedication, as we can see from the many religious holidays (St. Bartholomew's, Michaelmas) that ended in massacres, and the many massacres that ended in holidays.[2] It also explains why even crusaders, who set out from France singing hymns, began to commit atrocities by the time they reached Hungary or Italy, after their armies had gathered up so many devout followers of the Cross that eventually they acquired uncontrollable critical size. And it explains why even the most solemn processions or large funerals are in perpetual need of police protection. Protection from what? Always from the same danger—the atomic consequences of their own mass.

2. The Origin of Crime-condoning Philosophies

However, the sheer physical size of a social aggregation seems responsible not only for the number of crimes committed by its component individuals or groups; more significantly and dangerously, the frequency of crime, growing with the increasing size of the group, seems to be responsible also for the development of a corresponding frame of mind, a condoning philosophy. And a condoning philosophy,

[1] The following figures, taken from the *Municipal Yearbook*, 1951, give a clear picture of this progression: North Plainfield, N.J., with a population of 12,760, needs a police force of 15; Plainfield, N.J., with a population of 42,212: 78; Elisabeth, N.J., with a population of 112,675: 257; Buffalo, N.Y., with a population of 577,394: 1,398; Chicago, with a population of 3,606,439: 7,518; and New York City, with a population of 7,835,099: 19,521.

[2] Alexandre Dumas describes an incident well illustrating the massacre-holiday moods of crowds. After the fall of Napoleon in 1815, a number of citizens of Nîmes, shouting *vive le roi*, set out in search of an individual against whom they had a grudge. Unable to find him, 'and a victim being indispensable', they murdered his uncle instead and dragged his body into the street. In the terms of Dumas, 'the whole town came to see the body of the unfortunate man. Indeed the day which followed a massacre was always a holiday, everyone leaving his work undone and coming to stare at the slaughtered victims. In this case, a man wishing to amuse the crowd, took his pipe out of his mouth and put it between the teeth of the corpse—a joke which had a marvellous success, those present shrieking with laughter.' (Alexandre Dumas, *Celebrated Crimes*. New York: P. F. Collier and Son, 1910, vol. 2, p. 794.)

in turn, will invariably (as a secondary cause) exert an intensifying pressure on the frequency of crime. Hence the phenomenon by which, historically, every increase in the quantity of victims has normally resulted in a more than proportionate increase in the ferocity of persecution. This indicates that not only the frequency of persecution but even the philosophy of crime is determined less by a corrupting moral climate, as is so often believed, than by the physical element of mass, numbers, power and, in the last analysis, social size. As society and, with it, power grows, so grows its corrupting effect on the mind. Or, to rephrase slightly Lord Acton's famous statement, relative power corrupts relatively, and absolute power absolutely.

We shall understand this better if we visualize the successive stages through which socially condoned criminal action proceeds. As long as the victims of persecution are few, the method of execution or, to use a Marxian term, the *mode of production*, will consist in ceremonial knifings, hangings, or shootings, preceded by a semblance of legal process and followed by a semblance of civilized burial. The executioners, moreover, still not quite sure as to the sufficiency of their power and still feeling their wrong because of the singularity of their acts, will have an urge to apologize. But as the number of their victims increases, the time for apologies and even for indulging in guilt feelings begins to dwindle, and individual executions or burials not only become cumbersome but technically unfeasible. So new practices have to be initiated. Now the victims are led to wells, trenches, or rivers, executed on the spot, and then simply thrown in. This represents less an increase in viciousness than an adjustment to the requirements of new situations which could not be handled with previous means. Hence the spectacle in past or present of corpse-filled trenches in France, Germany, Russia, Korea, or wherever else the commission of mass slaughter demanded mass disposition of bodies. As the victims increase still further in number, even trench burial becomes impracticable. So we find corpses arranged in stacks, as was observed with irrational consternation in the concentration camps of the nazis, or blocking doors and carriage ways, as historians report with irrational surprise of the Paris of the sixteenth century.

Finally, when this, too, becomes impossible, the situation demands the last in the heretofore known modes of production—burning. With other methods falling short of the requirements of the task, the victims are now simply herded together, placed into a building, and set afire either *with* the building as in the mill at Carmes, where the techniques of mass cremation were as yet undeveloped, or *without* the building as in the modern crematoria of the nazis. In the future, use will un-doubtedly be made of atomic power, which not only suggests itself as the only efficient means of coping with the number of victims made available by our overpopulated modern mass societies, but is also by far the cheapest means of performing what is expected of it. Discussing the 'economics of extermination' the British mathematician and astrono-mer Fred Hoyle calculated that, while the cost of killing in World War II was still several thousand pounds per victim, the new atomic rate per corpse has been brought down to a single pound ($2.80).[1]

We see then that it is not atrocious design that breeds multiple slaughter, but multiple slaughter that breeds atrocious design. No per-sonal element needs to be involved in this wholly objective phenome-non. But there is yet another relationship of moral adjustment to physical magnitudes that demands attention. While the degree of atrocity reveals a natural as well as impersonal tendency to increase with every increase in the number of victims, the degree of human dis-approval, the philosophy of censure, reveals a proportionate and equally natural tendency to decline. Were this not so, the experience of witnessing mounting misery would soon overtax our compassion and kill us. In fact, the greater our decency and ability for compassion, the faster we would succumb.

But this was obviously not nature's intent. So, in the interest of our own survival, it has helped us to counteract the annihilating terror of mass atrocity by providing us with an adjustable cushion of moral numbness. As a result, instead of becoming more conscience-ridden as the rate of socially committed crimes rises, the ordinary human being is inclined to lose even the little conscience he may still have had so long as the victims were few. For as there is a *law of diminishing utility*, according to which each successive unit of a good, acquired at a given time, yields its owner less satisfaction than the preceding one, there seems also to be a *law of diminishing sensitivity*, according to which each successive commission of a crime burdens its perpetrator with less guilt feeling, and the people in general with less shock, than the pre-ceding one.[2] This goes so far that, when misbehaviour reaches the stage

[1] AP dispatch from London, 25 September 1952.

[2] This explains why the most genuinely felt shock registered by the world at nazi misdeeds was experienced at the very beginning of their rule, when their vic-tims were still few. The shock registered subsequently by Allied observers, when they saw bodies of victims by the wagon load, seems to have been largely artificial and propagandistic, to judge from the fact that hardly anyone registered shock at similar sights, some of them sketchily described in Chapter I, in countries whose alignment immunized them against unfriendly interpretation. This did not show

of mass perpetration, such general numbness and sophistication may set in that murderers lose all their sense of criminality, and onlookers all their sense of crime.

This is when the perpetrators begin to show a craftsman's pride in their accomplishments, express satisfaction for jobs well done, and expect promotions instead of punishment for duties meticulously performed. The bystanders, on the other hand, now begin to treat massacres as if they were holidays and, with the detachment that goes with disindividualized great numbers, to detect the scientific and commercial potentialities of the condition. Doctors suddenly see that the dying can be used for medical experiments; matrons, that tattooed skins look nice on lampshades; apothecaries, that human fat lends itself to the production of medicinal substances; and agriculturalists, that crushed bones furnish excellent fertilizer. So progressive is man's increasing insensitivity to the mounting intensity of atrocity that, in the end, mass murder becomes just like any other profession in which its practitioners assume all the attributes of honourable and honoured men, a culmination effectively portrayed by Charlie Chaplin in his elegant *Monsieur Verdoux*. No murderer of just a single person could ever be conceived as developing similar polish or noblesse. On the contrary. Not only will he be plagued by his own feeling of inadequacy; he will be treated with contempt even in the company of murderers. What a difference from the mass perpetrator who considers himself not only a master but a gentleman, and for whom even his antagonists will often feel a grudging admiration. This explains why, before they dispatched the war criminals, many of their captors seemed quite pleased to be photographed with them.

collusion, but it demonstrated that, contrary to the contentions of the obviously hard-boiled eye-witnesses and the meaning of such legal constructions as genocide, the frequency of commission never makes a crime seem worse. It merely normalizes it. We may appraise the degree to which our conscience has become blunted as a result of our familiarity with mass crimes, if we ask ourselves how many cocktails we have missed after reading accounts such as those concerning our Korean co-defenders of civilization. After calling the Korean conflict an 'ugly war', a correspondent of *Time* described it in these terms: 'This means not the usual, inevitable savagery of combat in the field, but savagery in detail—the blotting out of villages where the enemy *may* be hiding; the shooting and shelling of refugees who *may* include North Koreans . . . The South Korean police and the South Korean marines whom I observed in front line areas are brutal. They murder to save themselves the trouble of escorting prisoners to the rear; they murder civilians simply to get them out of the way.' (*Time*, 21 August 1950.) Our only redeeming feature is the fact that the law of diminishing sensitivity applies also to us, causing us to accept our large-scale atrocities as nonchalantly as the Germans accepted those of the nazis.

32

3. Critical Magnitudes

To sum up, the following conclusions appear to result from the foregoing:

(a) The principal immediate cause behind both the regularly recurring outbursts of mass criminality and the accompanying moral numbness in large sections of even the most civilized societies does not seem to lie in a perverted leadership or corrupted philosophy but in a purely physical element. It is linked with frequencies and numbers, which exert an intensifying effect, and with the possession of the critical quantity of power, which has a detonating effect. At a given volume a chain reaction of brutal acts and, in due course, the appropriate condoning philosophy will apparently result quite spontaneously.

(b) Though the critical volume of power is the immediate element leading to social barbarism, it is itself dependent on another physical element—a social mass of a given size. In a small society, the critical quantity of power can only rarely accumulate since, in the absence of great numerical weight, the cohesive force of the group is easily immobilized by the self-balancing centrifugal trends represented by the numerous competitive pursuits of its individuals.[1] In larger societies, on the other hand, the co-ordinating pressure of numbers may become such that competitive individual trends disappear and the danger of social fusion to the critical point is ever present. So, if critical power is the immediate cause of social evil, we may say that critical social size, being the breeding ground of critical power, is its ultimate or primary cause.

(c) In evaluating the critical size of a society, it is however not sufficient to think only in terms of the size of its population. Its density (correlating population with geographic area), and its velocity (reflecting the extent of its administrative integration and technological progress), must likewise be taken into account. If a population is thinly spread, it may be larger in numbers and occupy a bigger area, and yet constitute a smaller society than a less numerous but denser group. Similarly, a volatile and faster moving society may be larger than a more numerous but slower moving community. To understand this,

[1] The situation is somewhat different in a society which is *too* small and which, as a result, forces on its members a greater protective density than would be necessary in a society of optimum size. Too small and too large societies have therefore certain similarities. Moving and living more as collective organisms than as aggregations of individuals, too small societies can easily achieve critical size in relation to rejected and ostracized individuals. The basic difference between too small and too large societies is discussed in later chapters.

we need but think of the number of exits in a theatre. The same number may be sufficient for a crowd moving at its normal pace, but hopelessly inadequate if the crowd becomes excited and doubles its speed. The effect is then the same as if the crowd itself had doubled. However, in spite of these qualifying features, density, velocity, as well as the social integration which they necessitate, are not separate elements but consequences as well as determinants of the physical concept of social size. For if a given area fills up with an increasing population, its society becomes automatically more dense. As it becomes denser, it requires an increasing measure of integration. And integration of the distant parts of the community with its centre will gradually impart to an increasing number of citizens an increased velocity which, in turn, will grow in proportion to its technological progress. A progressive society will, therefore, be a more integrated and faster society, and a faster society will have the same power effect as if it were larger in number. But ultimately, other things such as area, technological progress, social integration, and natural resources being equal, the most powerful society will be the one with the largest population.

In view of all this, we are not only in a position to understand the full meaning of the alternative and more significant name we have given to our theory—*the size theory of social misery*; having diagnosed the origin and primary cause of the disease, we are moreover for the first time in a position to suggest a cure. For if socially produced brutality, be it on an individual or mass scale, is largely nothing but the spontaneous result of the critical volume of power generated whenever the human mass reaches a certain magnitude, it can be prevented only through a device that keeps power-breeding social size at a sub-critical level. This can be accomplished in two ways: through the *increase* of the controlling power to the level of the challenging power, or through attacking the problem at its root by bringing about a *decrease* in social size. The conventional method is to resort to the first alternative. It provides saturation police forces large enough to match at all times the latent power of the community. This is simple in small social units. But in large ones it is both difficult and dangerous. It is difficult because, as history has shown, social fusion in massive societies can unexpectedly reach such a degree that no police force on earth can check it. And it is dangerous because, as long as police power can check it, it possesses itself the critical volume so that, to the extent that it saves us from popular atrocities, it may present us with the subtler atrocities of a police state instead.

This leaves as the only reliable method of coping with large-scale brutality and criminality the second alternative: the establishment of a system of social units of such *small size* that accumulations and condensations of collective power to the danger point can simply not occur. The answer therefore is not increase in police power, but reduction of social size—the dismemberment of those units of society that have become too big. If we want to eliminate the Chicago rate of crime, we must not educate Chicago or populate it with members of the Salvation Army. We must eliminate communities of the *size* of Chicago. Similarly, if we want to discourage the development of crime-condoning attitudes and philosophies, we shall get nowhere by spreading the gospel. We must destroy those overgrown social units which, by their very nature, are governed not by the gospel but the number conditioned law of averages.

4. The Cause of War

If we now turn from the cause of society's principal internal, to that of its principal external, misery—the periodic eruption of aggressive warfare, we shall see that the power, atomic, or size theory will again furnish more satisfactory answers than the various other theories. The same causal relationships will reveal themselves once more. Again we shall find that the dreaded result of a society's behaviour is the consequence not of evil schemes or evil disposition but of the power that is generated by excessive social size. For whenever a nation becomes large enough to accumulate the critical mass of power, it will in the end accumulate it. And when it has acquired it, it will become an aggressor, its previous record and intentions to the contrary notwithstanding.

Because of the significance of these causal relationships and the use made throughout this book of their implications, let us define the nature of the critical volume of power and the role of its underlying social size once more, with its focus this time turned on external aggression rather than internal atrocity. In contrast to the sharply defined mass of power necessary to set off an atomic explosion, the critical mass of power necessary to produce war is again somewhat relative. As in the case of internal criminal outbursts, it varies with the sum of power available to any possible combination of opponents. But the moment it is greater than this sum *in the estimate* of those holding it, aggression seems to result automatically. Inversely, the moment the power of a nation declines to below the critical point, that nation will automatically become, not peace-*loving*, which, as we have seen, no nation is likely to be, but peace*ful*, which is just as good.

Moreover, the same law that causes an atom bomb to go off *spontaneously* when the fissionable material reaches the critical size, seems also to cause a nation to become *spontaneously* aggressive when its power reaches the critical volume. No determination of its leaders, no ideology, not even the Christian ideology of love and peace itself, can prevent it from exploding into warfare. By the same token, no aggressive desire and no ideology, not even the ideology of nazism or communism, as is pointed out later in this chapter, can drive a nation into attack as long as its power remains below the critical volume. It is always this physical element of power, dependent in its magnitude on the size of the community from which it flows, and generating at a given volume as its inevitable consequence aggression. It seems the cause of any and all wars, the only cause of wars, and always the cause of wars.

Even the most superficial historic survey confirms this relationship. There could be no gentler peoples on earth today than the Portuguese, the Swedes, the Norwegians, or the Danes. Yet, when they found themselves in possession of power, they lashed out against any and all comers with such fury that they conquered the world from horizon to horizon. This was not because, at the period of their national expansion, they were more aggressive than others. They were more powerful. At other times, the British and the French were the world's principal aggressors. When *they* had the critical volume of power that allowed them to get away with aggression, they too drove everything in front of them with fire and sword until a vast part of the earth's surface was theirs. The only thing that stopped them in the end was their inability, their lack of power, to go any further. At still other times, peoples such as the Dutch were peaceful in Europe where their power was subcritical, and aggressive in remote regions where their relative power was critical. More recently, and this is their only distinction and difference, Germany and Russia emerged as the champion aggressors. But the reason for their belligerence was still the same. Not their philosophy drove them to war but their suddenly acquired great power with which they did what every nation in similar condition had done previously—they used it for aggression.

However, as powerful Germany was as aggressive as others, weak Germany was as harmless. The same people that overran the world with the formidable soldiers of Hitler's formidable Reich, formed externally the most inoffensive of human societies as long as they lived divided into jealous and independent small psincipalities such as Anhalt-Bernburg, Schwarzburg-Sondershausen, Saxe-Weimar, or

Hohenzollern-Sigmaringen. They had their little wars, of course, but none that would have stamped them as different from the Italians of Parma, the French of Picardy, the English of Devonshire, or the Celts of Cornwall. Where they escaped the power-breeding unification of Bismarck, they remained peaceful even through the periods of the two world wars as was demonstrated by the inhabitants of Liechtenstein and Switzerland. Confining themselves within boundaries so narrow that they are unable by force of circumstance ever to acquire power unless they discover how to make atom bombs out of the pebbles of their mountain brooks, these two German tribes are for ever condemned to be as peoples amongst the most peaceful in spite of the fact that, as individuals, they may outrank even the Irish as lovers of a good brawl. And the Germans of the Reich itself, stripped of all power as they were after World War II, threatened to become again as peaceful in the nineteen-fifties as the Anhalters were a hundred years ago. Hence the extraordinary string of socialist election victories which were so puzzling to so many of our commentators who were unable to understand how a party in a *war-loving* country could win on an almost cantankerously anti-militarist platform. Clearly, deprived of power, even the aggressive Germans see no charm in a military destiny just as, endowed with power, even the saintly Indians have demonstrated in their bullying campaigns against Hyderabad, Kashmir, and Nepal, that they are not averse to the pleasures of warfare. Only in the face of the seemingly almighty Chinese and Russians do the disciples of Gandhi practise what they preach—love of peace.

We thus see that the phenomenon seems invariable as well as universal according to which the danger of aggression arises spontaneously, irrespective of nationality or disposition, the moment the power of a nation becomes so great that, in the *estimate* of its leaders, it has outgrown the power of its prospective adversaries. This *estimate*, which has already been mentioned but not stressed, seems to introduce a subjective and psychological element indicating that the objective fact of physical power alone is not all that is needed in order to cause its eruption into war. It must be coupled with the *belief* that the critical volume of strength has actually been reached, for, without such conviction, even the greatest power is no power while, with it, even inferior strength may provide the impetus of aggression. This is true, but should not obscure the fact that the source of aggressiveness lies nevertheless not in the psychological but in the physical realm. And it does so exclusively, since mere belief in power can obviously not be engendered without the reality of power; and the reality of power, on the other hand, is such that, at a given magnitude, it brings forth the corresponding belief in its existence and, with it, the corresponding aggressive ideology under any circumstances and even in the most timid of peoples. The only significance of the psychological factor is that it blurs the sharp outlines, surrounding the critical mass of power —in contrast to the precise weight limits of fissionable material—with a marginal area of some depth within which the aggressive explosion can occur anywhere, depending on whether the leaders are *more* or *less* certain of having acquired the necessary volume. The more confident will push their nations into war close to the inner boundary of the margin, and the more hesitant, in the belief of being more peace-loving while they are simply less confident, close to the outer boundary.

This subjective element which, created by power, and growing in proportion to its magnitude, acts within the limits of the critical margin as its detonator, explains why at times even a colossal power seems peaceful—when it is uncertain of its real strength. It also explains why at times several nations become aggressive simultaneously. This happens whenever, as in the case of the Franco-Prussian War, each gets the idea that it has become stronger than the other at the same time. At still other times, only one nation may become aggressive. This is the case when not only its own leaders think its power is invincible but the leaders of its victims as well. This happened in France under Napoleon, and in Germany under Hitler. It finally explains aggressions such as that of North Korea which became inevitable the moment the United States, by withdrawing from South Korea, produced the condition which turned the previously sub-critical mass of Northern power into a critical mass. Since the power theory would have made this aggression predictable with mathematical certainty, its acceptance might well have prevented this catastrophic advance battle of World War III.[1]

Thus we see that history is full of instances showing how previously peaceful peoples have suddenly and unaccountably become aggressive savages, and aggressors angelic defenders of peace. Not in a single case could their fateful change of heart be attributed to either barbarizing or civilizing influences. The mystery of their war-mindedness

[1] The power theory might also have averted the Anglo-French-Israeli invasion of Egypt which, as I predicted in a letter to the New York *Times* of 19 September 1956, paradoxically became inevitable after America declared she would not participate in it. This made it likely that Russia, not more anxious to get involved in world war than America, would stay on the sidelines too. Left to themselves, the power of not only England and France, but also of Israel, turned in relation to Egypt from sub-critical to critical with the result that within weeks Egypt was involved not in one but two wars.

was always their sudden acquisition of power, as the mystery of their conversion to the abandoned ways of peace was always their sudden loss of power. Nothing else ever counted.

5. *Lead us not into Temptation*

Unfortunately, as we have seen in Chapter I, all this contradicts accepted doctrine according to which power does not go off in the hands of just anybody. Only bad countries, bad men, or men infested with bad ideologies are supposed to yield to the temptation that comes from holding an explosive. The good would not. As a result, instead of attacking the problem in its physical aspect, which would suggest that the only way of preventing war is to prevent the organization of societies so large that they can accumulate the critical mass of power, most of our theorists and diplomats are still trying to attack it on a moral plane. They want to turn us all into good and decent fellows by giving us a sounder education or by conjuring up before our eyes the consequences of evil deeds. This accomplished, they feel the peace of the world would be ensured. They will not concede that, as the possession of power is the element that causes misbehaviour, its absence is the only element that ensures our virtue. For the thought of *throwing* the explosive does not come from our philosophic attitude but from the fact that we are *holding* it.

Though many of us refuse to accept the implications of this reasoning when thinking in political terms, in our everyday relations we have adopted them to such an extent that we would hardly consider them a great discovery. The Germans have described this cause-effect relationship in a meaningful saying: *Gelegenheit macht Diebe*—Opportunity creates Thieves—indicating that it is opportunity that causes us to misbehave, not any particular sort of depravity. And opportunity is, of course, nothing but another word for the seemingly critical volume of power. Even a confirmed thief will not steal if he has no chance of getting away with it. On the other hand, even an honest man will misbehave if he has the opportunity, the power to do so.

This explains why all of us, the good even more so than the bad, pray to the Lord not to lead us into temptation. For we know better than many a political theorist that our only safeguard from falling is not moral stature or threat of punishment, but the absence of opportunity. It also explains why mothers all over the world have long decided that the only way of protecting their jam from the hands of their children is to put it beyond the reach of their power. No story of the mythical boy who resisted the temptation of stealing an apple in an unobserved moment, and then was given it as a reward for his victory over himself, will ever produce similar results. True, some may develop an extraordinary will power and stay good because of sheer intellectual fortitude; but the mere fact that they, too, have to fight hard battles with the forces of opportunity shows the elementary character of these forces. The very first sin of man, the original sin, consisted in the use of the power to get hold of the one fruit of all that was forbidden. No warning, no appeal to reason, not the threat of the loss of paradise, prevented Eve from falling. And nothing has changed in this respect since the dawn of history. For virtue and vice are not internal qualities of the human soul that could be influenced by the mind except to an insignificant degree in the marginal area, but the automatic response to, and reflex of, a purely external condition—a given volume of power.

If we are still doubtful about this, we need only remember the little or large sins we have ourselves committed in the past. Who of us did not steal a sweetmeat as a child? As we grow older, we get wiser and conscious of moral behaviour, but the thing that makes us better is neither the process of ageing nor of training. It is the gradual disappearance of tempting opportunities. The moment an accidental opportunity falls into our lap even in later years, our primeval instincts are immediately at work again. That is when the worthiest of us begin to steal books, not from bookshops, where opportunities are few and consequences embarrassing, but from our best friends. Almost all of us have at some time or other gleefully cheated public transportation facilities of their dues, using other people's *non*transferable season tickets, or otherwise escaping payment whenever possible. I myself, along with a number of professorial colleagues, used to be a heavy offender in this respect.[1] Policemen who, being entrusted with the enforcement of the law, have also a unique chance of breaking it without

[1] Public facilities are always subject to cheating even on the part of the best such as the traditionally honest English public. Thus, when the British Post Office increased its telephone rates from two to three pence on 1 October 1951, it hoped to avoid losses from its inability to convert all its call boxes at once by putting the entire nation on its honour. But unofficial polls (UP dispatch from London of 30 September 1951) indicated that the Post Office was 'in for a beating. One newspaper said it found that cheating the tax collector is not considered a crime by many persons of otherwise unblemished integrity. And it found that the Post Office falls into the same category.' But above all it falls into the category of those institutions which offer a large measure of criminal opportunity which even persons of unblemished integrity have difficulty in resisting.

danger of detection, rank for this reason professionally amongst the worst violators of our criminal codes, as the regularly recurring police scandals in most of the world's big cities show. Bank clerks, however carefully chosen, are likewise so continually exposed to temptation that, according to President Truman, there were in 1951 'something like 600 defalcations and embezzlements' in this most conservative of all professions in the United States. 'One out of every 300 bank officers was found to be crooked.'[1] One should assume that at least the idealistic workers and delegates of the United Nations should be resistant to man's little dishonesties. Yet, they too seem not above the rest of us. According to a news item in *Time*, 'New York City's Board of Transportation reported that during 1946, while United Nations delegates met in the city, subway turnstiles had absorbed 101,200 foreign coins.'[2]

Thus, what Bernard Shaw said of a woman's morality, that it is merely her lack of opportunity, applies to all our virtues. We refrain from misbehaving only if, and so long as, opportunity is lacking. When it arises in an unequivocal shape, only the saints amongst us will be able to resist. And sometimes probably not even they, to judge from such incidents as the one reported from Pensacola, Florida, where 'Henry Moquin, a private detective and past president of an East Pensacola Heights civic club, pleaded guilty to stealing cigars from a blind man'.[3] When I was a boy, I was considered a paragon of virtue by my parents who must have been completely unaware of the secret joy I derived from smashing windows. I did not smash too many because the chances were not too abundant. But once a hailstorm broke some of our bedroom windows which consisted of countless small panes held together in a lovely mosaic pattern by a lattice-work of leaden frames such as one finds in churches. Being alone in the house, and with no one in the streets, I became suddenly aware that my power had reached critical mass. It was a magnificent opportunity. I collected a number of pebbles in the garden, went into the street, and then indulged in the most pleasant orgy of window smashing of my lifetime. When my parents returned, I naturally looked as innocent as one is supposed to be at that tender age, and agreed sorrowfully when my father complained that the storm seemed to have played havoc with

[1] President Truman, 29 September 1952.

[2] *Time*, 23 December 1946.

[3] *Time*, 3 December 1951. According to the *Washington News*, even United States Senators were found to consider it not beneath their dignity to take occasionally advantage of blind newsvendors in the entrance hall of the Senate building. Blindness, be it physical, moral, or administrative, is always an invitation to sin.

our house. Everything would have been perfect had I not overlooked a minor item. Hailstones melt, but pebbles do not. These were what my father found strewn over our bedroom floor. So I did not get away with my misdeed after all, but the point is that I thought I would. If I refrain from committing similar misdeeds now, it is not because my sense of morality and other people's property has improved. It is because it would look ridiculous for a professor of economics to be caught smashing the windows of his university. In other words, I have not really the power to do it. If I had . . .

As long as we think in terms of personal experience, we fully realize what critical power does to us. Though some may have been so lacking in opportunities that they never witnessed the thrill of their own reaction to the possession of power, certainly most of us have witnessed such reactions in others, as for instance in taxi drivers, elevator operators, shop assistants, or waiters during World War II. Once the extent of their authority over their customers dawned upon them, they turned from servants of the public into its insulting masters. Under the impact of the war-produced scarcity of their services and the resulting emergence of their power, I saw even officials of the YMCA, one of the most humble and Christian of all institutions, pervert themselves into Napoleons of aggressiveness, Hitlers of arrogance, and Himmlers of sadism, giving evidence in the most unexpected quarters of that vile and universal attitude which Shakespeare has so well described in Hamlet's great soliloquy as the *insolence of office*. The power that goes with office will turn any of us into Prussians.[1] And military power, a power great enough to give us reason to believe that it cannot be checked, will turn any of us into aggressors.

6. *Why Russia's Leaders are beyond the Reach of Reason*

To recognize this seems of vital importance. For, as long as we ignore the nature and role of power, we shall ascribe its consequences to the wrong causes such as the changeable disposition of the human mind, and search for its cure in the wrong direction. This is in fact what many of our diplomats under the influence of obsolete but tenacious theories are still doing. Having at last discovered that the present war danger no longer emanates from the Germans to whose doorsteps they have traced them until so recently, they are now

[1] I do not, of course, think that insolence of office is a particularly Prussian attitude. The term Prussian is used here in the misleading sense our authors have given it.

42

ascribing it to the Russians, and in particular to the depraved ambition and state of mind of an obstinately wicked group of communist leaders. As a result, they are trying again what, at one time, they have tried in vain with the nazi leaders. They are out to change their dangerous disposition by soothing appeasement, appeals to reason and humanity, force of argument and, if all fails, the threat of replacing them. But even if they should succeed along the entire line, the danger of war would not be more dissipated than it was by the removal of the nazi leaders. For Russia would follow the same policy of aggression if she were led by a group of saints, just as Germany was driven on the path of aggression not only by Hitler but also by Emperor Wilhelm who, unlike the uncouth and blasphemous Führer, was, if not exactly a saint, at least a devout believer and the head of his country's Protestant church. Russia, in her present power-breeding size, would be a danger to world peace even in the hands of an American proconsul, as ancient Gaul was a threat to Rome in the hands of anybody, particularly in the masterful hands of Rome's own generals.

The present danger to the peace of the world lies therefore not in an aggressive state of mind but in the existence of a near-critical mass of power which would have produced the aggressive state of mind even if it had not been in existence already. As a result, if the Russian leaders act as they do, it is not because they are bad, nor because they are communists, nor because they are Russians. They act aggressively because they have emerged from World War II with such a formidable degree of social power that they think they cannot be checked by any possible combination confronting them, or that there will be a time in the near future when they can no longer be checked. Wherever and whenever they had this conviction in the recent past, they attacked, invaded, and made war. Finland, Estonia, Latvia, Lithuania, Czechoslovakia, and the other satellites are all monuments to Russian *power*, not to Russian mentality or communist indoctrination. If Moscow has left other small states such as Greece, Iran, or Turkey unattacked, it is only because these countries are backed by the formidable power of the United States of which the masters of the Kremlin are not yet convinced that it can be challenged with impunity. But the moment they come to this conviction, World War III will have started.

It is said that the realistic rulers of the Kremlin would not repeat Hitler's error of waging war against the entire world. In fact the late Stalin himself has made this point. But Hitler, too, said he would not repeat the Kaiser's error of waging a war on two fronts at the same time, or Napoleon's error of letting himself be absorbed into the bottomless depth of Russia. Yet, in the end, he committed both. And Napoleon said he would not jeopardize his empire by attacking the Russian Tsar, with whom he thought at first it would be wiser to share rather than dispute the world. Yet, he did. Does this indicate that all these geniuses of conquest had suddenly lost their mental balance? By no means! It simply demonstrates that no vision, wisdom, or intelligence can restrain power once it has reached the critical volume. The only way of preventing aggression is then not by threatening destruction or appealing to the horse sense and humanity of leaders, but by putting the kettle, in which it simmers, away from the hob of power, even as the only way of preventing water from boiling once it has reached a certain temperature is not by appealing to its native coolness but by separating it from the source that has caused its condition—heat.

Both Napoleon and Hitler were thus probably quite sincere in their earlier declarations of restraint because, at the beginning of their wars, their power was not such that they would have been able to handle all comers. It had reached critical size only in relation to some states but not to the entire world. So they were at first aggressive only against those with whom they could deal safely. But each conquest increased their power until in the end it was so great that they had reason to believe that no hostile combination on earth was left to check them. That was the moment when both committed what earlier had seemed folly but was folly no longer. For the same reason the tough realists of the Kremlin will attempt world conquest in spite of the previous examples of failures and their own resolve to be wiser than their predecessors. When the power scales tip to their sides, the inevitable will occur. At the critical mass, Russian power will explode spontaneously even in the absence of a deliberate detonation by the Kremlin. The only chance to prevent this without deflating that power is to build up a containing power, a sort of saturation police force, of equal magnitude. This, in fact, is our present method of preserving peace. But on so vast a scale, the balance is so precarious that the detonation might occur in the containing power just as easily. For all that applies to Russia applies to the United States as well. That is why, in spite of our desire for peace, Russia is justly as apprehensive of American power as we are of hers, and her assertions of peace are quite possibly as genuine as ours.

It is thus always the critical mass of power that turns nations into aggressors, while the absence of critical power seems always the condition that makes them peaceful. Peacefulness is therefore not a mental attitude or an acquired quality that can be trained into us. It falls to us automatically as the result of physical weakness. The most savage tribes are peaceful when they are weak. But, for the same reason, civilized peoples become savages when they are strong. As an overdose of poison is safe in nobody's system, however sound and healthy he may be, so power is safe in nobody's hands, not even in those of a police force charged with the task of averting aggression.

But so as not to lose sight of the primary causal element, let us return from the power aspect, emphasized in the last few pages, to the size aspect of the theory explaining war, and recapitulate once more briefly the latter's meaning. Being a physical force, and depending for its magnitude on the magnitude of the society from which it flows, power can accumulate to the critical point only in a society of critical size. The question is, what do we exactly understand by social size? What is larger and what is smaller? Considering that *social* size is a function of *physical* size, and that the ultimate particle from which a unit of power can be extracted is the individual member of a given group, social size must be the greater the larger the number of the population. The socially largest society is the one with the physically greatest number of people. And the critical society is the one with a population larger than the sum of populations that can be aligned against it.

However, as long as various societies find themselves at different levels of development, a number of qualifying concepts must be introduced in the appraisal of the effective, or usable, or social, size of a group. For prior to the achievement of identical development levels, the social size of different communities is not necessarily equal to their physical size. As has been shown earlier, a denser society may then for a time be socially more effective and powerful than a numerically larger one; a progressive society larger than a retarded one; a faster society larger than a slower one; and a more highly organized society larger than a less organized one. This explains why a well-organized minority may socially frequently constitute a majority, or why less populous groups have historically often been more aggressive than more populous ones. For in times of transition, organization (as also density and velocity) acts as a multiplier of the population number, and an accelerator in the achievement of larger social size, extracting greater energy from an equal number of power-carrying particles by simply rearranging them in a more efficient manner. However, as nations continue to become more populous, density, velocity, and organization will in the end set in spontaneously even in the absence of a deliberate effort, so that in the last stage of development—such as is seemingly being reached by an increasing number of contemporary societies at the present time—social size will again equal physical size, with the numerically larger societies being the socially more powerful ones. And being more powerful, they will develop more readily the various social miseries and complexities, whose analysis is the subject of this study, than smaller societies.

A last modifying element which should be mentioned for the sake of completion in the evaluation of effective social power concerns the geographic distance of the place of its exercise from that of its origin. For effective power, like sound or light, diminishes as distance increases. This explains why empires, though they may retain their position as great powers at the centre, invariably begin to crumble at the periphery as result of even minor local power development. The American colonies, drawing from a relatively small population number, could therefore none the less develop critical superiority and attack British power which, though enormous in Europe, was only a ripple at the distance of three thousand miles. Had it not been for the fact that effective social power is inversely proportionate to the distance from its centre, the American colonists would hardly have begun to cultivate the idea that taxes with representation are more enjoyable than taxes without representation.

7. Objections to the Power Theory

There are many who will voice objections against the power or size theory of social misery on the ground that it sounds too much like a materialistic interpretation of history. And so it is. But there is nothing wrong with this fact. Simply because the materialistic interpretation was fathered by Marx does not mean that it is untenable. And not every materialistic interpretation is necessarily atheistic. This one is not. We live in a material universe, so why should there be anything strange in the idea that material circumstances have overpowering influences on our behaviour? God, not Karl Marx, created it that way. It is through our *senses* and through *matter* that He communicates to us the manifestations of His existence. His directions are conveyed to us through *things* and the laws embodied in *things*. To consider His physical creation as meaningless in the interpretation of human and social processes would thus seem much more blasphemous than the Marxian interpretation, which is unsatisfactory less because it is fallacious than because it is incomplete. It denies God, but at least it accepts the grandeur and meaningfulness of His design—which cannot always be said of its detractors. As Churchill has warned us, though we shape our buildings, our buildings shape us.

Nor does a materialistic interpretation of history deprive man of moral responsibility for his actions, or of his influence over historic development. Though our behaviour may be but a response to an external physical condition such as the magnitude of power or, more fundamentally, the size of society, we have both the intelligence and the freedom of action to determine the nature of the physical conditions producing our responses. If our intelligence tells us that a certain degree of power corrupts us all, we need but use our freedom of action and see to it that the corrupting volume of power will not come into our possession. And if we know that the corrupting volume of power can accumulate only in societies that have become too large, nothing prevents us from being wiser still and seeing to it that social aggregations do not grow beyond their critical limits. Ulysses, knowing that no human being could withstand the songs of the sirens, was not, therefore, doomed to become the hopeless victim of a bewitching physical circumstance. Applying his common sense and freedom of action, he plugged his sailors' ears so that they could not hear his commands. Then he deprived himself of the power to perform an otherwise inevitable act of insanity by having his robust body chained to a mast while passing the dangerous island. There is nothing in a materialistic interpretation of history that could be construed as an excuse for man's failure to apply his wit, and change a corrupting socio-physical environment in such manner that unwelcome human responses will automatically cease, and more appropriate responses automatically arise.

Though the theory submitted here represents a materialistic interpretation, it is thus neither amoral nor atheistic. Nor is it Marxian. According to Marx, the primary cause explaining both historic change and, along with it, our changing actions, attitudes, and institutions, is our *changing mode of production*. According to the theory underlying the analysis of this book, it is the *changing size of society*. If Marx's theory represents mainly an economic interpretation, the theory of this book represents mainly a social or, because of its emphasis on physical magnitudes, a physical, or socio-physical, interpretation of history. It tries to fill the gaps left open by the Marxian approach. This does not mean that the Marxian interpretation cannot explain a great deal. It does. In fact, it is one of the most lucid tools of understanding ever to be developed. But there are fundamental areas in which it fails.

Thus, while the Marxian *mode of production* gives a highly persuasive explanation of changes *within* given historic periods, it has never been able to explain satisfactorily changes *between* historic periods. Appearing always as a *deus ex machina*, it could reason out everything except the cause of its own emergence and decline. It offers no explanation, for example, why the self-sufficient subsistence mode of production of primitive societies should have given way to the interdependent methods of specialization. The size theory, on the other hand, makes the answer quite simple. For specialization appears to be nothing but the spontaneous adaptation of the mode of production to the possibilities and requirements of a society that has reached a certain physical magnitude. Again, viewing the charming still life and unchanging institutions of the Middle Ages against the background of the slowness of pace of the handicraft mode of production, the Marxian approach is full of subtleness. But once more it fails to offer a reason for the rise and prolonged application of the handicraft mode itself. Viewing the problem against the background of social size on the other hand, we can understand not only the social still life of the Middle Ages with all its implications of thought and habit, but the leisurely handicraft mode of production as well. For a leisurely way of life with its accompanying religiosity, its amiable courtesies, its respect for accomplishment and hierarchy, its concept of the just price, the fair wage, the sinfulness of interest, and lastly its unhurried method of gaining the means of its subsistence, are all characteristic reflexes not so much of economic activities as of life in *small* communities. Conversely, ideals such as equality, uniformity, socialism, easy divorce, which the Marxian interpretation attributes to the levelling effect of mass production and the interchangeability of human beings manipulating machines, can be much more easily understood if we think of them, along with the mass mode of production itself, as the consequence of the requirements of life in *large* societies and the levelling effect of *great* multitudes. Reaching the limit at which growing societies can no longer satisfy their needs by hand production, they automatically produce the equalizing, materialistic, semi-pagan, inventive climate of which the machine mode of production is not cause but consequence.

While there can be no doubt that the mode of production acts as an important secondary influence, a multiplier, and an accelerator of trends, and is therefore always useful in historic analysis, as a primary cause it appears to have no greater significance than Marx attributed to political ideas or legal institutions. As the preceding chapters have shown with regard to certain social miseries and philosophies, and as the following chapters will make increasingly clear with regard to a number of other areas of economic, cultural, political, and philosophic attitudes of good as well as of evil impact, the primary cause influencing human history and action will, in the ultimate analysis, nearly always appear to be the size of the group within which we live. Because Marx ignored this, his otherwise so brilliantly reasoned analysis led to those puzzling miscalculations which his opponents never tire of emphasizing (while at the same time only rarely giving evidence of grasping the connection themselves). He thought, for example, that socialism, evolving as the unwanted by-product of capitalist mass production, would first arise in the most advanced capitalist country. Actually it arose first in Russia, the most retarded. But Russia was the biggest— which explains the miscalculation. For socialism, with its integrating plans and social controls, is the natural by-product not of a mode of production but of a society whose extent and business units have become so large that the self-balancing mechanism of a multitude of competing individual activities has ceased to provide an orderly pattern.[1] Marx also thought that an increase in competition would lead to an end of competition, an increase in the accumulation of profit to an end of profit, an increase in capitalist production to the impossibility of selling the product, with the result that capitalism would be destroyed through its own pursuits. This seemed true of a number of large countries which, throughout the world, have shown a trend to increasing socialization. But it has not been true of small ones. Switzerland is as capitalist and sound as ever. And the reason for this is that the true germ of destruction is not competition but, as Marx himself must have sensed to judge from the phrasing of his famous capitalist contradictions, the *increase* in competition; not profit, but the *increase* in profit; not capitalism, but the unlimited *growth* of capitalism. But so that the germ may grow to the limit of destruction, it clearly requires a social hinterland large enough to permit such growth in the first place. The puzzling shortcomings of the Marxian analysis seem thus all resolved when we replace the mode of production by social size as the primary causal influence of historic development.

Many will object to the power or size theory also on the ground that it is based on an unduly pessimistic interpretation of *man*. They will

[1] As socialism is the natural system of excessively large societies it is natural also in societies which are too small. But the development possibilities are different. As they grow, a large society becomes more socialist and a too small society less so. In the former case, growth has a collectivizing, in the latter case, an individualizing effect. See the author's essay: 'Economic Systems and Social Size' in Robert Solo, *Economics and the Public Interest*, New Brunswick, Rutgers University Press, 1955.

claim that, far from being inspired and seduced by power, we are generally and predominantly animated by the ideals of decency, justice, magnanimity, and so forth. This is true, but only because most of the time we do not possess the critical power enabling us to get away with indecency. We behave simply because we know that crime does not pay and that, with the limited power at our disposal, it is more profitable to use it for good than for bad.

This assertion is however no more a slur against mankind than Adam Smith's concept that the capitalist business man is a cunning schemer with nothing in mind except his own interest, and conspiring whenever he can to enrich himself at the expense of the consumer. We just seem to be that way. Yet Adam Smith saw no reason to attack the freedom of capitalist individualism on this account. On the contrary, he was its staunchest defender. He knew that the individual's meanness was checked by the self-correcting device of competition which is nothing other than a mechanism to keep the business man's power down to proportions within which it can do no damage. It is because of his inability to do harm, not because of superior virtue, that the capitalist profit seeker will paradoxically behave as if *guided by an invisible hand* to serve society well. Since bad service would not yield profit, he becomes altruistic out of sheer egoism. But whenever he finds the opportunity of getting away with conspiracy against his fellow men, he will grasp it with relish, as has been shown by those who have succeeded in becoming monopolists. As a result of the large size of their business units, they alone in a competitive capitalist society have the power to misbehave with impunity, and promptly do so until checked by another power, the power of government drawing from still larger size.

Competitive capitalism thus does not seem to have suffered from putting trust more in the reliability of man's imperfections in pursuit of social aims than in the fiction of human goodness which has caused the disintegration of the idealistic plans of most social reformers. Nor has the Catholic Church, which was built on similar assumptions when Jesus chose not the gentle and saintly John as His successor, but earthly Peter, a man so full of weaknesses that he betrayed his own Master three times in a single night. And yet it was Peter whom his Master considered the rock on which to found the indestructible monument to His existence, not Saint John. Only socialists pay man the compliment of crediting him with an essentially good nature. But they, too, make this somewhat dependent on an external *social* condition, the absence of private property resulting from a given mode of production, as I suggested its dependence on an external *physical* condition, the absence of power resulting from a given size of the community. But the fact remains that capitalism, as long as it was based on the idea of competitive mischief, seems to have produced infinitely greater economic and spiritual values than socialism with its benign and unrealistic assumption that man's nature can be improved along with his economic environments.

One may say in fairness to socialism that it has not yet been given the chance and time to prove itself while capitalism has. But so has socialism. Man's first societies were socialist, and there were numerous attempts throughout history to establish idealistic cells for communal living freed from the degrading effects of private property. They all have had their chance and time, as the very fact proves that, in time, they all failed. And they failed not because of the eventual development of private property, but because from some of these properties, increasing in size, sprouted *power*. And it was power which broke socialist societies at their beginning, as it is power which threatens through the creation of monopolies to break up capitalist societies at their end.

Objections are finally due to arise from those who, like the ideological theorists of Chapter I, feel it would be dangerous to underestimate the role of ideas as the cause of social miseries such as aggressions and wars. However, the size or power theory does not underestimate ideas. All it maintains is that, as *primary* causal forces, they are irrelevant. An aggressive ideology such as fascism, nazism, or communism can do nothing to fulfil itself unless it has power—as contemporary Spain, Portugal, or San Marino amply illustrate. On the other hand, and this is the point of significance, if it possesses power, it becomes aggressive on that account, not because of its ideological content.

While thus denying the primary role of ideologies such as nazism or communism, the power or size theory does not contest their secondary significance. Though they cannot in themselves *cause* wars, they act—as already stated—as *accelerators* in the process of building up power to the point where it will explode spontaneously irrespective of how and by whom it has been created. But even in this respect, their effectiveness has become limited since, in the present stage of development, the critical mass can be accumulated only in very populous states. As a result, power philosophies, however incendiary they may be, can constitute no external problem if confined to small societies.

In large ones, however, they can indeed exert their influence. In Germany, for example, where the nazi ideology aspired to the critical volume of power not as an accidental by-product of growth but an end in itself, it managed to speed up the inevitable accumulation process (leading at a given magnitude to war) by perhaps a quarter of a century. But the more important point is that, because of her vast power potential over which she disposed since her unification in 1871—a potential that was destroyed neither in 1918 nor in 1945 when the Allies merely eliminated her then existing power but not the power-breeding unity of a state of more than sixty million people—Germany would have become aggressive after World War I even without nazism. The only difference would have been that, in the absence of a power philosophy, it would have taken longer, say until 1960 or 1970. She would have grown on the basis of her peace-directed instead of war-directed activities. But finally she would have exploded anyway, as a snowball on its descent from a mountain grows until it reaches proportions which are in themselves destructive, irrespective of whether it was set on its course by an innocent child or an evil schemer. What our peace planners must watch is, therefore, less the resurgence of *nazism* amongst the Germans, but of *power*—the very thing circumstances drive them to build up again. But power, unless kept at a sub-critical level—a difficult proposition once it has come close to it—will not be any safer in the hands of an Adenauer or an anti-militarist socialist leader than in the hands of a new Hitler, a German Stalin or, for that matter, an Allied overlord. Ideologies may either delay or hasten, but neither cause nor prevent.

8. Power and Size in the United States

A similar reasoning applies to the United States which so far has seemed to provide a spectacular exception to the size theory. Here we have one of the largest and, perhaps, the most powerful nation on earth, and yet she does not seem to be the world's principal aggressor as in theory she should be. Moreover, it would seem she is not aggressive at all.

This is quite true but, as we have seen, to become effective, power must be accompanied by the awareness of its magnitude. Within the limits of the marginal area, it is not only the physical mass that matters, but the state of mind that grows out of it. This state of mind, the *soul* of power, grows sometimes faster than the body in which it is contained and sometimes slower. The latter has been the case in the United States. Though she has been by far the greatest *physical* power on earth since before World War I, and has thus long ago entered the critical area, she has been overshadowed as a *political* and *military* power until relatively recently by all other great powers because she lacked the appropriate power state of mind. Her terrific but socially unco-ordinated energies could still be utilized in so many other directions that she saw no necessity of measuring her strength in international competition beyond the boundaries of the Western hemisphere. Thus, with an eagerness quite beyond the comprehension of European nations, she destroyed her military power after World War I as fast as she could and, instead of getting conquering ideas, became isolationist, losing completely the will of being a power anywhere outside the Americas. But within the Western hemisphere, even the United States developed attitudes that cannot always be held up as examples of gentleness. Here she *was* a power, whether she wanted or not, and *behaved* like one.

After World War II, a similar trend of destroying her own world power set in, at a pace however that was not only considerably slower. It has in the meantime been stopped altogether. There is no longer a possibility of the United States *not* being a great power. As a result, the corresponding state of mind, developing as a perhaps unwanted but unavoidable consequence, has begun to manifest itself already at numerous occasions as, for example, when President Truman's Secretary of Defence, Louis Johnson, indicated in 1950 the possibility of a preventive war, or when General Eisenhower, in an address before Congress in the same year, declared that united we can *lick* the world. The latter sounded more like a statement by the exuberant Kaiser of Germany than by the then President of Columbia University. Why should a defender of peace and democracy want to lick the world? Non-aggressively expressed, the statement would have been that, if we are united, the entire world cannot lick *us*. However, this shows how power breeds this peculiar state of mind, particularly in a man who, as a general must, knows the full extent of America's potential. It also shows that no ideology of peace, however strongly entrenched it may be in a country's traditions, can prevent war if a certain power condition has arisen. It may have a retarding and embellishing effect, but that is all, as the deceptive myth of preventive war indicates which advocates aggression for the solemnly declared purpose of avoiding it. It is as if someone would kill a man to save him the trouble of dying.

Yet, generally speaking, the mind of the United States, being so reluctantly carried into the inevitable, is still not completely that of the power she really is, at least not from an internal point of view. But some time she will be. When that time comes, we should not naïvely fool ourselves with pretensions of innocence. Power and aggressiveness are

inseparable twin phenomena in a state of near critical size, and innocence is a virtue only up to a certain point and age. If there ever should
be a powerful country without any desire to lick and dominate others,
it would not be a sign of virtue but of either overage or mongoloid
under-development. In the United States, neither is the case. So,
unless we insist once more that Cicero's definition of man does not
apply to us, the critical mass of power will go off in our hands, too.

With this we have for the second time arrived at the point where we
can suggest a cure for one of the most disturbing social miseries on the
basis of the power or size theory. Having found that the same element
which causes crime and criminality seems responsible also for war and
its resultant ideology of aggression, it appears that the same device
offered as the solution of the first problem must apply also to the
second. If wars are due to the accumulation of the critical mass of
power, and the critical mass of power can accumulate only in social
organisms of critical *size*, the problems of aggression, like those of
atrocity, can clearly again be solved in only one way—through the reduction of those organisms that have outgrown the proportions of
human control. As we have seen, in the case of internal social miseries,
already cities may constitute such overgrown units. In the case of external miseries, only states can acquire critical size. This means that, if the
world is to be relieved of some of the pressures of aggressive warfare,
we can do little by trying to unite it. We should but increase the terror
potential that comes from large size. What must be accomplished is the
very opposite: the dismemberment of the vast united national complexes commonly called the great powers. For they alone in the contemporary world have the social size that enables them to spread the
miseries we try to prevent, but cannot so long as we leave untouched
the power which produces them.

Chapter Three

DISUNION NOW

'I believe in the virtue of small nations.'
ANDRÉ GIDE

The new map of Europe. The solution of the problem of war by making war divisible. The automatic dissolution of minority problems. The dissolution of national hostility. Ineffectiveness of medieval small-scale wars. How the Truce of God made war divisible in time. The effect of Maximilian's Eternal Truce of God: great power wars. Terror of modern warfare. Causes of modern wars still as ridiculous as causes of medieval wars. Great power not productive of wisdom. The Duke of Sully and Saint Augustine on the misery of bigness and the greatness of small states.

THE unfortunate thing about the conclusions of the preceding analysis is that they are contrary to everything the twentieth century appears to be fighting for. All our statesmen seem to have in their mind in order to cope with the threat of atomic warfare is the unification of mankind. But where does this lead to? Exactly to where it did. Unification means the substitution of fewer units for many or, in political terms, of a few large powers for many small ones, with the result that by now not only the number of small states but even that of the large powers themselves has begun to shrink. Before World War II, there were still the Big Eight. After the war, there were the Big Five, then the Big Four, and now the Big Three. Soon there will be the Big Two, and finally the Big One—the single World State.

However, as we have seen by contemplating the physics of social size, and as we can see by simply looking from our windows at the political landscape of our own day, the process of unification, far from reducing the dangers of war, seems the very thing that increases them. For, the larger a power becomes, the more is it in a position to build up its strength to the point where it becomes *spontaneously* explosive. But not only does unification breed wars by creating war potentials; it *needs* war in the very process of its establishment. No great power complex in history has ever been created peacefully (except, perhaps, the Austro-Hungarian Empire which grew by marriage). And the greater the unity that emerged, the more numerous and terrible were the wars that were necessary to create it. Great Britain, France, Italy, Germany—they all were the result of a series of wars amongst the very members subsequently composing them as their conquered, not their voluntary, parts. The League of Nations was the product of World War I, and the United Nations of World War II. None of these glorified vast-scale organizations was ever worth its price, and it makes one shudder to think of the price of an ultimate single World State.

But even if a single United Nations World State would come into existence, it would solve nothing. It would still be composed of the reduced number of state organisms crystallizing around the remaining great powers. Not a single advocate of world unity in a position of political authority has as yet visualized a world organization in which the United States, Great Britain, France, or Russia would dissolve to the extent that they would lose their identity. Thus, whatever form the United Nations take, there will still be the great powers, and there is no reason to believe that they would behave differently united than they do disunited. As the Korean or Egyptian campaigns have shown, they wage wars against each other as members of a world organization as uninhibitedly as they did as non-members, and always for the same reason: where there is a critically large volume of power, there is aggression, and as long as there is critical power, so long will there be aggression. As Professor Henry C. Simons wrote with singular clarity:

'War is a collectivizing process, and large-scale collectivism is inherently warlike. If not militarist by national tradition, highly centralized states must become so by the very necessity of sustaining at home an inordinate, "unnatural" power concentration, by the threat of their governmental mobilization as felt by other nations, and by their almost inevitable transformation of commercial intercourse into organized economic warfare among great economic-political blocs. There can be no real peace or solid world order in a world of a few great, centralized powers.'[1]

[1] Henry C. Simons, *Economic Policy for a Free Society*. The University of Chicago Press, Chicago, 1948, p. 21.

Having seen where the unifiers have brought us—nowhere—let us apply the philosophy of the size theory and see what solution the opposite direction might hold for us. Instead of union, let us have disunion now. Instead of fusing the small, let us dismember the big. Instead of creating fewer and larger states, let us create more and smaller ones. For from all we have seen until now, this seems the only way by which power can be pushed back to dimensions where it can do no spectacular harm, at least in its external effects.

1. *Europe's New Political Map*

So let us divide the big and envisage the possible consequences! For the sake of a simplified illustration, the principle of division shall in the following be applied only to Europe and, to make it simpler still, to Europe minus Russia. Since the main complexities of our time have their historic origin there, a continental European study provides the same variety of aspects and arguments as a discussion of the entire globe.

This, then, would be the new political map of Europe. With the great powers of France, Great Britain, Italy, and Germany eliminated, we now find in their place a multitude of small states such as Burgundy, Picardy, Normandy, Navarre, Alsace, Lorraine, Saar, Savoy, Lombardy, Naples, Venice, a Papal State, Bavaria, Baden, Hesse, Hanover, Brunswick, Wales, Scotland, Cornwall, and so forth.

A division of the great powers alone, however, would not be enough. With France, Italy, Germany, and Great Britain dissolved, the present medium powers such as Spain, Yugoslavia, Czechoslovakia, Rumania, and Poland would loom disproportionately large in the new set-up of nations. This means that, if left intact, they would no longer be medium but large powers. Their sub-critical mass would have become critical and nothing would have been gained by dividing the others. So these must be divided too, and as a result another crop of small states appears on our new map such as Aragon, Valencia, Catalonia, Castile, Galicia, Warsaw, Bohemia, Moravia, Slovakia, Ruthenia, Slavonia, Slovenia, Croatia, Serbia, Macedonia, Transylvania, Moldavia, Walachia, Bessarabia, and so forth.

From this extensive list, one fact emerges already now. There is nothing artificial in this new map. It is, in fact, Europe's natural and original landscape. Not a single name had to be invented. They are all still there and, as the numerous autonomy movements of the Macedonians, Sicilians, Basques, Catalans, Scots, Bavarians, Welsh, Slovaks, or Normans show, still very much alive. The great powers are the ones which are artificial structures and which, because they are artificial, need such consuming efforts to maintain themselves. As they did not come into existence by natural development but by conquest, so they cannot maintain themselves except by conquest—the constant reconquest of their own citizens through a flow of patriotic propaganda setting in at the cradle and ending only at the grave.

But nothing that needs so colossal an effort for its survival is natural. If a Celtic-speaking inhabitant of Brittany knew by instinct or tradition that he is of the same French nationality as the German-speaking Alsatian, the French-speaking Burgundian, or the Catalan-speaking inhabitant of the South of France, he would not have to be told so all his life. Even so, the various groups composing the great powers grasp every opportunity of freeing themselves of the propagandized glory of greatness, trying instead to recede, whenever they can, into the narrow limits of their valleys and provinces, where alone they feel at home. Hundreds of years of joint living and great power propaganda could neither erase sentiments of autonomy nor accomplish what every small state has achieved without effort—natural loyalty and meaningful nationality.

Hence, the division of the great powers, whatever it might signify, would not constitute a return of Europe to an artificial, but to its natural, state. But this does not touch our main problem. The principal question still is: would such a Europe be more peaceful?

2. The Elimination of War Causes

Yes, indeed! This is the second point that emerges from the mere enumeration of the names of small states. Nearly all wars have been fought for unification, and unification has always been represented as pacification. So, paradoxically, nearly all wars have been, and in fact still are, fought for unity and peace, which means that, if we were not such determined unionists and pacifists, we might have considerably fewer wars. The most terrible war of the United States, the Civil War, was fought for the preservation of unity. In Europe, unification usually meant that a larger state wanted to unify with its territory a smaller one. This process began to radiate from various centres at the same time with the result that the small states were gradually absorbed by the broadening central states until the now emerging great powers reached common frontiers. With every chance for further extension gone, they began to dispute each other's latest acquisitions, their *border territories*.

But what are the names of these border territories which were originally small sovereign states, and became the cause of major disputes not in their own right but as a result of their absorption by major powers? They are the same names we have encountered in our new map—Alsace, Lorraine, Saar, Slesvig, Holstein, Macedonia, Transylvania, Trieste, Slovakia, Savoy, Corsica, South Tyrol, and a host of others. They are the very states for whose possession the vast majority of European wars were fought. Ever since they lost their independence they became synonymous not with progress but with conflict. As a result, they have never been fully absorbed by the powers now dominating them, and they will therefore for ever be areas of irritation in anybody's flesh except their own.

The re-establishment of small-state sovereignty would thus not only satisfy the never extinguished desire of these states for the restoration of their autonomy; it would disintegrate the cause of most wars as if by magic. There would no longer be a question of whether disputed Alsace should be united with France or Germany. With neither a France nor a Germany left to claim it, she would be Alsatian. She would be flanked by Baden and Burgundy, themselves then little states with no chance of disputing her existence. There would be no longer a question of whether Macedonia should be Yugoslav, Bulgarian, or Greek—she would be Macedonian; whether Transylvania should be Hungarian or Rumanian—she would be Transylvanian; or whether Northern Ireland should be part of Eire or Britain; she would be nobody's part. She would be North Irish. With all states small, they would cease to be mere border regions of ambitious neighbours. Each would be too big to be devoured by the other. The entire system would thus function as an automatic stabilizer.

Together with the problem of contested border areas, a small-state Europe would automatically dissolve a second source of constant conflict—the problem of *minorities*. Since from a political point of view there is no limit to how small a sovereign state can be, each minority, however little and on whatever ground it wishes to be separate, could be the sovereign master of its own house, talk its own language when and where it pleased, and be happy in its own fashion. Switzerland, so wise in the science and practice of government, has shown how she solved the problems of minorities by means of creating minority *states* rather than minority *rights*. In spite of the fact that her cantons are already quite minuscule, three of them were subdivided into sovereign halves completely independent from one another when internal differences developed that would have created minority problems and necessitated a greater degree of mutual submission than could be reconciled with the ideals of democratic freedom. Hence, tiny *Unterwalden* was subdivided into *Obwalden* and *Nidwalden* as far back as the thirteenth century, each following an independent course in Swiss politics ever since. In 1597, under the impact of the Reformation, the canton of *Appenzell*, rather than forcing her hostile groups into a continued but now unwanted unity, divided herself into the Catholic and predominantly pastoral *Inner Rhoden* and the Protestant and mainly industrial *Ausser Rhoden*. Again in 1833, the canton of Basel subdivided itself into the now independent half-cantons of *Basel-City* and *Basel-Land*, after the rural districts had revolted against the undemocratic rule of the urban trade guilds. Division, not union, was the device by which the Swiss preserved their unity and peace, solving at the same time, as one of the few nations to accomplish this, their minority problems.

Finally, a third of the world's most bothersome problems would disintegrate of themselves. A small-state Europe would mean the end of the devastating and pathological proportions of *national hostility* which can only thrive on the collectivized power mentality of large nation-states. Germans, Frenchmen, and Italians, weighed down by the perverting influence of their history of blood and gore, will always hate each other. But no Bavarian ever hated a Basque, no Burgundian a Brunswicker, no Sicilian a Hessian, no Scot a Catalan. No insult mars the history of their loose and distant relations. There would still be rivalries and jealousies, but none of the consuming hatreds so characteristic of the perpetually humourless and mentally underdeveloped big.

3. Harmlessness of Small-state Wars

Here, objections become audible. Is it not ridiculous to maintain that a small-state world would eliminate wars? What about the dark Middle Ages during which both small states and uninterrupted warfare prevailed?

Quite. But the purpose of this analysis is not to furnish another of those fantastic plans for eternal peace so peculiar to our time. It is to find a *solution* to our worst social evils, not a way to *eliminate* them. The problem of war in modern times is not its occurrence, but its scale, its devastating magnitude. Wars as such will, of course, always be fought —in a world of great powers as well as in a world of little states. A small-state world dissolves the most vexing but not all of the causes of wars. It does not eradicate aggressiveness or any other of the inborn evils of human nature. Nor does it eliminate the possibility that even small social organisms might develop occasionally a laboratory quantity of critical power leading to their release. But what it can do is to bring them under control, reduce their effectiveness, deprive them of their sting, and make them bearable.

From the point of view of war, this is all there is to the virtue of a small-state world. It reduces the problems which overpower the great to proportions within which they can be checked even by the little. Since every problem assumes the proportions of the body in which it is embedded, the proud and great powers are terrorized by the dangers which the little states take unfearingly in their stride. It is for this reason that a great-power world clings so pathetically to the hopeless illusion of the *good* man with all his better sides, and strives so pitifully for eternal peace. For every minor wickedness and every slightest and peripheral disturbance scares the wits out of its bulky brain, and shakes it in its very foundations. A little-state world is untroubled by all this. Its wars mean little, and are as little as the states between which they are fought. Its hatreds whittle down to rivalries, and it never suffers the double heartbreak of the great-power world which is constantly out to achieve the unachievable, and then invariably succumbs to the unpreventable.

It is thus quite true that a small-state world might not be peaceful at all, but constantly bubbling with wars such as characterized the Middle Ages. But what were these famous medieval wars like? The Duke of Tyrol would declare war on the Margrave of Bavaria because somebody's horse had been stolen. The war lasted two weeks. There were one dead and six wounded. A village was captured, and all the wine drunk that was in the cellar of the inn. Peace was made, and the sum of a hundred thalers was paid in reparations. The adjoining Archbishopric of Salzburg and the Principality of Liechtenstein learned of the event a few weeks later and the rest of Europe never heard of it at all. In the Middle Ages, there was war in some corner of Europe almost every day. But they were little wars with little effects because the powers waging them were little and their resources small. Since every battlefield could be surveyed from a hill, opposing generals would sometimes end a fight without a single casualty, and without ever giving the signal to attack, as when they realized that the enemy had hopelessly outsmarted them. Hence the term *manœuvre wars* which, bloodless as they were, were as real wars as any. What a contrast to the modern giant-scale conflicts which are so beyond the vision of even the greatest generals that, like blind colossi, they have no other alternative, if they want to discover the prospective winner, than to fight to their gasping ends.

The great thing about the earlier condition was that war as well as peace was *divisible*. To hear this praised as an advantage will undoubtedly shock the theorists of our unitarian age. Yet it was an advantage. The small-state world with its incredible parcellation of sovereign territories allowed conflicts to remain localized and, whenever war did break out, prevented its spread across the entire continent. The numerous boundaries acted constantly as insulators against the expansion of a conflict even as the parcellation of an atomic pile into a composite of small bricks acts as a barrier, not to the occurrence of an atomic explosion which, within such narrow limits, is harmless and controllable, but to the devastating and uncontrollable chain reaction which would occur if the brick sovereignties were unified into a single frame as in the atom bomb.

The paradoxical result of the constant occurrence of warfare during the Middle Ages was the simultaneous prevalence of peace. We fail to realize this because history records primarily *disturbances* of peace rather than the *existence* of peace. As a result we see the medieval wars as we see the Milky Way, which appears so dense with stars only because we view this disc-shaped galaxy from its outer regions at a horizontal angle. Hence, we know all about a war between Bavaria and Tyrol in some specific year while ignoring the fact that at the same time there was peace in Bohemia, Hungary, Carinthia, Salzburg, Flanders, Burgundy, Parma, Venice, Denmark, Galicia, and where not. The war picture of the Middle Ages is thus one of bubbling numerous little waves washing over this and that region, but never unifying its particles into the proportions of a tidal wave rolling over the entire continent. And what strikes one upon closer study are less the wars than the frequent conditions of peace. As many a nostalgic traveller through Europe discovers, the Middle Ages built much more than they destroyed—which would hardly have been possible if our war picture of that era were correct. As in so many other respects, the *dark* ages of medieval times were even in their war aspects more advanced than our modern age with all its peace desires and its smug detractors of medieval backwardness.

4. *The Truce of God*

The Middle Ages enjoyed such relatively numerous periods of peace not only by making peace and war divisible *in space* as a result of the boundary-ridden small-state system. With a true touch of genius, they made them divisible also *in time*. Their leaders never believed in the unattainable nonsense of an eternal peace, and therefore never wasted their energy in trying to establish it. Knowing the substance of which man was made, they wisely based their systems on his shortcomings, not his pretensions. Unable to prevent war, they did the next best thing. They tried to control it. And in this they succeeded signally through an institution which they called *Treuga Dei*, the *Truce of God*.[1]

This truce was based on the concept that war, as it was divisible regionally, was divisible also into separate actions and periods. According to its original provisions, all warfare had to be interrupted on Saturday noon and could not be resumed until Monday morning in order to ensure the undisturbed worship of the Lord on Sunday. Subsequently, the period of truce was extended to include Thursday in honour of Christ's ascension, Friday in reverent commemoration of the crucifixion, and all of Saturday in memory of His entombment. In addition to these time limitations, a number of places were declared immune from military action. Thus, even in the midst of war, neither churches and churchyards, nor fields at harvest time could be made the scene of battle. Finally, entire groups of persons such as women, children, old people, or farmers working in fields were placed under special protection and had to be left unmolested. Infractions of the Truce of God were punished by the Church as well as the State, and particularly severe violations with long years of exile in Jerusalem.

All this was very trying to the unhappy warriors who found their chances of fight reduced to three days per week and so atomized that, sometimes, they had to break off battles after they had hardly shot their first arrows. At other times, the prolonged week-end interruption had such a dissipating effect that they failed to resume their hostilities altogether. But the main feature of this singular institution was always in evidence: in spite of the numerous enforced periods of peace, there was a sprinkling of days when war was legitimate. Care was taken that the safety valve through which aggressiveness could blow itself out in small and controllable bursts was never plugged. That is, never until Emperor Maximilian I of the Holy Roman Empire made a fateful step.

[1] The first documentary evidence of the Truce of God dates back to the year 1041, when several French bishops communicated its outlines for acceptance to the Italian clergy. In 1042, Duke William promulgated it in Normandy. In 1095, Pope Urban II confirmed it as a general institution at the Council of Clermont. In 1234 its rules were codified by Pope Gregory IX, and incorporated in the *Corpus juris canonici*.

Maximilian, ruling from 1493 to 1519 when the Middle Ages gave way to the modern epoch of history, was a great idealist, and is often referred to as the *Last Knight*. It would be better to call him the *First Modernist*. For, as is typical of modern theorists, he felt that great ideals and grand concepts could be established by imperfect man in this imperfect world in uncompromising completion. So he calculated, if peace could be preserved on church ground and farm lands, why not everywhere? If it could be respected with regard to old men, women, and children, why not with regard to all men? And if it could be maintained from Thursdays to Mondays, why not on all days, in all weeks, in all years? Why not make peace *indivisible*?

This is what he tried. He promulgated the *Eternal Truce of God*. As the statesmen of our own day—likewise delighting in totalities such as total triumphs, total surrenders, total peace—were to do centuries later, Maximilian outlawed warfare for all time to come. And what was the result? After the promulgation of the *Eternal* Truce of God, wars were fought not only on Mondays, Tuesdays, and Wednesdays, but on Thursdays, Fridays, Saturdays, and Sundays as well; not only on permitted battle grounds, but in wheatfields and in churchyards; and not only against soldiers, but against women, children, and old men as well. Something had indeed become total—but not peace.

Viewing the small-state world of the Middle Ages, we thus find that it provided by no means heavenly perfection. On the contrary, it was full of shortcomings and weaknesses, and full of the problems confronting life in general. But—and this was its great virtue—it was never terrorized by them since, on a small scale, even the most difficult problem dwindles to insignificant proportions. This is what Saint Augustine had in mind when, contemplating the clumsy misery of hugeness, he asked in the *City of God* (Book III, Chapter X):

'Why should any empire make disquiet the scale unto greatness? In this little world of man's body, is it not better to have a mean stature with an unmoved health, than a huge bigness with intolerable sickness? To take no rest at the point where thou shouldst rest, the end, but still to confound the greater growth with the greater grief?'

or when he quotes Sallust who wrote in praise of the power-free world that appears to have existed at the dawn of history:

'Kings in the beginning were diverse in their goodness: some exercised their corporal powers, some their spiritual, and men's lives in those times were without all exorbitance of habit or affect, each one keeping in his own compass.'

As the kings in the beginning, so the 'reactionary' Middle Ages were characterized by the fact that, in spite of their weaknesses and conflicts, they were 'without all exorbitance or affect', and that every problem could be contained with the narrow limits of its 'own compass'.

5. The Curse of Unification

Now let us turn our back on the Middle Ages, and see what happened when the small-state world with its ever-feuding parts and operetta wars gave way to our modern large-power system. The reason and apology with which it introduced itself to historians was the pacification of large regions previously torn by tribal warfare. In this it unquestionably succeeded and, because most of us grunt with delight whenever we hear the word *peace*, it is applauded on this account to this very day. But was the result of this regional pacification peace? Hardly. For as soon as the new nation states had established themselves on firm ground and pacified their new dominions into reliable and well-co-ordinated units, their natural aggressiveness began to assert itself in exactly the same manner as was the case with their smaller predecessors whom they had wiped out because of their peace-disturbing quarrelsomeness. Once their acquisitions were properly digested, they looked again beyond their boundaries for outlets of their energies—and a new cycle of wars began, wars, however, that were qualitatively different from the earlier ones.

These wars which, from the establishment of the Eternal Truce of God onwards, characterize the evolution of modern times, had one element in their favour. They occurred at longer intervals than the medieval wars. This is why we are often deluded into thinking that the pacification of large regions and their organization as great powers was beneficial to mankind after all. Even if wars were not completely eliminated, their number was greatly reduced. But it is not the quantity that matters. It is the quality that counts. Being waged by great powers, these wars were no longer little conflicts with their inevitable crop of a few casualties, and their tendency to recur with the regularity of seasons. There were now prolonged spells of peace, with no casualties at all. But when wars finally did break out, they sucked into their maelstrom each time a major part of the world. What might have been saved in the prolonged spells of peace, was now destroyed with a terrifying multiplier. A single month of a modern great-power war costs more in life and wealth than the sum total of casualties and destruction of several centuries of medieval warfare put together.

The great powers, instead of pacifying the world, merely eliminated the much ridiculed operetta wars of the *dark* ages, giving us the
real thing instead. Otherwise, their establishment changed nothing.
The causes of war are still as ridiculous as they always were because
great powers, while they have become fatter than their predecessors,
have not become wiser. Previously, when two customs officials on the
bridge across the Rhine linking Strassburg and Kehl engaged in a
brawl, and each claimed that his country's uniform had been shamed
and must be avenged, the worst that could happen was a war between
Baden and Alsace. The states fifty miles in the rear on either side were
left in peace. Not being united with the belligerents, they would have
considered it silly to take offence at an insult directed at neighbours
with whom they had, politically, nothing in common. The same incident occurring in our time will still produce war, and even more so
since the big are touchier than the small. But this war will not stop at
the boundaries of Alsace and Baden, which are no longer the states on
either side of the Rhine. Today, these states are France and Germany,
two great powers. This means that into a brawl of two customs officials
on a distant bridge on the Rhine will now be drawn the people of Normandy living on the Atlantic, the people of Corsica living on an island
in the Mediterranean, the people of Mecklenburg living on the shores
of the Baltic, and the people of Bavaria living in the Alps. And because
the famous great powers have less confidence in their ability to handle
their conflicts alone than have small states and are, therefore, in their
perpetual scare, perpetually allied with other powers, great and little,
an exchange of slaps between two customs officials at Strassburg will
almost immediately be followed by a similar exchange between officials
at Vladivostok or Yokohama. With the isolating boundaries of little
states removed in the interest of unity, every minor cause of dispute is
likely to produce a chain reaction of global proportions. War has become indivisible.

Thus, the fact that modern wars are fewer in number can hardly be
considered a praiseworthy contribution to peace if we take into account
the misery they spread from one end of the world to the other. No
small-state world could ever have produced similar effects, as the history of the Middle Ages shows, or even the contemporary history of
the only large area where a small-state arrangement still exists—
South America. There are always wars and revolutions going on in that
continent, wars that nobody notices, which come and go like spring
showers, which are settled without the expensive apparatus of a United
Nations or a continental super-government, and which can be dismissed

from the calendar of events by an editorial. The very fact that they inspire composers of operettas rather than profound political thinkers who would be indignant to be bothered with such trifles, shows their harmless nature. But one wonders whether a people would not prefer to be the victim of a ridiculous operetta war that creates a sensation in Hollywood to being the participant in a pompous modern great-power war that creates a sensation in our history books.

The great powers, arising in the guise of pacifiers, have thus given the world nothing but aches. They represent no progress. Instead of solving the problems of small states, they have magnified them to such unbearable proportions that only divine power, and no longer the ability of mortal man, could cope with them. This is why already Aristotle warned that 'to the size of states there is a limit, as there is to other things, plants, animals, implements', and that

'. . . a great city is not to be confounded with a populous one. Moreover, experience shows that a very populous city can rarely, if ever, be well governed; since all cities which have a reputation for good government have a limit of population. We may argue on grounds of reason, and the same result will follow. For law is order, and good law is good order; but a very great multitude cannot be orderly: to introduce order into the unlimited is the work of a divine power—of such power as holds together the universe.'[1]

A similar conclusion was drawn by the Duke of Sully, the Prime Minister of Henry IV of France, who wrote in his *Memoirs* that 'It may be generally observed that the larger the extent of kingdoms, the more they are subject to great revolutions and misfortunes.'[2] In logical application of his convictions he elaborated together with his king what has since become known as the *Great Design*. The purport of this plan was 'to divide Europe equally among a certain number of powers, in such a manner that none of them might have cause either of envy or fear from the possessions or power of the others'.[3] There were to be fifteen states of equal size—six hereditary monarchies: France, Spain, England or Britain, Denmark, Sweden, and Lombardy; five elective monarchies: the Holy Roman Empire, the Papacy or Pontificate, Poland, Hungary, and Bohemia; and four republics: Venice, Italy,

[1] W. D. Ross, *The Student's Oxford Aristotle*. London, New York, Toronto: Oxford University Press, 1942, vol. 6, 1326 a.

[2] Duke of Sully, *Memoirs*. London: Henry G. Bohn, 1856, vol. 4, p. 225.

[3] Ibid., p. 244.

Switzerland, and Belgium. The main victim of this reorganization of Europe was to be the overpowering family empire of the Habsburgs.

No one, however, has exposed the shortcomings and misery of excessive social size, and castigated its worshippers, more scathingly than Saint Augustine. Advocating in a famous passage (*The City of God*, Book III, Chapter XV) that there should be in the world as many kingdoms as there are many families in a city, he lashes out at the glorifiers of the big in these words (Book IV, Chapter III):

'Now then let us examine the nature of this spaciousness, and continuance of empire, which these men give their gods such great thanks for; . . . But first, I would make a little inquiry, seeing you cannot show such estates to be anyway happy, as are in continual wars, being still in terror, trouble, and guilt of shedding human blood, though it be their foes'; what reason then, or what wisdom shall any man show in glorying in the largeness of empire, all their joy being but as a glass, bright and brittle, and evermore in fear and danger of breaking?'

What reason indeed shall any man show in glorying in great powers whose only virtue is that they are big? And this, as the world has painfully discovered, is not a virtue. It produces neither strength nor courage. Being 'evermore in fear and danger of breaking', the policy of the big is considerably less daring or inspiring than that of the small states. In the pre-World-War-II struggle with Hitler, only little states such as the Netherlands, Austria, or Switzerland dared to challenge the mighty man. They claimed their independence by virtue of their existence, not by the dictator's gracious offers of guarantees, which they turned proudly down. On the other hand, the great powers, in abject though justified fear of developing cracks in their huge immobile hulks at the slightest disturbance, betrayed all their principles for the sake of unprincipled expediency, accepting, as in the case of France, gratefully the indignity of being 'guaranteed' by a foreigner.

If the great powers had at least produced superior leadership in their process of growing so that they could have matched the magnitude of the problems which they produced! But here, too, they failed because, as Gulliver observed, 'Reason did not extend itself with the Bulk of the Body.'[1] Political wisdom, like many another virtue, seems to thrive

[1] Jonathan Swift, op. cit., p. 140.

only on smallness, as we shall see later on. Little states produce greater wisdom in their policies because they are weak. Their leaders could not get away with stupidity, not even in the short run. It is not by accident that the politically and socially most advanced countries of the world today are states such as Switzerland (4 million inhabitants), Denmark (4 million), Sweden (7 million), Norway (3 million), Iceland (less than 160 thousand). Large powers, on the other hand, can get away with stupidity for prolonged periods. But who amongst us, if he feels that he can get away with stupidity, which can be had so effortlessly, will ever take the trouble and pains of being wise?

For all this the great powers, which have grown by destroying the small, giving us nothing in return except problems which even they can no longer handle in spite of the vastness of their strength, must at last themselves be destroyed if we are to get anywhere at all. *They* are the world's principal peace disturbers, not the small whom they are ever so ready to blame. What Saint Augustine reasoned seems, therefore, still as sound today as it appeared to him when he contemplated the meaningless vastness of Ancient Rome: that 'the world would be most happily governed if it consisted not of a few aggregations secured by wars of conquest, with their accompaniments of despotism and tyrannic rule, but of a society of small States living together in amity, not transgressing each other's limits, unbroken by jealousies'.[1]

[1] This summary of Saint Augustine's views is from John Neville Figgis, *The Political Aspects of S. Augustine's 'City of God'*. London: Longmans, Green and Co., 1921, p. 58.

Chapter Four

TYRANNY IN A SMALL-STATE WORLD

'Kings in the beginning were diverse in their goodness . . .
and men's lives in those times were without all exorbitance
of habit or affect, each one keeping in his own compass.'

SAINT AUGUSTINE

*In miniature all is soluble. The effect of the small-state pattern
on dictatorship. It either shortens dictatorial government or
enlightens it. It prevents the spread of the dictatorial germ.
What would have happened if Hitler had succeeded in his beer-
hall putsch and become a petty tyrant in Bavaria. Huey Long's
limited power and shortened life span due to a small-state pattern
existing in the United States. Small-state principle solves the
power problem of huge Labour Unions and Monopolies. The
mattress principle.*

As the preceding chapters have shown, neither the problems of war
nor those relating to the purely internal criminality of societies
disappear in a small-state world; they are merely reduced to
bearable proportions. Instead of hopelessly trying to blow up man's
limited talents to a magnitude that could cope with hugeness, hugeness
is cut down to a size where it can be managed even with man's limited
talents. In miniature, problems lose both their terror and significance,
which is all that society can ever hope for. Our choice seems therefore
not between crime and virtue but between big crime and small crime;
not between war and peace, but between great wars and little wars,
between indivisible total and divisible local wars.

But not only the problems of war or crime become soluble on a
small scale. *Every* vice shrinks in significance with the shrinking size of
the social unit in which it develops. This is particularly true of a social
misery which seems to many as unwelcome as war itself. Tyranny!

There is nothing in the constitution of men or states that can prevent the rise of dictators, fascist or otherwise. Power maniacs exist every-where, and every community will at some time or other pass through a phase of tyranny. The only difference lies in the *degree* of tyrannical government which, in turn, depends once more on the *size* and *power* of the countries falling victim to it.

Having just shaken ourselves free of the tyranny of nazism, and being contemporaries of the tyranny of communism, we need not strain our imagination to visualize both the internal as well as the external consequences of the establishment of dictatorial power in a large state. Internally, the machine at the disposal of the dictator is so colossal that only the insane see any sense in being brave. The vast majority is con-demned either to a life of misery or of heil-yelling uniformity. But his power has also external effects. It spills over boundaries, overshadow-ing small as well as powerful neighbours. The small because, in spite of their formal independence, they have no chance to resist, and the powerful because they have no way of knowing whether a challenge to the dictator would usher in his or their destruction. So they, too, will do the dictator's bidding. Whenever he moves, the entire world reverberates from the distant thunders of his brewing designs. Only a costly and uncertain war could liberate it from its awesome suspense.

Since great power is by definition an element that can single-handedly throw the world from its balance, a single dictator in a large state is sufficient to disturb the peace of mind of all. As a result, a great-power world is safe and secure only if the government of *each* great power is in the hands of wise and good men (a combination that is rare even in democracies). As things are, however, great power attracts by its very nature the strong rather than the wise, and autocrats rather than democrats. So it is not surprising that, of the eight great powers exist-ing before World War II, not one but four were under dictatorial rule: Germany, Italy, Japan, and Russia; and of the Big Four of the post-war world, two—Russia and China. And though there are only two great-power dictatorships at the present time, there is not a corner on the globe remote enough to escape the terror of their existence.

1. *The Limitation of Evil*

Now let us trace the effects of the same problem in a small-state world. If a power maniac gets hold of a government there, both the internal and external consequences are vastly different. Since a small state is by nature weak, its government, which can draw the measure of its strength only from the measure of the country over which it rules, must likewise be weak. And if government is weak, so must be its dictator. And if a dictator is weak, he can be overthrown with the same leisurely effort which he himself had to apply in order to overthrow the preceding government. If he becomes too arrogant, he will hang on a lamp-post or lie in a gutter before he has time to awaken to the fact that he has lost power. No police force in a little state can be great enough to protect him from even minor rebellions.

The first and most important benefit derived from a small-state arrangement is thus the shortening of a dictator's life span or, at least, of his term of office—unless he decides to be wise rather than to engage in self-destructive assertions of his power. And this is the second benefit. Since arrogance and bullying are dangerous in a small state, a dictator cherishing his life is practically driven into a rule beneficial to the public. Deprived of the opportunity of glorying in the pleasures of vice, he will do the next best thing and glory in the more subtle satisfactions of virtue. He will employ architects and painters rather than generals and hangmen, and improve the lot of the workers rather than the glamour of his soldiers' uniforms.

History shows that the short-lived as well as the good dictatorship are phenomena that have existed primarily in little states. The first never mattered because of its brief existence, and the second because of the actual benefits the world derived from a good dictator's rule. The history of the ancient Greek city-states, the medieval Italian and German principalities, and the modern South American republics abounds in examples of both these categories of petty tyrants, the short-lived and the good. If the theorists of unity use again the term *comic opera figures* to describe them, they characterize them exactly as what they are—men who are ineffectual even if they are bad. The only thing that seems out of place in such operatic designations is their contemptuous undertone. Ineffectualness means the lack of power to tyrannize mankind—a condition for which the 'comic opera' rulers should be blessed, not castigated. When will our theorists realize that the greatest blessing our statesmen could give us would be to transform the stark and worthy tragedies of modern mass existence back into the ridiculous problems of an operetta?

Thus, *internally*, with the small power supplied by a small state not even the worst dictator is able to frighten his subjects into the kind of creeping submissiveness which even the best dictator commands in a large power. For though also the small-state dictator outranks his subjects, he can never out-tower them.

However, what is still more important as regards the world outside, the small-state dictator is *completely* ineffectual *externally*. Unlike the might of Hitler which made itself felt in an uneasy France years before he actually attacked her and she was still considered a great power, a small-state dictator's sway ends at his country's border creeks. Being hardly able to frighten anyone at home, he can frighten nobody at all abroad. His manias are limited to his own territory whose narrow confines act like the cushioned walls of an isolation ward in a lunatic asylum. Any chain reaction of folly is bound to fizzle out when it reaches the boundaries. Communism, which is such a terrible tool in the hands of a great-power dictator, is externally so ineffectual in the little Republic of San Marino that most of us do not even known that there *is* a communist state also this side of the Iron Curtain. But what the might of the United Nations cannot contain within Russia, a dozen Italian gendarmes can contain within San Marino.

One might say that, although a small-state world limits a dictator's power to his own territory, the dictatorial germ itself might spread and gradually infect others. This is possible, but this, too, would be harmless because in that case dictatorial governments would merely multiply in number, but not grow in bulk or external threat, since the states in which they could develop represent competing interests and, therefore, tend to balance each other. They cannot be used for fusion and aggregation of power. Moreover, since a world consisting of hundreds of small sovereignties with a multitude of differing political systems would constantly react to different forces and trends at different times, the spread of dictatorial influences would be matched by the spread of democratic influences elsewhere. By the time they reached the extremity of the map, they would in all likelihood have begun to fade away in the regions where they originated. In a small-state world, there is a constant breathing and sneezing and changing that never permits the development of gigantic sub-surface forces. These can arise only in a large-power arrangement which provides prolonged periods of peace and allows powers to inhale with their formidable chests for entire decades, only to blow down everything in front of them when, at last, they begin to exhale their hurricanes.

2. *Hitler in Bavaria and Long in Louisiana*

We all know what happened to the world when Hitler became master of the great power of Germany. It made Germany terrible even in peace, and her neighbours were as afraid of her assertions of friendship as of her threats. But let us assume that the same man had managed

73

to obtain dictatorial power only in Bavaria as he attempted in his famous beer-hall putsch of 1923. It may have been a catastrophe for the world that this early attempt failed.

In 1923, at least part of Germany was still organized on a small-state pattern. Life in little states being more individualistic than in large powers, people do not, as a rule, act as if shell-shocked when they have to deal with government. Consequently, Hitler might either have met the fate of Kurt Eisner, Bavaria's communist dictator, who preceded him in the experiment and was promptly assassinated. Or he might have been granted a few years of rule that could not have extended beyond Bavaria's small territory. The neighbouring states, with the natural reaction towards the success of a competing government in a competing state, would have been on double guard against the staging of a similar putsch on their soil while Hitler, unable to satisfy his power complex in a little state, would have frustrated himself into impotence by the sheer paradox of his condition. As dictator of Bavaria, he might never have become dictator of Germany. He might have remained a crude amateur and petty tyrant with an abbreviated life span, considering that small states can organize the downfall of a dictator overnight. But unfortunately he failed in Bavaria and acquired mastery of the great power of Germany instead. The result was that he not only became virtually irremovable; he forced the greatest minds of his generation to take issue with what they previously called romantic or criminal lunacy, making them wonder whether he was not actually the super-genius Goebbels claimed him to be. In Bavaria, he might for lack of other outlets have decided to annoy or enchant the world, as a Grandma-Moses-sort of primitive from the Inn Valley, with his pictures. In Germany, the same man was able to shatter it like a Napoleonic apparition with his wars. In Bavaria, the neighbouring Wurtemberg or Austria would have been able to cope with him—as, indeed, they did. In Germany, the combined power of Great Britain, France, the United States and the Soviet Union could not prevent the nazi dam from bursting.

But we do not need to confine ourselves to hypothetical speculations in visualizing the always harmless effects of dictatorship in small states. In the United States, where we actually do have a small-state organization, the problem of regional dictatorship has never reached unmanageable proportions. Some will say that Americans are too free a people to submit to tyranny, or that we are too educated to produce dictators, and that *this* is the reason why dictatorship constitutes no problem here. Neither opinion seems valid. There have been dictators, and, by logical consequence, there have been submissions even here. Our good fortune is not that dictators cannot arise, but that they cannot spread. Their influence is neatly arrested at the state boundaries, and no federal military intervention is required to stop them there. Whatever degree of governmental authority local tyrants may possess in their own states, they can be of no danger to others. Huey Long was as obnoxious a figure, and had as absolute aspirations, as Hitler. If he was ineffectual, it was only because he was a small-state boss, as Hitler would have been had he won in Bavaria. Being without power, there were limits to the effects of his designs. True, the dictatorial germ did spread but Huey could not spread, and even the germ could not go far because of the slowing-down action of boundaries.[1] At present, the germ has reached a stage of virulence in Georgia, but again it is neatly confined and, by the time it might reach Florida, it will in all likelihood have expired in Georgia. But even where dictatorships do exist in states of the American union, they are so weak that they are unable to scare anyone except the government officials in the state in question.

But let us assume that, in the place of the many little states, there had been only one great and powerful Southern state. Huey Long, as he succeeded in Louisiana, might just as well have succeeded there. But he could no longer have been overthrown so easily as he actually was. He would have ceased to be a comic opera figure. He would have been an arrogant lord not only to the citizens of his own state, but of all the

[1] Sir George Thomson, in an article in the *Listener* of 23 March 1950, describing the conditions bringing forth an atomic chain reaction, furnishes in the following an analysis which is as revealing of the problems of the social world as it is regarding those of the world of atoms: 'The process (of the chain reaction) is enormously rapid once it really gets going and the result is a violent explosion. It is really rather like the spread of a disease with the atoms in the role of patients and the neutrons acting like germs. Now just as the disease will spread better if people are living close together in a city than if they are widely scattered, so here one needs to have a lot of plutonium together to make it go off. If there is only a little, or if it is spread out too sparsely, the neutrons will escape into space without finding an atom to infect, and the epidemic will die out at an early stage. In fact, there are always neutrons in the air and a piece of plutonium is always being slightly infected, but nothing much happens unless there is enough material in a mass to allow the chain reaction to spread—and then the bomb goes off. So the act of firing the bomb consists in bringing pieces of the material together till they form a mass exceeding what is called the critical size.' Similarly, the infected germ of dictatorship cannot produce much harm in a small-state world whose separating boundaries prevent the accumulation of 'enough mass' for a chain reaction to take place. If there are only small states, or states with sparse populations, which amounts to the same thing, the dictatorial germ, like a neutron, will escape into space without finding enough human atoms to infect.

states of the continent. His morning moods would have been the object of hope and concern from New York to Los Angeles. Instead of being castigated and ridiculed, he would have been decorated and honoured. And his safety would have been protected against an assassin's bullets by an army of SS guards such as could never be afforded by little Louisiana.

But there would have been a worse sequel than this. For large-scale tyranny becomes not only respectable and practically irremovable because of the impressive physical force it is able to muster in its defence; it becomes doubly so by breeding at a critical magnitude in the people the appropriate philosophy of submission. In previous applications of the power or size theory of social misery we have found that a criminal mental climate is not cause but consequence of the mass commission of crime, and the aggressive state of mind not cause but consequence of the acquisition of aggressive power. For the same reason, it is not submissive disposition that leads to the misery of tyranny, but tyrannical power, growing in proportion to the size of the community, that leads at a critical magnitude to the condoning spirit of submission. Submissiveness is thus not a human quality that could be explained to a significant extent as the result of upbringing, tradition, national character, or the mode of production. Like most other social attitudes, it is the adaptive reflex reaction with which man responds to power. Its degree varies directly with the degree of power, just as its opposite reaction, the assertion of freedom, varies inversely with it. Where there is power, there is submission, and where there is no submission, there is no power. This is why, historically, the seemingly most freedom-loving peoples have accepted tyranny as submissively as the seemingly most submissive ones,[1] or why it is safe to say that even Americans

[1] This contradicts the flattering self-portrait of many but not the facts of history. It is said, for example, that the seemingly freedom-loving French would never submit to tyranny in the measure shown by the Germans. Yet, when the nazis extended their sway over them, they—as also the Danes, Dutch, or Poles—proved as submissive to their tyranny as the Germans. While there were resistance movements, as a mass phenomenon they were characteristic of post-war development, not of the period of actual German domination. Then even nazis discovered they were resisters. Though the French had a series of revolutions, these were never directed against strong governments. Under Louis XIV and XV, they accepted the most outrageous degree of royal exploitation, waste, arrogance, intolerance, and immorality without a murmur. But when the throne fell into the hands of Louis XVI, a perfectly charming, impotent, humble, and well-meaning king whose greatest extravagance was his tender affection for flowers, they at last staged the revolution that still overwhelms posterity with its exalted principles that were not French, and its daring that was not great. (Liberty, equality, fraternity, being practised for centuries in the mountains of Switzerland and Tyrol,

would submit if our federal structure permitted the accumulation of the necessary volume of governmental power. For, as young Boswell confided so touchingly to his *London Journal*, 'when the mind knows it cannot help itself by struggling, it quietly and patiently submits to *whatever* load is laid upon it' (italics mine).

3. The Mattress Principle

Fortunately, however, the United States is internally not an uneasy assembly of great powers, such as would have permitted critical accumulations, but of small states. As a result she benefits from the smooth flexibility that characterizes all small-cell organisms, rendering them capable of adaptation to constantly changing human and social conditions. A small-cell union has the same advantages, and has them for the same reasons, as the newly developed and much advertised mattresses which are built on the principle of the coexistence of a great multitude of *small independent* springs, rather than on the principle of unitarian construction where all springs are tightly interlocked. As a result, only those springs are compressed which are actually touched by the body, giving the whole a resiliency and duration that had never before been possible. With the previous unitarian and interlocking construction, on the other hand, the depression of a single spring pressed all the others down as well, producing eventually an unregenerative sleeping hole, ruining even those springs that were left unused.

But not in all her relationships is the United States a small-state complex, and where it is not, we see a repetition of the same problems

were so alien to France, that it was not until 1789 that they were introduced. And even then they were practised only at brief intervals until they prevailed in 1871.) Hardly had they guillotined their king, they accepted submissively the tyranny of Napoleon, following him with a devotion matched only by that displayed by the nazis under Hitler. True, they also rebelled against Napoleon, but only after he had been hopelessly defeated in the field, and rebellion meant no longer love of freedom but treason. Peoples never revolt against tyrants. They only revolt against the weak. If the Germans had no great romantic revolution, it is not, as popular theory has it, that they are more submissive than others. It is because the historically necessary precondition to every popular uprising, the sudden weakening of a previously strong government, only rarely materialized in their case. When it did, as in 1918, they rebelled as lustily as their neighbours, dethroning not only one sovereign, the Kaiser, but all their kings, grand dukes, dukes, and princes. Space forbids us to present the mass of material, amusing and disenchanting, showing how all peoples, the English, the French, the Czechs, the Germans, have always been submissive to governmental power in proportion to its magnitude, not in proportion to their feelings of liberty or their national character.

of size which are typical of all large-area or large-power organizations. Thus, private economic power, unlike the political power of the states, is *not* limited by state boundaries. As a result, we find that a number of economic powers and enterprises have been organized on a large-scale, coast-to-coast, basis. This means that each of them is in a position to throw the entire nation, not just a single state, off its balance if mood or ambition should counsel such a course.

Nowhere is this unchallengeable great-power domination more dramatically evident than in the vast national labour unions. A raising of John L. Lewis's formidable eyebrows may paralyse the vital coal-mining industry, not in one state or two, but in all the states of the union. A frown on his forehead may mean a cold winter for 165 million people. A word from his lips may stop trains and arrest the wheels of hundreds of industries. It may deprive us of gas and light. A single gesture of John L. Lewis or of any of a number of important labour leaders may spell catastrophe to the nation. Organized on a continental basis, unions have become utterly unmanageable because of the formidable power they are able to acquire, a power wholly unnecessary for the realization of labour's aims, or rather one that *would* be unnecessary if the small-state system had been applied also economically. As long as this is not done, giant enterprises will exist, and as long as there are giant enterprises, the law of balance will demand giant unions.

It is easy to visualize the insignificance of union-management difficulties in an *economic* small-state world. John L. Lewis, as Governor Long did with his state, would still dominate a union, but a union whose power would end at the state boundaries. During the course of a year, there would be strikes just as there are now, in several or all states, but, according to the mattress principle, they would not be linked or interlocked. They would remain individual, and individual problems are always more easily solved than intertwined mass problems. The workers would still get what they want because employers —now likewise unable to form interstate combines—would not be more daring in their refusals of concessions simply because they have to deal with local instead of national unions. On the contrary, they would be more amenable because they, too, would now be weaker. Life, after all, is lived locally, and local pressures are the ones that count. Problems of industrial strife would thus still exist, but they could not get out of hand. They could be solved with a volume of power that would be moderate and yet bring satisfaction to labour without becoming a problem in its own right, that is to say, without becoming power problems in addition to being labour problems.

The same is true with regard to the vast aggregations of power on the side of employers, though, in their case, the small-cell or mattress principle needs less argument because we have long been familiarized with the dangers inherent in employers' unions and unifications. The moment we talk of monopolies, combines, holding companies, or cartels, we realize what the concentration of vast economic power in the hands of a few means. So our legislators have never ceased studying the question of how to cut down their size. But the simplest method, instead of enacting futile prohibitions, would have been to establish the small-state or federal principle, which has succeeded so superbly politically, also economically. With all economic power of a private nature, and serving private purposes, ending at the state boundaries, the monster of size would vanish by itself. And with it would vanish the need of those monstrously powerful labour unions whose sole valid justification is that the enterprises with which they have to deal are likewise monstrously powerful. As our state boundaries constitute no *traffic* barriers, this would not mean the establishment of *tariff* barriers. Nor would a reduction of economic *power* mean a reduction of economic *productivity* and, with it, a lowering of the standard of living. In fact, as Chapter VIII will show, it would mean the opposite.

Thus we see that a small-state world would not only solve the problems of social brutality and war; it would solve the equally terrible problems of oppression and tyranny. It would solve all problems arising from power. Indeed, there is no misery on earth that cannot be successfully handled on a small scale as, conversely, there is no misery on earth that can be handled at all *except* on a small scale. In vastness, everything crumbles, even the good, because, as will increasingly become evident, the world's one and only problem is not wickedness but bigness; and not the thing that is big, whatever it may be, but bigness itself. This is why through union or unification, which enlarges bulk and size and power, nothing can be solved. On the contrary, the possibility of finding solutions recedes in the ratio at which the process of union advances. Yet all our collectivized and collectivizing efforts seem to be directed towards this one fantastic goal—unification. Which, of course, is a solution, too. The solution of spontaneous collapse.

Chapter Five

THE PHYSICS OF POLITICS

'Guid gear comes in wee bulk.'
SCOTS PROVERB
'Care is taken that the trees do not scrape the skies.'
GERMAN PROVERB

Limitation to all growth. The universe as a microcosmos. Lucretius's primal particles and Planck's quanta. Fred Hoyle's theory of the origin of the earth. Instability of the too large. Correction through fission. Balance versus unity. Schrödinger on why atoms are small. Small-cell principle basic to mobile balance. Mobile versus stable balance. Disturbances of balance due to development of large aggregations. The principle of division. Division as the principle of progress and health. The organization of hell.

The Philosophic Argument

UNTIL now we have dealt with the idea of dividing the great powers from the point of view of expediency. Reduced to smallness, we have found, states lose their terror potentialities, problems their difficulties, and vice much of its significance.

This is no accident, for smallness is not only a convenience. It is the design of God. The entire universe is built on it. We live in a microcosmos, not in a macrocosmos. Perfection has been granted only to the little. Only in the direction of the minuscule do we ever come to an end, to a finite, a boundary, where we can conceive the ultimate mystery of existence. In the direction of the colossal we arrive nowhere. We may add and multiply, and produce increasingly vaster figures and substances, but never an end, as there is nothing that cannot always again be doubled, though doubling in the physical sense soon means collapse, disintegration, catastrophe. There is an invisible barrier to size beyond which matter cannot accumulate. Only non-existing mathematical shadows can penetrate further. Division, on the other hand, brings us eventually to the existing, though unseen, ultimate substance of all things, to particles which defy any further division. They are the only substances which creation has endowed with unity. They alone are indivisible, indestructible, eternal. Lucretius has called these the *first bodies* or *primal particles* and, in an unsurpassed piece of reasoning, has argued in the *Nature of Things* (Bk. I, vv. 610 ff.) that they alone

> Are solid in their singleness, close packed
> And dense with their least parts, yet never framed
> By union of those parts, but holding fast
> In their eternal oneness; nor one jot
> Does nature suffer to be torn away
> Therefrom, or be removed, keeping them safe
> As seeds of things. Besides, if there were not
> Some smallest thing, each tiniest body must
> Of infinite parts consist, since halves of halves
> Will still have halves, nor aught will set a bound.
> How then will differ the full sum of things
> From least of things? No difference thou wilt find;
> For, hold the sum unbounded as thou wilt,
> Each tiniest thing will equally be formed
> Of infinite parts. But since true reason crieth
> That this is false, forbidding mind belief,
> So must thou yield forthwith and own the truth:
> That there exist those things which must be formed
> With nature truly least. Since these are such,
> Thou must confess the primal particles
> Are solid and eternal.[1]

All other things are combinations of these primal particles, combinations and aggregations that are infinite in number and variety, but always stemming from the same unchanging particles. It is a testimony to the unique perception and deductive powers of ancient philosophers such as Lucretius or his great predecessors Democritus and Epicurus that modern science, with all its resources and laboratory facilities, could do no more than *prove* what they had *reasoned* while lying daydreaming in the shadow of a poplar. Thus Max Planck, in his famous Quantum Theory which, together with Einstein's Relativity Theory, forms the basis of modern physics, confirmed experimentally in the twentieth century in what has been called one of the great discoveries

[1] Lucretius, *On the Nature of Things*. New York: Walter J. Black, 1946, pp. 30 ff.

of all time, that the universe does not consist of vast unified entities infinite in both extremes but of discontinuous particles radiating in small bundles, the *quanta*. As he himself phrased it: 'Radiant heat is not a continuous flow and indefinitely divisible. It must be defined as a discontinuous mass made up of units all of which are similar to one another.' Though these units, the quanta or indivisible primal particles, vary with the frequency of their radiation, they are nevertheless all reducible to *Planck's Constant*, the perpetual and apparently only absolute element in the physical universe. It is defined as equal to 6·55 billion-billion-billionth erg-seconds.

It was the knowledge derived from the Quantum Theory that has enabled us to penetrate the secret of the atom and, with it, of the entire universe. We found the key to the big by searching for the small, and it is not without significance that our age, which has developed such perverse yearnings for social colossalism and world-embracing organizations, is not named the colossal or unitarian age, but the atomic age, not after the largest but after one of the smallest aggregations of matter.

1. Smallness, the Basis of Stability

Whatever we investigate, the vast universe or the little atom, we find that creation has manifested itself in manifold littleness rather than in the simplicity of huge bulk. Everything is small, limited, discontinuous, disunited. Only relatively small bodies—though not the smallest, as we shall see—have stability. Below a certain size, everything fuses, joins, or accumulates. But beyond a certain size, everything collapses or explodes.

We need only look into the night sky to realize how there is a limit to everything, and a very narrow limit at that. The most gigantic stars are mere specks in space, and the vastest galaxies mere discs which our eyes can hold in a single glance. Fred Hoyle gives us a picture of celestial proportions when he pictures the sun as a ball six inches in diameter, and then asks:

'Now how far away are the planets from our ball? Not a few feet or one or two yards, as many people seem to imagine in their subconscious picture of the solar system, but very much more. Mercury is about 7 yards away, Venus about 13 yards away, the Earth 18 yards away, Mars 27 yards, Jupiter 90 yards, Saturn 179 yards, Uranus about 350 yards, Neptune 540 yards, and Pluto 710 yards. On this scale the

Earth is represented by a speck of dust and the nearest stars are about 2,000 miles away.'[1]

Individually, heavenly bodies may seem huge, but what are they in relation to space? True, they do sometimes grow into what astronomers call supergiants, but from that moment on they are on the road not of conquest but of destruction. Instead of *generating* energy they now begin—as do the great powers in the political universe—to *absorb* it. Their very effort of existence forces them to consume more than they receive. In the description of Fred Hoyle, they begin to live off their capital until, in their terrific spurt of power expansion, their supply of hydrogen becomes exhausted. Then their brief spasm of grandeur revenges itself. They collapse. But this is not the entire story. In the process of collapsing, their internal forces, set up by rotation, increase to such an extent that eventually a stage is reached 'at which the rotary forces become comparable with gravity itself'.[2] This is when the giants of the universe break up in the fantastic spectacles of explosion which we call *supernovae*. Fred Hoyle maintains that the planets of our own solar system are the remnants of a twin star to the Sun that 'must have been appreciably more massive than the Sun' itself.[3] As a result it exploded and instead of the luminous giant it hoped to be, it is now a *black dwarf* floating in outer darkness, and recognized not even by its own descendants. Giant size does not fit the pattern of creation. Whenever it develops, it destroys itself in violence and disaster.

This does not mean that the ideal size of existing things ought to be the *very* smallest. If that were the case, the universe would and should consist of nothing but atoms and quanta. But this was obviously not the purpose of creation either. To judge from the overwhelming variety of forms and substances, which could develop only on the basis of a myriad of aggregations, combinations, and fusions, it is in aggregations and combinations that life finds its true fulfilment, not in simple unitarian one-cell structures. As a result, things can be too little as they can be too large, with instability adhering to both developmental stages. This is why the universe, as long as it consisted of nothing but atomized dust, was an unstable chaos that had to find stability by combining and condensing its particles into the form of stars and other bodies of considerable weight and solidity.

However, this very process shows that the instability of the too small is not only a minor problem; it is also of a fundamentally different

[1] Fred Hoyle, *The Nature of the Universe*. Oxford: Basil Blackwell, 1950, p. 16.
[2] Ibid., p. 77.   [3] Ibid., p. 75.

character from that of the instability of the too large. It is a *constructive* instability for which nature has provided a self-regulating device in the mechanism of growth. Through this, aggregations and fusions are automatically fostered until a proper and stable size is reached, until their function-determined form is fulfilled.[1] This accomplished, they come to an equally automatic end. Thus, apart from cases of freak developments, no one needs ever to worry about things that are too little.

The instability of the too large, on the other hand, is a *destructive* one. Instead of being *stabilized* by growth, its instability is *emphasized* by it. The same process, so beneficial below a certain size, now no longer leads to maturity but to disintegration. This effect has been utilized by plant specialists who kill some kinds of weed not by laboriously trying to prevent their form-fulfilling growth but by trickily fostering the much deadlier process of overgrowth, making what they want to annihilate, too big. Sir George Thomson has described the phenomenon of the instability and self-destructiveness of bigness in an analogy which is all the more interesting as it tries to illustrate a physical process by drawing a comparison from the political field as this book tries to illustrate a political process by drawing a comparison from the physical field:

'Atoms of middle weight are stable and inert, but the light as well as the heavy atoms have stores of energy. If one thinks of the heaviest atoms as overgrown empires which are ripe for dissolution and only

---

[1] The only question is: what is the *proper* size of things? This depends on their function or, as D'Arcy Wentworth Thompson explains in his brilliant and exhaustive study *On Growth and Form* (Cambridge: University Press, 1942, p. 24): 'The effect of *scale* depends not on a thing in itself, but in relation to its whole environment or milieu; it is in conformity with the thing's "place in Nature", its field of action and reaction in the Universe. Everywhere Nature works true to scale, and everything has its proper size accordingly. Men and trees, birds and fishes, stars and star-systems, have their appropriate dimensions, and their more or less narrow range of absolute magnitudes. The scale of human observation lies with . . . in the narrow bounds of inches, feet or miles, all measured in terms drawn from our own selves or our own doings. Scales which include light-years, parsecs, Angström units, or atomic and sub-atomic magnitudes, belong to other orders of things and other principles of cognition.' But whatever the magnitude, in relation to the whole of creation even things measured in light-years are of limited dimensions. It is thus never a question of large or small, but of more or less *small*, of the 'more or less *narrow* range of absolute magnitudes', depending on the function things have to perform. This applies also to states. Being not celestial but human aggregations, their magnitudes must be drawn from the stature of man, and be measured in miles and years, not in parsecs and eternities.

held together by special efforts, or perhaps by a genius, one may think, on the other hand, of the lightest of the atoms as individuals which run together naturally for mutual help and readily coalesce to form stable tribes and communities.'[1]

It is always the same revelation: only *small* things, be they atoms, individuals, or communities, can be combined in search of a more stable existence, and even they will coalesce *naturally* only up to a point. Beyond that, what previously helped to fulfil their form, now bursts it, with the result that, as they continue to grow, they become heavier and clumsier until the only thing they do naturally is—fall apart. This is why neither Sir George Thomson's political nor my physical comparisons are really analogies. They are homologies. They are two different manifestations of one and the same principle: the universal principle by which stability and soundness adhere only to bodies of *middle weight* or, to put emphasis where it belongs, to bodies that are relatively *small*.

2. Unity versus Balance

Physics thus seems to demonstrate quite clearly that the universe is neither unitarian nor simple, but multitudinous and complex. Instead of being composed of a small finite number of near-infinite masses of matter which could be kept together only through the conscious assistance of God Himself, it consists of an infinite number of finite little realms which need neither 'special efforts' nor a 'genius' to remain in And they accomplish this incredible feat by an arrangement which, equilibrium. But what holds them together then? They themselves! like so many other devices of creation, is nowadays considered a reprehensible sign of reactionary scheming: by balance—the balance of substances, forces, powers, or whatever one may call it.

There are two ways by which equilibrium and order can be achieved. One is by means of a stable and the other by means of a mobile balance. When in their proper element, both are self-regulatory. The *stable balance* is the balance of the stagnant and the huge. It creates equilibrium by bringing two objects into a fixed and unchanging relationship with each other such as a house with its ground, or a mountain with its plain. Instead of creating harmony, it moulds its diverse parts into unity. Being the balance of the rigid and fixed, it could be

[1] Sir George Thomson, 'The Hydrogen Bomb: a Scientist's View'. *The Listener*, 23 March 1950.

conceived as a *universal* principle only if the universe were still, non-moving, lifeless. Then the existence of only a few large bodies would make sense and, for that matter, even the existence of a single one. But in the bottomless vastness of the abyss of creation, it could be maintained only by the ever-conscious will of God Himself who, in order to prevent it from dropping into nowhere, would have to do nothing less than hold it perpetually in His hands.

Since this was obviously not His intent, He created instead a moving, breathing, and dynamic universe, maintained in order not by unity but harmony, and based not on the stable balance of the dead, but the *mobile balance* of the living. In contrast to the stable balance, this balance is self-regulatory not because of the fixity of its relationships but because of the coexistence of countless mobile little parts of which no one is ever allowed to accumulate enough mass to disturb the harmony of the whole.

This means that smallness is not an accidental whim of creation. It fulfils a most profound purpose. It is the basis of stability and duration, of a graceful harmonious existence that needs no master. For little bodies, countless in number and for ever moving, for ever rearrange themselves in the incalculable pattern of a mobile balance whose function in a dynamic universe is to create orderly systems and organisms without the necessity of interfering with the anarchic freedom of movement granted to their component particles. Erwin Schrödinger, analysing the intrinsic reason for the smallness as well as the infinite number of atoms as the prerequisite to all physical orderliness and the accuracy of all physical laws, has well explained this when he writes:

'And why could all this not be fulfilled in the case of an organism composed of a moderate number of atoms only and sensitive already to the impact of one or a few atoms only?

'Because we know all atoms to perform all the time a completely disorderly heat motion, which, so to speak, opposes itself to their orderly behaviour and does not allow the events that happen between a small number of atoms to enrol themselves according to any recognizable laws. Only in the co-operation of an enormously large number of atoms do statistical laws begin to operate and control the behaviour of these *assemblées* with an accuracy increasing as the number of atoms involved increases. It is in that way that the events acquire truly orderly features. All the physical and chemical laws that are known to play an important part in the life of organisms are of this statistical kind; any other kind of lawfulness and orderliness that one might think of is being perpetually disturbed and made inoperative by the unceasing heat motion of the atoms.'[1]

3. The Physics of Politics

The mobile principle of balance, transforming as it does the anarchy of free particles into systems of high orderliness because of the statistical accuracy arising invariably from the chance interaction of bodies that are both countless and minute, is so evidently the device that keeps the universe from disintegrating that it seems extraordinary that so many of our political theorists, apparently on the assumption that the social universe follows a different order, should have come forth with a battle cry against it. Whenever they encounter it in its political variation as the principle of balance of power, they reject it not only as intriguish and Machiavellian, but also as outmoded and dangerous to peace. In its place they want unity, though this exists nowhere except in unstable primal particles or in the fixity of death. What they actually, though not deliberately, advocate, however, is *disbalance*, since this, not unity, is the only logical alternative to balance. So determined are they in their convictions that even today, in spite of the disturbances produced by their unification efforts, one is looked upon as either irresponsible or mad, or both, if one dares to see wisdom in balance of power instead.

This is the more astounding as everything around us reveals in the most unmistakable manner that there is absolutely nothing that is *not* built on balance. Our solar system is balanced by the sun and the planets. Our galaxy is balanced by a multitude of other galaxies. On our earth the mountains are balanced by the valleys, land by water, seasons by seasons, heat by cold, darkness by light, mosquitoes by birds, silences by sounds, animals by vegetables, age by youth and, the most enchanting of all balances, men by women. Everything, everywhere points to balance, nothing to unity. Without balance we cannot even walk. So overwhelmingly manifest is this principle that many of us conceive even God not only as a Unity but as a Trinity.

If it were for no other reason than this, the conclusion would seem justified that a principle which so obviously applies throughout physical creation should have validity also in the very physical world of politics. This should be particularly evident to analysts living in democracies, considering that there is no system so opposed to the concept of unity as democracy with its careful pattern of balancing

[1] Erwin Schrödinger, *What Is Life?* Cambridge: University Press, 1951, p. 8.

parties and balancing divided powers. No American interested in his safety will rise in a convention of the Republican Party and say: 'For the sake of unity, let us all join the Democrats.' And few would support a President if, in the interest of administrative efficiency and unity, he should suddenly abandon as reactionary the balance-of-power principle and demand the unification of the judicial and legislative branches of government with the executive. Only the totalitarian delights in oneness and unity rather than in the harmony produced by balanced diversity. And what does he gain by it? Casting aside the self-regulatory system of balances, he now needs the special effort of a stabilizer, a genius, a dictator who must consciously hold together what previously arranged itself automatically. For even unity must still be balanced.

4. Mobile versus Stable Balance

As a result, the true problem also in the world of politics—which, after all, is as much subject to the physical interaction of its determinants as the world of atoms or of stars—is not one of balance of power versus unity, but of a *bad* balance versus a *good* one. It is in this direction that our theorists should have extended their research. For what seems wrong with our political universe is, of course, not that it is *balanced*, but that it is *badly* balanced. And it is badly balanced because, unlike the physical universe, it is no longer composed of a *great* number of *small* mobile units which, as we have seen, are essential to an orderly pattern of behaviour, but of a *small* and shrinking number of immobile, though still moving, *huge* units—the great powers. With their emergence, the mobile balance, dependent on manifold littleness, could no longer function satisfactorily, and had to be replaced by a stable balance.

This does not mean that a stable balance is without merit. To be adequate, a balance must furnish an *automatic* equilibrium which relieves its creators of the absorbing and sterile task of keeping it under constant supervision. It must rest in itself. In a world of dead matter, a stable balance meets this requirement to perfection. In fact, it is the only form of balance that keeps inanimate things in their fixed relationships. But, while it fulfils the requirement of adequacy in an inanimate, non-moving world, it loses its self-regulatory character when applied to a moving and living system such as a society of nations. Here a mobile balance is required to ensure proper operation and the necessary correlation of perpetually occurring changes. But a mobile balance, as we have just seen, is dependent on a multitudinous small-cell arrangement which is disrupted when cell unifications take place and large solidified organisms are created in the form of big powers in the political body or of cancerous overgrowth in the human body.

Cell unification, being the characteristic feature of disease as well as of ageing, produces the effect that, whenever it sets in, the rhythm of life is slowed down. What was previously flexible and swift, now becomes slow and rigid. But the balance of the *rigid* is a stable balance. However, even a rigidified big-power system is still moving and living though, like an old man, at a very reduced speed. And this is where the difficulty arises. A mobile balance has become impossible because of the loss of swift energy and the resulting accumulation of massive bulk. And a stable balance is inadequate because even a slow-moving system is still moving, and even an old man is not yet dead. Yet it is the only balance that can be applied under these conditions. But it can no longer function automatically, as a sound system of balances should. Separated from its proper element—the world of the rigid and the dead—a stable balance in the world of politics can be maintained only by conscious and continuous guidance. Every time a movement occurs in an over-aged social system, a powerful authority is needed to rearrange its hardened unified cells in a new balance. Hence the fanatical attempts of the statesmen of our time to create majestic super-governments in the form of League of Nations, United Nations, or World States, betraying that what the despised small-state world could do so effortlessly, the glorified big-power world cannot do at all: govern itself. It requires an external controlling agent.

And this is its added tragedy. Though in desperate need of such an organ, there is no genius to compensate for the loss of automaticity, as there is no human intelligence that could ever for any length of time have power and wisdom enough to furnish the balancing forces necessary to cope even with minor changes of position effected by the helpless hulks of overgrown empires. This is why, even when a chance alliance seems occasionally to provide the necessary power, the result is a balance, a peace, which is distinguished only by everybody doubting the world's ability to maintain it. For its very preservation needs a perpetual effort of such titanic proportions that the effort itself, if miscalculated, might bring about its end. And every effort of such magnitude will eventually be miscalculated, as was so pitifully demonstrated by the United Nations whose collection of peace lovers have produced the disbalance of war more often during their brief existence, and faster, than any previous assembly of men.

The chief symptom of a *bad* balance is thus not that it is either mobile or stable, but that it needs a conscious regulating authority. This happens whenever it is out of place, as when the mobile balance of change is imposed on things that are rigid or a stable balance of rigidity on a dynamic system of change. As a result, a *good* balance in a living, breathing, and changing arrangement—be it a system of stars, states, or men—must be a *mobile* balance, a balance whose self-regulatory feature is derived from the independent existence of a great number of small component parts held together not in tight unity but elastic harmony.

In this lies the subtly soothing charm of the so-called *mobiles* which artists, perhaps in instinctive yearning for the lost bliss of the past, have recently begun to produce: tender structures of many parts and unforeseeable interactions. When one breathes into them, countless exquisite movements and rustling sounds set in, disturbing the position of every eerie limb without for an instant disturbing the harmony of the whole. For in contrast to *unity*, whose slightest disbalance threatens to crack it irreparably asunder, disturbances of *harmony*, even if they were severe —which is mechanically and logically impossible because of the smallness of the parts involved—immediately bring forth such a multitude of internal correcting movements that they re-establish a new equilibrium as a result of their very disequilibrium. The same is true of the political *mobile* of a small-state world. Its disturbances can be much more easily handled than those of a large-power set-up, even as with scales on which there are a great many little weights a disturbed balance can be more easily restored than if there are only a few large ones. In the one case we merely have to manipulate a pebble, in the other a block. But the problem in the latter case is that it may be impossible for us to find a large enough block to match the requirement of balance, or a large enough force to move the block.

5. Division—the Principle of Progress

In the world of politics it is thus not the much maligned principle of balance of power that is at fault, but the loss of its automaticity resulting from the emergence of an immobile big-power world whose increasing calcification causes everything to crack, including the principle on which the universe itself seems built. The task confronting us appears, therefore, clear. Instead of discarding the balance of power and replacing it with the unity of a world state, we must discard our bad balance and replace it with a good one. But how can this be done?

If the mobile balance, necessary to all living systems, deteriorates as a result of the overgrowth of cells, or of the fusion of parts into solid gluts, it follows that it can be restored to proper functioning only through the break-up of its overgrown units and the reintroduction of a flexible small-cell arrangement. In other words, if smallness represents nature's mysterious principle of health, and bigness its principle of disease, *division*—the transformation of a controlled stable into a self-regulatory mobile balance through the splitting of its parts—must of necessity represent its principle of cure. But this is not all, for increasing mobility in moving systems means more than mere restoration of health. It means *improvement* over the less mobile. As a result, division (or multiplication, which exerts a similar reducing effect on the size of things) represents not only the principle of cure but of progress, while unification, which looks so progressive to so many, represents by contrast not only the principle of disease but of primitivism. In terms of politics, the only way of restoring a healthy balance to the world's diseased conditions seems thus through the application of the device which the social considerations of the previous chapters offered as an expedient, and which the physical considerations of the present chapter now impose as a requirement: through the division of those social units which have outgrown manageable proportions; through the dismemberment of the great powers.

If this should still appear as an invitation to retrogression, we need but cast a random look at some of life's other patterns to realize how everywhere, at a given point, the fullness of existence is enhanced through the process not of unification but division. Books are improved by being divided into many chapters. The day—by being broken down into hours for many different pursuits. Languages—through the division of sounds until every nuance is expressed by a different word. Only the primitive is content with a vocabulary consisting of a single Tarzan's yell. The usable area of a house is increased not by eliminating but by erecting walls, not by the unification but the division of living space. An unfenced garden seems to contain nothing: a walled-in little spot of land—the universe. Parties may be saved from boredom not by having all the guests assembled in a single circle dominated by a magnetic personality, but by dissolving the dreaded pattern of unity into a number of small groups sparkling by themselves. Slabs of stone, useless when too big, may be reassembled into delicate mosaics or lofty cathedrals if broken down into small parts. Even cancer, the most dreaded of all unification problems, could be cured if doctors would find a way by which the successful big-power maniacs amongst the body's cells could either be divided or pushed back into the limiting narrowness of their original boundaries.[1]

Similarly in technology, it is the indication not of worsening but of improving design when forces and complexes are divided, and parts are multiplied and reduced in size. Battleships are made virtually unsinkable through the division of their previously unitarian hulk into a number of isolated small compartments. Mountain torrents are tamed through the division of their water masses. United they devastate the land. Disunited into small channels, they irrigate and fertilize it. Ball bearings have solved the problem of friction through the simple but revolutionary device of substituting many small rolling elements for a few large ones. In a modern engine the process of multiplication and division has been carried so far that any single part, as in a small-state world any single state, may get out of order without damaging the system as a whole. An airplane, once dependent on undivided motor power, is now balanced in the sky by four or six engines. Its switchboard has become a maze of buttons and levers, and its structure a composite not of hundreds but thousands of parts. And yet how much safer it is compared to its unitarian ancestor. It is in their stage of crudity that mechanical devices consist only of a few, large, unified parts, balancing uneasily the forces they try to co-ordinate, and breaking down when a single piece fails. On the other hand, the more numerous the parts, the more self-balancing and advanced becomes a

[1] Though for a time growth diseases can be balanced either internally through the body adapting its mechanism to heavier tasks, or externally through the help of doctors, we cannot be really at peace unless the growth is exterminated. For, in spite of the new balance, we know that balance at the level of the big is not only precarious but is bound to collapse under its own strain. Instead of recovering health, we merely acquire another disease—a disease of adaptation. The dangers arising from excessive internal balancing efforts necessary to counteract infection (the unbalanced growth of certain blood cells) have been well demonstrated by H. Selye. After exposing animals to non-specific noxious agents, he observed in each case an ordered march of events: (1) 'The alarm reaction'; (2) 'The stage of resistance'; and (3) 'The stage of exhaustion'. 'The first phase was characterized by a state of shock and the second by an outpouring of adrenocortical hormones which resulted in a fair degree of stability; the third phase was a terminal phenomenon due to wearing-off of the adaptive mechanism.' This means that once a resistance effort of excessive proportions is imposed on the body, the very effort to maintain the now difficult balance between alignments that have become too large on both sides leads to its undoing. For 'the organism ultimately becomes damaged by its own excessive defences and in the end is destroyed by them' in a queer sort of 'biological suicide'. Hence Selye's term 'Diseases of Adaptation'. See *Quarterly Bulletin* of the British Psychological Society, vol. 2, no. 17, July 1952, p. 87.

mechanism. And the more elaborate its pattern of smallness, the more does it begin to resemble the human brain (which likewise seems to have developed the balancing sparks of thought and consciousness as almost automatic reflexes once its substance had become so finely divided that the number of its individual cells began to run into the billions).

The most revealing illustration of the evolutionary and progressive character of the principle of smallness and division, however, is furnished by the story not of mechanical but of organic progress. Modern biology has shown more clearly than any other science that, whenever nature itself improves the design of life, it does so not by uniting but by splitting. Julian Huxley has given this process the appropriate name of *adaptive radiation* or *deployment*. By branching off into a number of different forms, orders, classes, and subclasses, an originally unified group diversifies itself with the result that, instead of finding life more difficult in consequence of the lessening co-operation of its members, it is enabled 'to exploit its new environment much more extensively' and economically than if it had remained uniform and unified.[1] This means that *deployment* is not just mutation. It is improvement, advance, progress. The first step towards *higher* forms of life was accomplished when 'living substance differentiated into four kinds of chemical mechanisms', green plants, bacteria, fungi, and animals. Further progress was achieved when each of these main branches deployed in its turn into countless numbers of species, types, and groups, each new division making the emerging specialized forms 'increasingly efficient in dealing with their particular sector of the environment'. Animals alone subdivided into filter feeders, tentacle feeders, vegetable feeders, pursuers of prey, earth-swallowers, and parasites, and 'if any of them had not evolved, some of the available food-resources would have gone to waste'. As a striking example of improvement through division, Huxley points to

'the groundfinches of the Galapagos Islands, the Geospizidae, which more than anything else persuaded Darwin of the fact of evolution. They are a small group of song-birds, undoubtedly derived from some species of New World finch which got blown out from the mainland and succeeded in establishing itself on this oceanic archipelago. The group now consists of four distinct genera and fourteen separate species, adapted for many distinct modes of life. Some

[1] The quotations in this paragraph and the following footnote are from Julian Huxley, 'Biological Improvement', *The Listener*, 1 November 1951, pp. 739 ff.

are seed-eaters, others omnivorous ground-feeders, others insectivorous, others leaf- and bud-eaters, while one has gone in for a woodpecker type of life.'

Though, with extraordinary disregard for the results and significance of his own research, Huxley concludes that man is different from all other groups, advancing for unspecified reasons not in nature's normal way through separation, division, or divergence, but through the creation of variety-in-unity, fusion, and convergence, historic development indicates that the human race constitutes no exception.[1] For man, too, just like the groundfinches of the Galapagos Islands, has not united but differentiated in order to progress and to enrich his possibilities. Instead of remaining an ever-growing and increasingly integrated entity, he split into races and nationalities. And to emphasize his division, he developed, in addition, different cultures and languages, each of which was necessary if all the available material and intellectual resources were to be utilized. Had all men become Americans, the supportable human population would be very much smaller, and much of life's beauty would have gone unenjoyed. For which American would have wanted life on an ice cap, or in the magnificence of the barren altitudes of Central Asia? By branching off also into Eskimos and Tibetans

---

[1] It is a strange habit of even the most eminent of modern scientists to contradict in their afterthoughts what they have tried to prove in their monumental previous work. Marx, who reasoned most convincingly that every system breeds the germs of its own destruction, made an exception in the case of his own preferred system, socialism. Arnold Toynbee, after showing how every civilization disintegrates when it reaches the stage of a universal state, and how every civilization as yet has reached that fateful stage, comes to the conclusion that Western Civilization, which happens to be his own, seems to be the one exception. And Julian Huxley, after showing in a superb series of studies how nature improves its form of life by an unending process of splitting, division, adaptive radiation, deployment, discontinuity, divergence, comes forth in his final argument with the concept that in the case of the human species, which also happens to be his own, it operates differently. By coming to this conclusion he illustrates his own contention that 'the human sciences today are somewhat in the position occupied by the biological sciences in the early 1800s'. For whatever he discovered as a biologist, he throws overboard as a human scientist, in which capacity he simply rationalizes the unitarian prejudices of our time. If his thoroughly convincing analysis of the evolutionary process is correct, the cause of human misery must obviously lie in man's perpetual effort to make an exception of himself. If deployment and differentiation constitute nature's way of advancing and of utilizing in an increasingly efficient manner environment, why should man's progress be accomplished by exactly the opposite method of integration, 'co-operation of integrated individual personalities', or the idea of making every task a community enterprise?

it was not only possible for more men to live; the new varieties increased the pleasures of the old. And what loss would human culture have suffered if, fulfilling the unitarian's ideal, all of us had spoken only one language, and always understood each other. No Shakespeare would have been necessary to follow a Sophocles, no Goethe a Shakespeare.

6. Summation and Hell

The evidence of science thus indicates that not only cultural and mechanical but also biological improvement is achieved through an unending process of division which sees to it that nothing ever becomes too big. It also reveals that in the entire universe there seems no problem of significance which is not basically a problem of size or, to be more to the point, a problem or oversize, of bigness, since, as we have seen, the problem of smallness is automatically taken care of by the process of growth. True, nature solves also the problem of bigness automatically, leading the overgrown to spontaneous destruction. But while cure by annihilation is a perfectly adequate solution in the insensible world of physics, it is far from satisfactory if applied to social and personal problems. Here we must, therefore, seek solution in division and, instead of passively looking on as things get out of hand, reduce their size to proportions adjusted to the stature of man. For on a small scale, everything becomes flexible, healthy, manageable, and delightful, even a baby's ferocious bite. On a large scale, on the other hand, everything becomes unstable and assumes the proportions of terror, even the good. Love turns into possessiveness; freedom into tyranny. Harmony, based on the interplay of countless different, little, and vivacious individual actions, is replaced by unity, based on magnetized rigidity and maintained by laborious co-ordination and organization. This is why the great hero of the age of bigness is neither the artist, nor the philosopher, nor the lover. It is the great organizer.

Which brings me to the story of the professor of statistics who, after his demise, with briefcase in hand, appears before the Lord complaining about the poor and archaic manner in which He had organized the world. 'I have an infinitely better plan than yours,' he says unfolding his charts and diagrams. 'As things are now, life is divided into too many repetitious little tasks and activities. We arise in the morning after eight hours of sleep. We spend fifteen minutes in the bath. We chat for five minutes with our families. We read ten minutes, and eat for fifteen minutes. Then we spend half an hour walking to our office.

We work four hours. We eat again for ten minutes. We nap half an hour. We use another half-hour walking home; another hour chatting with our families; half an hour for another meal and, finally, retire for another eight hours of sleep.

'All this splitting up of one's lifetime is extremely wasteful. I have calculated that the average man spends twenty-three years sleeping, two years eating, three years walking, five years talking, four years reading, two years suffering, ten years playing, and six months making love. Now why not organize the world simply? Why not let man engage in these various activities in single chunks of sustained action, beginning with the unpleasant two years of suffering, and ending with a pleasant six months of love making?'

The Lord, as the story goes, permits the professor to try out his plan. But it fails dismally and, as penalty, the statistician is expelled from heaven. Arriving in hell, he immediately asks to be brought before Satan and, hoping for better results this time, submits a similar plan.

'Satan,' he begins, unpacking again his charts and diagrams, 'I have a plan for organizing hell.'

At this Satan interrupts with laughter that shakes every rock in the fiery caves of the underworld.

'Organize hell?' he roars; 'my dear professor, organization *is* hell!'[1]

And so is unity, which organization creates, and from which it results!

[1] The story is retold by memory from a story by the pre-Hitler publisher of the Munich *Simplicissimus*.

Chapter Six

INDIVIDUAL AND AVERAGE MAN

'The average man . . . is to history
what sea-level is to geography.'
ORTEGA Y GASSET

*The natural internal democracy of a small state. Position of
the individual in the small state. The mass state and its political particle, the average man. The passive form of speech of the
mass-state citizen. Transformation of quantity into quality.
Mass and Man. The greater personal dignity of the small-
state citizen. Aristotle on the ideal size of the political community. External democracy of a small-state world. Possibility
for multitudes of political systems to exist side by side. Freedom
from issues. The Tower of Babel. The blasphemy of union.*

The Political Argument

CHAPTER V attempted to show that the small-cell principle is not,
as so many political theorists tell us, a reactionary concept as
compared with the modern concept of unification but, on the
contrary, a principle of advance and progress or, better still, the principle on which the entire universe is built. As a result, it seems justified
to deduce that what is applicable in the universe as a whole as well as
in all special fields such as biology, technology, art, or physics, should
be applicable also in the field of politics. If large bodies are inherently
unstable in the physical universe, they are in all likelihood unstable
also in the social universe. If large cells are cancer in the human body,
they would appear to be cancer also in the political body. And if
health and proper balance demand their destruction in our physical
systems, they would seem to demand their destruction also in our
social systems.

If we recognize this, we shall understand the purpose of a small-state
concept with considerably greater appreciation than was possible

before. At the beginning of our analysis we viewed it simply as a device of expediency which would make a number of obnoxious social problems such as war soluble. Now we see that it seems not only a matter of expediency but of divine plan, and that it is on *this* account that it makes everything soluble. It constitutes, in fact, nothing but the political application of the most basic organizing and balancing device of nature. The deeper we penetrate into its mystery, the more are we able to understand why the primary cause of historic change—explaining our changing institutions, forms of government, economic systems, philosophies, and cultures—lies not in the mode of production, the will of leaders, or human disposition, but in the size of the society within which we live. If a society is too large, it breeds, as we have seen, social miseries such as aggressiveness, crime, or tyranny as a result of its very size. But also social *blessings* are concomitants of social size— *small size*. This is why only a small-state system is able to ensure both internally and externally ideals such as democratic freedom and cultural enlightenment, or why, as the following chapters will show, the worst of small states provides greater happiness to man than the best of large ones.

1. *Internal Democracy*

The reason for this seems clear. Man's greatest happiness lies in his freedom as an individual. This is inseparably connected with political democracy. But democracy, in turn, is inseparably connected with the smallness of the collective organism of which the individual is part— the state. In a small state democracy will, as a rule, assert itself irrespective of whether it is organized as a monarchy or republic, or even as an autocracy. Paradoxical as this may sound, we do not need to go to great length to realize the truth of this proposition.

The small state is by nature *internally* democratic. In it the individual can never be outranked impressively by the power of government whose strength is limited by the smallness of the body from which it is derived. He must recognize the authority of the state, of course, but always as what it is. This is why in a small state he will never be floored by the glamour of government. He is physically too close to forget the purpose of its existence: that it is here to serve him, the individual, and has no other function whatever. The rulers of a small state, if they can be called that, are the citizen's neighbours. Since he knows them closely, they will never be able to hide themselves in mysterious shrouds under whose cover they might take on the dim and aloof appearance of supermen. Even where government rests in the hands of an absolute prince, the citizen will have no difficulty in asserting his will, if the state is small. Whatever his official designation, he will never be a *subject*. The gap between him and government is so narrow, and the political forces are in so fluctuating and mobile a balance, that he is always able either to span the gap with a determined leap, or to move through the governmental orbit himself. This is, for instance, the case in San Marino where they choose two consuls every six months with the result that practically every citizen functions at some time during his life as his country's chief of state. Since the citizen is always strong, governmental power is always weak and can, therefore, easily be wrested from those holding it. And this, too, is an essential requirement of democracy.

While every kind of small state, whether republic or monarchy, is thus by nature democratic, every kind of large state is by nature undemocratic. This is true even if it is a declared republic and democracy. It is therefore by no means unnatural that some of the world's greatest tyrants such as Caesar, Napoleon, Hitler, or Stalin arose on the soil of great states at the very moment when republicanism and democracy seemed to have reached a pinnacle of development. French coins bore the inscription: *République Française, Napoleon Empereur,* which was a contradiction only on the surface. Any government in a great power must be strong, and any great multitude must be ruled centrally. But to the extent that government is strong, the individual is weak, with the result that even if his title is *citizen*, his position is that of *subject*. The mobile balance maintained amongst the individuals of the small state translates itself in a large power into the heavy stable balance maintained by the colossal and dangerous mass of people on the one side, and the equally colossal and dangerous power of government on the other.

A citizen of the Principality of Liechtenstein, whose population numbers less than fourteen thousand, desirous to see His Serene Highness the Prince and Sovereign, Bearer of many exalted orders and Defender of many exalted things, can do so by ringing the bell at his castle gate. However serene His Highness may be, he is never an inaccessible stranger. A citizen of the massive American republic, on the other hand, encounters untold obstacles in a similar enterprise. Trying to see his fellow citizen President, whose function is to be his servant, not his master, he may be sent to an insane asylum for observation or, if found sane, to a court on charges of disorderly conduct. Both happened in 1950. In 1951, a citizen spent $1,800 in eleven months in an effort 'to get the President's attention'[1]—in vain. You will say that in a large power such as the United States informal relationships such as exist between government and citizen in small countries are technically unfeasible. This is quite true. But this is exactly it. Democracy in its full meaning is impossible in a large state which, as Aristotle already observed, is 'almost incapable of constitutional government'.[2]

2. The Average Man

The chief danger to the spirit of democracy in a large power stems from this technical impossibility of asserting itself informally. In mass states, personal influences can make themselves felt only if channelled through forms, formulas, and organizations. It is these latter rather than the individual who become increasingly the true agents and asserters of political sovereignty, so that we should speak of a group or party democracy rather than of an individualistic democracy. As a result, the individual declines, and in his place emerges the glorified average man of whom Ortega y Gasset writes that 'he is to history what sea-level is to geography'.[3] An individual can now have his will only to the extent that he comes close to this mystical average, and it is on the strength of his being an average, not an individual, that his desires can be satisfied. There is no average citizen in Liechtenstein. What citizen Burger gets is not what some average citizen wants, but what citizen Burger wants. In a large state, even a democracy such as ours, everything is patterned after citizen average, and what citizen Thomas Murphy is able to get is only what citizen average wants. 'Anybody who is not like everybody,' to quote again Ortega y Gasset, 'who does not think like everybody, runs the risk of being eliminated.'[4]

But who is this mystical, glorified, flattered, wooed, famous, inarticulate, faceless average man? If he is neither one individual, nor all individuals, he is no individual at all. And if he is not an individual, he can

---

[1] *New York Times*, 13 November 1951. Another incident concerned Dewey Williams, a marine cook, who was arrested in a Chicago railway station and fined $10.00 on disorderly conduct charges after he had placed a telephone call to the White House and insisted on talking to President Truman in the hope of getting his job back. (*New York Times*, 16 September 1951.) In 1952, Lieutenant Robert P. Hasbrook was reported to the air police by a San Antonio (Texas) hotel detective who had overheard him trying to telephone President Truman. (*New York Times*, 15 April 1952.)   [2] Aristotle, op. cit., 1326 b.

[3] Ortega y Gasset, *The Revolt of the Masses*. New York: The American Library, 1950, p. 17.   [4] Ibid., p. 12.

only be one thing, the representative or reflex of the community, of society, of the masses. What we worship in the individualistic fiction of the average man is nothing but the god of collectivism. No wonder that we overflow with emotion when we hear of government of, for, and by the *people*, by which we express our adherence to the ideals of group or mass democracy, while as true democrats we should have nothing in mind but government of, for, and by the *individual*.

Thus, however democratic a large power may try to be, it cannot possibly be a democracy in the real (though not original) meaning and glory of the term—a governmental system serving the *individual*. Large powers must serve *society* and, as a result, all genuine ideals of democracy become reversed. Their life rhythm can no longer depend on the freedom and interplay of individuals. Instead they become dependent on organization. But good organization presupposes totalitarian uniformity and not democratic diversity. If everybody were to follow his own way in a large state, society would soon collapse. Individuals must therefore be magnetized into a few groupings within which they must stand as stiffly at attention as tube travellers during rush hours when they are likewise forced into directed, synchronized and magnetized behaviour by the condition of crowding. Man the individual, the active, is replaced in mass states by man the type, the passive.[1] Nothing illustrates more tellingly this transformation than our increasing preference for the passive voice in our speech. We no longer fly to London. With a touch of pride we now say that we are flown there by the government or an air line. We no longer eat, but are fed. We are housed, entertained, schooled, evacuated, and taken care of in many important respects by mother government and father state. Previously we allowed ourselves to be treated as passives only as babies, invalids, or corpses. Now we are treated in this manner all our lives and, instead of resenting it, actually demand it. Our intelligence seems to have become collectivized along with the necessary collectivization of modern mass states, and lodged itself in the government which is taking charge of managing our lives in an ever-increasing degree. Painful as we may think this is, the mass state leaves us no other choice. The law of crowd living is organization, and other words for organization are militarism, socialism, or communism, whichever we prefer.

This condition must by necessity produce a fundamental change in the outlook of the citizen of the mass state. Finding himself perpetually

---

[1] Typical of this transition is the rise of such new symbols and terms as: Mother of the Year, Boy of the Month, Anystreet, etc.

living in the midst of formidable crowds it is only natural that he should begin to see greatness in what to the inhabitant of a small state is a stifling nightmare. He becomes obsessed with a mass complex. He becomes number struck and cheers whenever another million is added to the population figure. He falls into the error against which Aristotle has warned, and confounds a populous state with a great one. Quantity suddenly turns before his dazzled eyes into quality. Platitudes, pronounced in chorus by the multitudes, turn into hymns. A new, red, bloodshot sun arises out of a fiery dawn—the community, the people, the nation, humanity, or whatever he may call the monster whose only sign of existen e seems its voracious appetite for human sacrifice. Ecstatically he announces that the new thing that has formed itself out of our collective flesh is *greater* than the sum of us all, though this greater thing is completely illiterate, has never been able to pronounce a single word, has never written a poem or expressed a thought, and has never given anyone a fond pat on the shoulder. It depends on government as its constant interpreter because in its mongoloid development it has not even been able to master its own language. After thousands of years, Dr. Gallup has at last succeeded in endowing it with a vocabulary of two words: *yes* and *no*. Till Eulenspiegel, the medieval prankster, accomplished that much with a donkey.

3. The Collectivization of Individuals in Large States

Yet our mass-state citizen has invested this grunting low-grade organism with the attribute of divinity. In contradiction to all the meaning of creation, he has begun to place aggregates above the individual and to worship what should worship him. The nation to him is no longer simply something apart from the individual but something superior, on whose orders one must sacrifice all those who are less numerous such as wife, children, or oneself. Its symbols such as national anthems or flags become sacrosanct, and its offices become more dignified than the persons who occupy them. When President Roosevelt, during his last inauguration, stood on a platform whose railings were draped in the national colours, he was insulted and accused of infamy by a group of citizens on the ground that he, a mere individual, had dared to place himself above the flag, while the code demands that the flag, representing the nation, must at all times fly *above* the heads of individuals. And when President Truman, in a healthy outburst of an offended father, wrote a violent letter to a newspaperman who had criticized his daughter's singing, he was taken to task even by some of his friends who thought that the dignity of the presidential office ought not to be subordinated to personal feelings.

But all this worship of the masses, the people, the nation, and of the institutions representing them, is collectivism under whatever name it goes. And collectivism is irreconcilable with the ideals of democracy which, like Western civilization, is inseparably linked with individualism. It is logical nonsense to accuse the Marxists of collectivist thinking because they place society above man, and then proclaim ourselves that the nation stands above the individual. Either no community ranks above the individual, or all do, be it the people, the state, the empire, the class, the party, the proletariat, the organization, or the nation. The difference between the individualist and the collectivist is not that the one denies the existence of the group and the other of the individual. Their difference lies in the value which they assign to the one in relation to the other. The collectivist thinks that the organism whose purpose we must fulfil is society, and that man's significance is a derived one—derived from the measure of his service to the community. Hence the latter's justification for demanding continually the most promiscuous assertions of affection and loyalty from its members. The individualist, on the other hand, thinks that we have our own purpose for which we live, and that the purpose of society is a derived one—derived from its usefulness to man, not man the type, but man the individual. To the individualist, the nation and all its symbols therefore stand not above but below himself, and he will serve it not because it represents value in its own right but because serving it means to serve his own ideals, as he will shine his shoes not in order to worship their beauty, but because well-shined shoes enhance his own appearance. To an individualist, therefore, President Truman's much blamed threat to punch the face of a music critic to pulp was not an indignity to the high office he occupies, but a laudable assertion of the still lingering democratic individualism in American life according to which no office of the nation, however exalted it may be, can ever outrank the infinitely superior position of being the father of a beloved daughter.

However, populous, large, powerful nations cannot withstand the collectivizing trends of crowded living indefinitely. Weak as the individual is, he is by nature at first oppressed and then impressed by physical strength. Representing an infinitesimally small share of his country's sovereignty, he has no chance of resisting the influence and spectacle of mass deployment which must eventually swallow him up in an orgiastic cloud of panting nationalism. Being outclassed, out-towered, outnumbered, and out-awed on all sides by packs and groups and gangs and clans, he will at last lose faith in his own significance and replace it with a new faith—faith in the significance of the organized group. The happiness he found previously in his home and in the circle of his friends, he now finds in parades and brigades, and in the excitement of continuous communion with the multitudes. The new man of, for, and by the people, having for ever the welfare of humanity in his infected mind, becomes a callous brute to his friends and family when they venture to claim a personal share of his existence. When he hears the bugle call from the masses, he gets up from his dinner table, grabs his overcoat and flag, and steps over the arms of his crying children into the arms of his new mistress, the people, to whom he belongs and to whom he thinks he owes primary allegiance. If humanity demands it, he will slaughter all objects of his individual affection, and his fortitude and choice will be entered on the heroic pages of history as we have done with that virtuous Roman general whom we are still taught to admire because he executed his own son on the ground that, though he had won a great victory, he had done so by disobeying orders.

4. *The Meaning of Neighbourhood*

No such development can occur in a small state, in which the organized power of the people can never become strong enough to frighten the individual out of his faith in the personal existence and destiny of man. In contrast to his counterpart in great, populous states, the small-state citizen has much greater personal dignity, representing, as he does, not an infinitesimally small share of the state sovereignty, but a proportion that can defiantly assert itself. Since the concept of sovereignty does not increase in quality with the increase in population—as even our political theorists still concede by granting precedence amongst states to alphabetical position rather than political and military rank—the effect of increasing population is the diminution of individual importance. A Liechtensteiner's share in sovereignty is 1/13,000th, a Russian's 1/200,000,000th.

Thus, the greater the aggregation, the more dwarfish becomes man. But this is not all, for along with the decline of a person's share in sovereignty goes a decline in his share in government. Since *effective* legislatures cannot expand their membership in proportion to the growth of their countries, increasing population must ultimately lessen democratic representation. In 1790, the average constituency of a member of the House of Representatives in the United States comprised

33,000 citizens. If this ratio were still to prevail, the membership of the House would today be in the neighbourhood of 4,560, a figure that would make any sensible legislative action all but impossible. As a result, as our population increased, adjustment had to be made by increasing not the *number* but the *burden* of representatives, so that to-day the constituency of an American congressman contains on the average almost 350,000, and in some instances more than 900,000 people. By contrast, as the following figures show, the burden of representation is lessened and its effectiveness increased as the population of a country is smaller. Thus the average constituency comprises 81,000 citizens in Great Britain, 66,000 in France, 42,000 in Belgium, 30,000 in Sweden, 24,000 in Switzerland, and 11,000 in Israel.[1]

All this shows that only the small state fulfils the requirements of both individualistic and democratic existence. It is *individualistic* because it fits the small physical size of man so much better than the colossal robes of large powers which, far from clothing and protecting the individual, smother him. And it is *democratic* because of its physical inability to overwhelm the citizen, who is at all times capable not only of participating in government but also of resisting governmental encroachments without the intermediary of powerful organizations. The citizen can go his own way in pursuit of his happiness without needing to conform to organized opinions and ways of life simply because they are upheld by the multitudes. He is free, not because freedom is laid down as one of his constitutional rights but because no authority disposes of enough power to impede his freedom, which is much safer. He will never be annihilated by the 'dignity' of offices whose purpose is to be at his disposal, and whose sight will hardly delude him into believing in the functional superiority of those whose constitutional task it is to be his inferiors. It is quite different in large states, where we begin to address the public lavatory attendant, once his lavatories add up to impressive enough totals, as His Excellency and call him Minister of Public Hygiene, from whom we consider it an honour if he lets us wait not more than fifteen minutes.

Finally—and this is again because of our small physical stature—we can find the fulfilment of our happiness only within relatively narrow geographic limits. We may sing expansively 'From the Mountains to the Oceans', but we need only put a patriotic mountaineer to the ocean for which he clamours, or the seafarer into a peaceful Alpine haystack, to realize the magnitude of their misery and the meaninglessness of vast

[1] The figures of this paragraph are taken from Emanuel Celler, 'Can a Congressman Serve 900,000 People?', *The New York Times Magazine*, 11 March 1951.

area concepts when it comes to the question of personal happiness. What we love is not distance but neighbourhood. They alone have a personal meaning for us. This is why the President of the United States will for ever go to his Hydepark, Independence, or Gettysburg, if he wants to be truly happy. To be President in Washington, in spite of all the glamour and power of his office, is an exacting burden. There is no charm in his relations with his people, who must be fed with a continuous outpouring of oratory, prayers, and citations of God. But to be President of the United States in Independence amongst neighbours and friends, with whom one does not orate but chat, that is something quite different. The burden becomes pleasure, as everything becomes light and bearable within narrow limits. Only within small units can man, in his small bulk, feel at home.

5. The Ideal Size of States

There is one other question to answer in connection with the problem of a state's internal democracy. What is its ideal size? Up to what point can a political community grow without endangering the sovereignty of the individual? And conversely, down to what point can it shrink without defeating the purpose of its existence? Is it possible that a state might be too little as well as too large?

The size of everything, as we have seen, is determined by the function it fulfils. The function of the state is to furnish its members with protection and certain other social advantages which could not be obtained in a solitary pioneer existence. This indicates that a state composed, let us say, of only five or six families, might indeed be too little. But we have already seen that this constitutes no serious problem, for whenever things, be they physical or social atoms, are too small or lack in density, they begin to form aggregations and 'run together naturally for mutual help and readily coalesce to form stable tribes and communities'. The question is, when does a community become stable?

From a political point of view, it begins to fulfil its purpose at a population figure that may conceivably be lower than a hundred. Any group that can form a village, can form a stable and sovereign society. A country such as Andorra, with a present population of less than seven thousand, has led a perfectly healthy and undisturbed existence since the time of Charlemagne. However, a community has not only political purposes. It has also a cultural function to perform. While it may produce an ideal democracy at its smallest density, this is not sufficient to provide the variety of different individuals, talents, tastes, and tasks to bring out civilization as well. From a cultural point of view, the optimum size of a population must therefore be somewhat larger. Economically, it is big enough when it can furnish food, plumbing, highways, and fire trucks; politically, when it can furnish the tools of justice and defence; and culturally, when it can afford theatres, academies, universities, and inns. But even if it is to fulfil this extended purpose, a population needs hardly to number more than ten or twenty thousand to judge from the early Greek, Italian, or German city-states. With a population of less than a hundred thousand, the Archbishopric of Salzburg produced magnificent churches, a university, several other schools of higher learning, and half a dozen theatres in its little capital city alone. Thus we can say that though there is a lower limit to the ideal size of a community, it is hardly of any practical significance, particularly if we have only its economic and political purpose in mind.

The main question, as always, concerns the upper limit. Aristotle has answered this with clarity and precision in the following passage from his *Politics* (VII, 3):

'A state, then, only begins to exist when it has attained a population sufficient for a good life in the political community: it may indeed, if it somewhat exceed this number, be a greater state. But, as I was saying, there must be a limit. What should be the limit will be easily ascertained by experience. For both governors and governed have duties to perform. The special functions of a governor are to command and judge. But if the citizens of a state are to judge and to distribute offices according to merit, then they must know each other's character: where they do not possess this knowledge, both the election to offices and the decision of lawsuits will go wrong. When the population is very large they are manifestly settled at haphazard, which clearly ought not to be. Besides, in an overpopulous state foreigners and metics will readily acquire the rights of citizens, for who will find them out? Clearly then the best limit of the population of a state is the largest number which suffices for the purposes of life, and can be taken in at a single view.'[1]

From a political as well as a cultural point of view, this is indeed the ideal limit to the size of a state, a limit that provides a population large enough 'for a good life in the political community', and yet small enough to be well governed since it 'can be taken in at a single

[1] Aristotle, op. cit., 1326 b.

view'.[1] It is this kind of state that exists in a number of Swiss cantons where alone we can still find the old and cherished institution of direct democracy. They are so small that their problems can be surveyed from every church tower and, as a result, be solved by every peasant without the befuddling assistance of profound theories and glamorous guessers. However, modern techniques have given some elasticity to the concept of what can be taken in at a single view, extending the population limit of healthy and manageable societies from hundreds of thousands to perhaps eight or ten million. But beyond this, our vision becomes blurred and our instruments of social control begin to develop defects which neither the physical nor the social sciences can surmount. For at that point, we come face to face with the instability which nature has imposed on oversize. Fortunately, there are few tribes on earth numbering even that much, considering that the great powers are not homogeneous tribe states but, with the exception of the United States, artificially fused conglomerates. And even the United States, though a homogeneous large power, is composed of a number of small states which may ultimately break down its present homogeneity.

6. External Democracy

So far, this chapter has discussed the inherent *internal* democracy of small states. If, in addition, we now assume not only the existence of individual small states, but of a small-state *system*, imposing a lacework pattern of littleness on entire continents, democracy becomes a reality also from an *external* point of view, bringing its benefits not only to various individuals but also to various groups and societies. It is quite obvious that the multitude of different individual and regional wills and preferences can be much better served in a small-state world than

[1] Many other political philosophers and reformers were more specific though less profound than Aristotle in defining the ideal size of their communities. But it is interesting to find how many placed so great a value on the smallness of the social unit. Plato thought a population of 5,040 was the best. Thomas More's towns in Utopia held 6,000 families. Charles Fourier's *phalansteries* contained 400 to 600 families or 1,500 and 1,600 individuals. Robert Owen's *parallelograms* comprised 500 to 2,000 members, and Horace Greeley's *associations* were to number from 'some hundreds to some thousands of persons'. William Morris envisaged a return to a society from which all big cities had disappeared, and London dissolved into a number of villages separated by woods. It is also significant that so many ideal societies such as More's Utopia, Campanella's City of the Sun, or Bacon's New Atlantis, were placed on islands whose enchantment our imagination invariably attributes to their seclusion and the narrowness of their confines. As Marlowe says, there are 'infinite riches in a little room'.

in a large-power system or, worse still, in one super-colossal single world state. In a tightly united one-power continent, for instance, embracing three or four hundred million people, the form of state must either be republican or monarchical in its entire expanse. Its form of government must either be democratic or totalitarian. Its economic system either socialist or capitalist. In each case, the system existing in one corner of the map must exist also in the opposite corner. A huge mass of people must accept one special system though nearly half of it may be opposed to it. When Italy voted to become a republic after World War II, the entire southern part of the country, though voting overwhelmingly in favour of the monarchy, had to go along against its political wishes with the rest of the country because it was inseparably linked with a predominantly republican North that outvoted not only its own monarchists, but the entire population of a different external geographic region—the South. The flexible adaptability to multitudes of individual desires, which is such an essential feature of true democracy, is thus completely lacking in the rigid framework of large-power organization whose very oneness represents a smothering totalitarian characteristic.

Now let us see how the picture of the same political landscape looks if organized on a small-state pattern. A mountain-valley state decides to go anarchist and abolish government altogether. A city-state wants to be a republic; another wants to be ruled by a hereditary prince; a third by an archbishop; a fourth by triumvirs; a fifth by two consuls; a sixth by a constitutional king; a seventh by oligarchs; an eighth by a president to be chosen every three years and endowed with semi-dictatorial powers; a ninth by a president chosen every seven years and with no function other than to receive foreign diplomats and kiss their ladies' hands; a tenth wants to combine socialism with monarchy and democracy; an eleventh communism with monarchy and absolutism; and a twelfth a co-operative system with a sprinkling of aristocracy.

If man had not manifested so many different political temperaments and economic desires, history would not have known so many governmental and economic systems. None of these has any inherent superiority over others. Their only value is that they are chosen by their peoples. Since no absolute value adheres to any single institution, why should not as many individuals have as many different institutions as they like instead of having all to use a single costume which half of them might consider not to their taste? If freedom of choice is considered an advantage economically, why not also politically? For, with a great multitude of systems prevailing in an area inhabited by hundreds of millions of people, it becomes mathematically inevitable that far more individuals are able to obtain what their hearts desire than if the same region were to permit only a single system, even as in a restaurant many more people can obtain satisfaction if the menu includes a great variety of dishes rather than a single one which can be made palatable to all only through the propaganda of the cook. Since variety and change are essential prerequisites of democracy, uniform systems, however excellent they may be, spreading over vast regions, are necessarily totalitarian in space and, since it is almost impossible to change them, totalitarian also in time.

But the chief blessing of a small-state system is perhaps less its flexible ability to create satisfying political conditions for a much greater number of individuals than is possible in large-state set-ups; it is its gift of a freedom which hardly ever registers if it is pronounced because it is of a kind that seems to have become extinct long ago. We no longer feel its absence, so accustomed have we become to the nightmares of our day. It is the *freedom from issues*.

7. Freedom from Issues

Ninety per cent of our intellectual miseries are due to the fact that almost everything in our lives has become an ism, an issue. When we want to build a house or a street, we face the issue of city planning which is a battle-ground between traditional and modern schools, functional and artistic designs, American or Russian concepts. When we talk of education, we face the issue of pragmatism or great bookism. When we talk of children, we face the issue of inhibitionism or disinhibitionism. When we talk of sex, it is Freud versus Jung. When we discuss politics, we cannot pronounce a single word that is not an issue. Artists get into guilt tantrums if they find they have painted something that has nothing to do with the social issues weighing down on our cocktail hours. Professors get upset when they discover they have served the truth instead of the commonwealth. Our life's efforts seem to be committed exclusively to the task of discovering where we stand in what battle raging about what issue.

But what are issues? Sparks kindled by some spontaneous combustion of minds and flitting aimlessly through people's brains which act as involuntary conductors because in modern crowd life we stand too closely together to escape infection. They are uncontrollable phenomena of large-scale existence, transmitting themselves across the entire surface of the globe and creating the necessity in those they brush of participating intellectually in whatever movement may arise in whatever corner of whatever continent. If a Korean soldier crosses the 38th Parallel, we are hit by shock waves in New Jersey, and if a Siberian Eskimo sneezes near the North Pole, some Chileans and Englishmen will be jerked into battle positions off the shores of Argentina. The littlest causes sweep like tidal waves over the world from one end to the other, forcing us to take sides wherever we are, to debate them at lunch with our friends in a hundred languages, and to start divorce proceedings against our wives if we disagree on them in our beds. In the intellectual oneness of our world community, we react to every force like the interlocked springs in those old mattresses. Even if we are not immediately touched, we are depressed by them. Every damn thing in this world has become everybody's issue.

The blessing of a small-state world now seems quite clear. With its countless isolating boundaries, the problems of remote regions remain remote. They cannot transmit themselves universally because they are held back by the autochthonous problems of other little regions which, confined within narrow limits, cannot become issues. Instead of being in a perpetual state of war, one will now be intellectually involved in it only if it comes to one's own boundaries—which happens relatively rarely. Instead of being the involuntary participant in daily bloodshed, murder, massacres, which is the cause of our hellish existence, we shall become their witnesses only when they happen next door—which again happens only rarely. Instead of being reduced to perpetual mourning by our forced participation in everybody else's passing, we shall be free to enjoy the pleasures of life, experiencing the sorrows of death only when it strikes near us—which again happens only rarely. A small-state world, by dividing our universal, permanent, impersonal miseries into small, discontinuous, and personal incidents, thus returns us from the misty sombreness of an existence in which we are nothing but ghostly shadows of meaningless issues, to the bliss of reality which we can find only in our neighbours and our neighbourhoods. There alone, love is love, and sex is sex, and passion is passion. If we hate a man, it is not because he is a communist but because he is nasty, and if we love him it is not because he is a patriot but because he is a gentleman. In neighbourhoods everything becomes part of our personal experience. Nothing remains an impersonal issue. The tabloids with their delight in printing unadulterated detective, sex, and crime stories in a world in which everything else has become a part of highbrow social attitudes show our still lingering yearning for the one freedom which no political theorist ever seems to appreciate and which never-theless was the chief reason of the happiness of past generations even in the absence of other freedoms—the freedom from issues.

8. *The Unifiers, Aristotle, Shaw, and God*

We have seen in this chapter that the only chance for democracy and its underlying individualist principles, without which Western civiliza-tion is unthinkable, lies in the little state and a little-state system, and that the principal danger to our cherished heritage of personal free-dom lies, not in our disunion which preserves littleness, but in the process of union which obliterates it. Yet it is precisely this which our schoolmasters prescribe for us. Crushed by the intellect-killing but emotionally appealing weight of great physical power, they have drawn their scornful daggers against the small and placed everything that has size, bulk, or mass on glittering altars. They have persuaded us to wor-ship the colossal and then were amazed that we worshipped Hitler who was nothing—but he was colossal. They have praised to the heavens the enormity of the Roman empire and were amazed that we worshipped Mussolini along with the ancient Caesars who were nothing—but they were enormous. They have praised the develop-ment of massive powers, of the unification of East and West, of the creation of first two worlds and, finally, glory of glories if it comes, of the one world, though the one-state world is nothing but totalitarian-ism projected into the international plane.

They cannot see that the great word *unity*, which they pronounce with such solemnity and preach down to us from every pulpit, is to a true democrat what to a boxer's eye is his adversary's fist. If driven too far, it not only destroys the individual but the state as well, as Aristotle, to quote once more this most lucid of all political theorists, so con-cisely reasoned when he wrote in another passage of his *Politics* (II, 2):

'Is it not obvious that a state may at length attain such a degree of unity as to be no longer a state?—since the nature of a state is to be a plurality, and in tending to greater unity, from being a state, it becomes a family, and from being a family, an individual. So that we ought not to attain this greatest unity even if we could, for it would be the destruction of the state. Again, a state is not made up only of so many men, but of different kinds of men; for similars do not constitute a state. It is not like a military alliance . . . Again, in another point of view, this extreme unification of a state is clearly not good; for a family is more self-sufficient than an individual, and a city than a family, and a city comes into being when the community is large enough to be self-sufficing. If then self-sufficiency is to be desired, the lesser degree of unity is more desirable than the greater.'

Only in a time of crisis has unity sense, when individuals and peoples are bound to live in a 'military alliance' and many of our ideals must temporarily be suspended. But in all other periods unity, which is the great ideal of the totalitarians and collectivists, is the principal danger confronting the democrats. They do not want to have single parties but several parties, not single states but many states. Their principles are based on diversity and balance, not on unity and its natural concomitant, tyranny. It is for this reason that the British, once World War II was won, closed their ears to the appeals for continuing their superbly functioning war-time unity, and chose instead a much less efficient and much more bungling party government. Similarly, the American electorate, in a healthy assertion of democratic principles, rejected in the presidential elections of 1948 the candidate who campaigned loftily on the platform of national unity. With the war over, they saw no reason why they should not return to their customary ways of partisanship and bungling in government which, as long as it can be afforded, is always a guarantee of freedom from governmental interference into one's personal life.

Unity, to a democrat, is a dangerous vice. It obliterates the sovereignty of the individual. But beyond this, as the preceding chapter has shown, it is contrary to all purposes of creation. The law of the universe is harmony, not unity, which, even intellectually, we are almost unable to grasp. Whenever we lay our hands on something that appears as a unity, a oneness, it seems to dissolve. We may lay our hands on space, and suddenly it melts away into the fathomless depth of time. We may hold something as a piece of dead matter, and suddenly it disappears in a flash and vibrates in form of energy.

So contrary to man's purpose are the concepts of union and unity that attempts at establishing one-world systems seem almost blasphemous. It would be a good thing if our modern unifiers would re-read the story of the Tower of Babel to learn what God Himself thought of union. It might cure at least some of them of their mental affliction. In the dawn of history, as in our day, men became obsessed with a mania for unification, and they wanted not only to live in a single state, but in a single giant tower that was to be taller than even the new headquarters of the United Nations in New York. But unlike our modern politicians and many a bishop, God was not at all pleased with this. He considered it an arrogant challenge to His design. Having created men as sparkling individuals in His own image, He justly resented their wanting nothing more ambitious than to exist as mass-men in the depersonalized animal warmth of a communal hive. So, instead of praising them, He considered their undertaking blasphemy, and punished them by taking away even the little unity they had possessed up till then, the unity of language.

And this is what unification still constitutes today—blasphemy, leading, as all blasphemy must, not to rewards but punishment. The nations have been created to live apart, not together, as otherwise they would obviously not have created themselves in the first place. Such was even the opinion of the Secretary General of the League of Nations, not the real one, of course, but the one of Bernard Shaw's play *Geneva* who, when contemplating the terrors of unity, mused:

'The organization of nations is the organization of world war. If two men want to fight how do you prevent them: by keeping them apart, not by bringing them together. When the nations kept apart, war was an occasional and exceptional thing: now the League hangs over Europe like a perpetual war cloud.'[1]

[1] George Bernard Shaw, *Geneva, Cymbeline Refinished, Good King Charles.* New York: Dodd, Mead Co., 1947, p. 61.

Chapter Seven

THE GLORY OF THE SMALL

'Yet it was here in the nameless constellation of
city states on the mainland east of the Aegean . . .
that for the first time and almost the last time in
history all the major problems of human society
to seem have been simultaneously solved.'

SETON LLOYD

What drives small-state rulers to become patrons of the arts?
Wolf Dietrich of Salzburg. Reason why small states provide
time and leisure for artistic activity. Exacting social demands
of large powers. Why large powers honour their mechanics
rather than their poets. Toynbee on the withdrawal of creative
individuals from social life. Why small states give greater
opportunity for acquiring knowledge than large ones. Modern
specialized talents, ancient universal genius. Historic examples
of small-state productivity: Greek city-states, Italian city-
states, German city-states. English civilization created in
period of England's political smallness. End of cultural pro-
ductivity as a result of political unification. Toynbee on politi-
cal unification as a token of cultural decline.

The Cultural Argument

THE only impressive thing in great powers is their excessive
physical strength. As a result they can claim a place of honour
only in a world that has greater veneration for physical prowess
than for intellectual values, and is basically collectivist rather than
individualist. To an individualist excessive strength signifies nothing
but a threat to his integrity, and an invitation to ignore the development of his intellect. He abhors physical power beyond the degree
that is necessary for the enjoyment of a healthy life. He will delight in
the strength that enables him to engage in athletic competition or in

fights such as those fought by medieval knights, which were noble because they were personal. But he will find no enchantment in the accumulation of massive power such as is produced by well-organized, mindless masses, and is capable of running against other well-organized, mindless masses.

Wherever the element of mass is introduced, the individual is killed even if he survives physically. Man's life lies in the spirit, and the spirit can develop only in the unoppressive shelter of a small society. It is no coincidence, therefore, that the world's culture has been produced in little states. Not *by* little states—a point that cannot be enough emphasized in our community-worshipping age, since states, communities, nations, or people of any sort, form, or size are here to furnish us with street cars or sewage-disposal plants, not with thoughts; with material facilities, not with ideas—but *in* little states. This is their greatness and their glory. And there are several reasons for this.

1. *Cultural Diversion of Aggressive Energies*

The citizen of a small state is not *by nature* either better or wiser than his counterpart in a large power. He, too, is a man full of imperfections, ambitions, and social vices. But he lacks the power with which he could gratify them in a dangerous manner, since even the most powerful organization from which he could derive his strength —the state—is permanently reduced to relative ineffectualness. While the wings of his imagination remain untouched, the wings of his vicious deeds are clipped. A small-state individual may still murder, attack, or rape, but not in the voracious and unbalanced way possible in large powers, since he is kept in easy check during most of his lifetime by numerous and always ready and mobile balancing forces.

Political power games in small states are, therefore, rarely anything but actual games, never absorbing the ambitions of individuals to the exclusion of all other interests. What if someone succeeds in intriguing himself into the position of president, prince, prime minister, or dictator? He cannot do very much with it, however great his title. He would, of course, adore to shake the world in the grand historic manner, creating terror and futile horror as did Hitler or Stalin—if he only could. But, *hélas*, he can not. Where should he get the weapons? Where the armies? He may be able to stage a few murders with impunity, but even that would not make him a historic figure, and could not occupy his talents long enough to save him from boredom. He is a master, but has not enough submissive citizens to master. A barmaid will have enough courage to resist his advances if he should rely on his power instead of his gallantry. And there will be few of his prospective victims who, like Dante, Schiller, or Wagner, could not withdraw themselves from his jurisdiction by walking or riding a few miles by night, arriving an hour later in a different state. The job of exercising *power* in grand style in a little state carries little satisfaction.

But human ambition ravages in the small-state politician's heart none the less. Seeing the conventional road to historic eminence blocked, such as the road of battle glory for which one needs no mind at all, and which can be trodden without intellectual equipment by an Afghan water-carrier, an Austrian paperhanger, or a Byzantine whore as successfully as by a graduate from any military academy, he has no other way of sneaking into the coveted pages of history than by applying his intelligence to man's *higher* aspirations. This is harder, but it is the only chance of obtaining honourable mention besides the conquerors.

Thus Wolf Dietrich, a famous prince-archbishop of Salzburg—to give one of a myriad of examples—reputedly put the torch to his cathedral as Goering did to the Reichstag, not to create an issue, however, but to build a monument to his taste that should outlast the victories of Alexander. With no chance of enlarging his possessions, his aggressiveness was diverted into the construction of a magnificent Renaissance cathedral whose façade became the incomparable backdrop of *Everyman*, the still flourishing central attraction of the Salzburg festivals. His successors built other churches, all wholly unnecessary but each more beautiful than the other, blew tunnels through rocks, hewed theatres out of mountainsides, built lovely fountains and gorgeous marble pools in which their horses could bathe in the heat of summer, and lovingly created enchanting forest castles for their fertile mistresses. They turned Salzburg, the tiny capital of a state of less than two hundred thousand inhabitants, into one of the world's architectural gems. This is nothing, of course, compared with the construction of autostradas, Maginot and Siegfried lines, battle cruisers, rockets, or atom bombs, producible only in large powers which, because they *can* produce them, seem to be driven into producing nothing elss.

The first reason for the intense cultural productiveness found in little states lies thus in the fact that the absence of power will almost invariably turn rulers who might otherwise have become common arsonists and aggressors into patrons of learning and the arts. They cannot afford the maintenance of an army of soldiers, but the maintenance of a dozen artists is within the fiscal reach of even the poorest local prince. And since in a small-state world, every country is surrounded by multitudes of other small states, each artistic achievement in one will kindle in all the others the fierce flame of jealousy that cannot be quenched except by accomplishments which surpass those of all the neighbours. Since this, in turn, produces new jealousies, the process of creative production can never come to an end in a small-state system. To realize this we need only glance at Europe's countless little cities. It is there, not in the great metropolitan additions in which some of them have been drowned, that we find the main part of our cultural heritage, since nearly every little city has at one time or other been the capital of a sovereign state. The overwhelming number, splendour, and wealth in palaces, bridges, theatres, museums, cathedrals, universities, and libraries we do not owe to the magnanimity of great empire builders or world unifiers, who usually prided themselves on their ascetic modes of life, but to those ever-feuding rulers who wanted to turn their capital into another Athens or another Rome. And since each of them imposed the imprint of his particular personality on his creations, we find, instead of the giant dullness and uniformity of later colossalism, as many fascinating differences in architectural pattern and artistic styles as there were rulers and little states.

2. Relief from Social Servitude

A second reason for their cultural fertility is that small states, with their narrow dimensions and insignificant problems of communal living, give their citizens the time and leisure without which no great art could be developed. So negligible is the business of government that only a fraction of an individual's energies needs to be diverted into the channel of social service. Society runs almost on its own momentum and thus permits the dedication of the principal part of the citizen's life to the improvement of the individual rather than to the service of the state.

This is quite different in the case of large powers whose enormous social demands are such that they consume practically all the available energy not only of their direct servants but of the citizens as well in the mere task of keeping their immobile, clumsy societies going, and preventing their social services from collapsing. Forever afraid of breaking underneath their own weight, they can never release their populations from the servitude of pressing their collective shoulders to the wheels of their stupendous enterprise. Their purpose must by force of circumstance turn away from the grace of individual living to the puritan virtue of co-operation which is the law of some highly efficient animal societies but was not originally meant to be the primary concern of human living.

As a result, in large powers it is no longer the cultivation of learning and art in an atmosphere free of the issues of the day that counts, but the breeding of social analysts, mass specialists, efficiency experts, and engineers. It is no longer the great poet or great architect who reaps society's principal honours, but the socially useful mechanic, the organizer or what is so appropriately called the engineer of human relations.

True, artists and writers may still share in the applause of the masses, but only if they produce things of *social* significance. If they fail to do so, if they cannot be interpreted except in the antiquated terms of individual accomplishment, they are considered reckless parasites. A singer may still be appreciated, but only if he produces mass swooning. His art, whatever it is, is then obviously socially important, affecting as it does such vast numbers. But the principal honours will be reserved to those who acquit themselves of the chief task of a large society, which is: to keep it *materially* alive. This is not unjustified, because this is indeed a task which, as Aristotle said, is in a large power comparable to the job of 'holding together the universe'. With our dependence on massive existence for individual survival, every occupation disposing of a multiplying element becomes important on that account alone, while quality ceases to be a criterion of value altogether. A public utility director, whose task would be considered menial in a little state, thus emerges as a social leader of first rank in a large one. A raiser of livestock, if the number of his cattle exceeds five hundred, ceases to be a peasant and takes on the glamour of royalty. A washroom attendant, as already pointed out, dresses in tails, rents a box at the opera, and assumes the title of Excellency if the number of toilet seats he has to maintain in hygienic condition runs into the millions. Even crooks, if they cheat in impressive totals, are treated with awestruck respect, which again brings to mind Saint Augustine, that saintly deprecator of the big, who tells in the *City of God* (Book IV, Chapter IV) the following charming story:

'. . . for elegant and excellent was that pirate's answer to the great Macedonian Alexander, who had taken him: the king asking him how he durst molest the seas so, he replied with a free spirit, "How darest thou molest the whole world? But because I do it with a little ship only, I am called a thief; thou doing it with a great navy, art called an emperor."

With modern society so completely absorbed by the task of surviving physically the choking crowd conditions it has created, it is
not surprising that it should consider the achievements in the fields of
the social sciences, technology, hygiene, and so forth, as the ultimate
accomplishment of civilization.[1] But civilization has nothing to do with
this. Tubes, furnaces, and bathrooms are all essential and useful for
material comfort and collective vitality, but they are not monuments of
what we call culture. Culture is the portrait of an angel or a street
urchin, which a modern would be allowed to paint only with a heavy
social issue in mind but which a true artist paints for its own sake.
Culture lies in cathedrals and lofty spires whose sole purpose is to be
beautiful. Socially they are completely useless. One cannot use their
floor space as a garage, nor their wind-swept rooms high in the towers
as offices, nor their weird gargoyles as iced-water fountains. So they
can no longer be built, for where could anyone find the time and
leisure in our exacting age to create something whose sole value is the
pleasure it gives to the discerning eyes of his maker or his God? The
few monuments which mass society still does sponsor—and even these
are not for the glory of God but its own glorification, such as the monuments it erects to those who died so that the community might live,
and who are symbolized characteristically not by some heart-broken
mother's son but by a callously depersonalized *unknown* soldier—must
be utilitarian in nature. So, instead of baroque fountains wasting
precious water, or statues wasting precious metals, we now build
memorial hospitals, memorial parks, and memorial community halls.
Everything, everything has to be subordinated to social needs. Culturally, vast-scale living has become sterile. What the populous nations
of the world still possess in true civilization is not their own creation
but the heritage of a past that granted the essentials to artistic creation:
time for musing, slowness of pace, and, above all, relief from stultify-
ing social service.

Arnold J. Toynbee, in his *A Study of History*, has indicated this vital
connection between cultural productivity and relief from exacting social
tasks by tracing the development of intellectual greatness not to participation in, but withdrawals from, social living. He finds this to be the case

'. . . in the lives of mystics and saints and statesmen and soldiers and
historians and philosophers and poets, as well as in the histories of

[1] 'For that reason,' writes Ortega y Gasset, 'as Spengler has very well observed,
it was necessary, just as in our day, to construct enormous buildings. The epoch
of the masses is the epoch of the colossal. We are living then under the brutal
empire of the masses.' (Op. cit., p. 13.)

nations and states and churches. Walter Bagehot expressed the truth we are seeking to establish when he wrote: "All the great nations have been prepared in privacy and in secret. They have been composed far away from all distraction." [1]

In other words, all that is great in great nations is not the product of their period of power which kept them busy with occupying the limelight on the stage of history, but of the time when they were insignificant and little. No powerful country, being itself the chief distraction, could, of course, have stayed away from 'all distraction' or developed any genius 'in privacy and in secret'.

Toynbee mentions as examples of his theory men such as Saint Paul, Saint Benedict, Saint Gregory the Great, Buddha, Mohammed, Machiavelli, Dante, and he might have added practically every great artist up to Gauguin or Shaw. The *ivory tower*, from which our time wants to drag every artist so that he may earn his living by facing the issues of the day and contributing to the collective efforts of war and peace or whatever else it may be, is nothing but the place of withdrawal where the true monuments of civilization are created in defiance of the clamour of the masses.

3. The Variety of Human Experience

There is a third reason for the intense cultural productivity of the small, and the intellectual sterility of the large, state. This is the most important reason of all. Societies may have patrons of the arts as rulers. But even so they could do little without artists. And they may provide the facilities for leisure and musing. But, again, these alone might not produce the creative impulse. What is needed in addition is the opportunity for creative individuals to learn the truth without which neither art, nor literature, nor philosophy can be developed. But to learn the truth in a world that is as manifold as ours and which manifests itself in such countless forms, incidents, and relationships, a creative individual must be able to participate in a great variety of personal experiences. Not in a great number, but in a great variety. And this is infinitely easier in a little state than a large one.

In a large state, we are forced to live in tightly specialized compartments, since populous societies not only make large-scale specialization

---

[1] Arnold J. Toynbee, *A Study of History*, abridged version. New York: Oxford University Press, 1947, p. 224.

possible but also necessary.[1] As a result, our life's experience is confined to a narrow segment whose borders we almost never cross, but within which we become great single-purpose experts. Shattered into the spectrum's varied colours, we begin to see life as all red, all blue, or all green, while it appears in its true colour, white, only to those who sit on the high controlling towers of government and are alone in a position to see the wheel of society actually turning. But they are so busy with the task of co-ordination that they cannot communicate to us the facts they perceive. The rest of us are condemned to be segment dwellers, unblended and unblending, moving on moving particles which we consider motionless, and knowing the screw we shape but not the engine of which it is part.

Instead of experiencing many different things within surveyable limits, as did our enviable ancestors, we experience only one thing on a colossal plane. But this we experience innumerable times. Mechanics now meet only mechanics, doctors doctors, commercial artists commercial artists, garment workers garment workers, journalists journalists. Furnishing an existence within functionalized homogeneous little subnationalities, our modern labour unions and professional organizations pride themselves that their members can nowadays have everything from entertainment to education, hospitalization, vacations, and burial without ever stepping outside the cosy shelter of their organizations. It is considered snobbish, indecent, or treasonable to mix with anyone not of one's kind. If a historian knows a psychoanalyst, he is suspected of being a lunatic. If a business man knows a sculptor, he is suspected of being a sex pervert. If an engineer knows a philosopher, he is suspected of being a spy. If an economist makes a pronouncement on a question which, by definition, belongs to the field of political science, he is considered a fake. One of my own students accused me in open class of fraud when I ventured to correct a statement by him concerning a fact of English political life. He rejected my correction by stating sternly that an economist could not possibly have authoritative knowledge in a field outside his own. If he claimed this nevertheless, he was either a genius or an impostor, indicating strongly that he considered me the latter. And he was right, of course. Even as an economist I am a fraud. The only field in which I

---

[1] This does not mean that specialization as such is undesirable. On the contrary, the purpose of every community, as indicated in the preceding chapter, is to foster it. But when it begins to obliterate the diversity of man which, at a lesser degree of perfection, it cultivates, its advantage turns into ruin. This happens in the excessive large-scale specialization made possible in large states.

really know something concerns the documentation of international customs unions. There, I know everything, and, meaningless as it is, am probably the world's foremost authority. In every other field I have to trust to what other specialists have dug out.

Because modern life makes it technically impossible to participate in manifold experiences, anything written nowadays in the massive crowd states is drawn not from life, but from the co-ordinated *study* of life. The world no longer crosses an author's path. He must go out of his way and discover it indirectly and laboriously from encyclopedias and monographs, or from the writings of other hard-working students. If he can afford it, he keeps a staff of researchers who do the learning and experiencing for him without knowing what all their work is for, while he himself does nothing but act as the mechanical computer of the figures which are fed into his system and whose results are as much of a surprise to him as to anybody.[1] No single individual, unless he is indeed a supergenius, has the opportunity to experience the multitude of social and human problems that constitute life. But since culture is the product of individual perception of the whole scope of existence, the large state, which deprives the creative individual of his fullness and dimensions in favour of a mechanically efficient but intellectually sterile community, can never be the proper soil on which true civilization can flourish.

The great advantage of the little state then is that, once it has 'attained a population sufficient for a good life in the political community', it offers not only the advantages of a reasonable degree of specialization but also the opportunity for everybody to experience everything simply by looking out of the window. There is no passion or problem disturbing the heart of man or the peace of a large empire that would not exist also in a small country. But in contrast to the large

[1] A characteristic illustration of the new ways in which modern authors tackle the task of writing a book has been provided in the following account by Ramon Cuthrie, a friend and associate of Sinclair Lewis, describing the latter's effort to write a novel on the problems of labour: 'It was in 1929 that Red [Sinclair Lewis] made his first attempt to write the labour novel. He and Dorothy were living on their farm in Vermont. A number of authorities on labour, economics, etc. were in residence as a consultant staff. One of the experts was the late Ben Stolberg; I have forgotten who the others were. Everybody except Red was buckled down to the job of writing the book. Red himself seemed rather baffled and disconcerted by the invasion. He would take naps, go for walks, read detective stories, get quietly but purposefully drunk, turn out pot-boilers for "The Saturday Evening Post", while the board of experts sat in solemn conclave laying out the novel.' (Ramon Cuthrie, 'The Labor Novel that Sinclair Lewis Never Wrote', *New York Herald Tribune Book Review*, 10 February 1952.

empire, where their meaning lies hidden under the weight of countless duplications and in a multitude of disjointed specialized realms, they unfold themselves without the intermediary of analysts and experts before the eyes of everybody, and with a clarity of outline and purpose that cannot be perceived elsewhere. A small state has the same governmental problems as the most monumental power on earth, even as a small circle has the same number of degrees as a large one. But what in the latter cannot be discerned by an army of statisticians and specialized interpreters, could be perceived by every leisurely stroller in ancient Athens. As a result, if we really want to go to the bottom of things, we have even today no other recourse after having tried Harvard and Oxford than to take down from their dusty shelves Plato or Aristotle. Indeed, the worth of Harvard and Oxford lies largely in the fact that they keep on their shelves the great men of little states.

Yet these were no supermen. The secret of their wisdom was that they lived in a small society that displayed all the secrets of life before everybody's eyes. They saw each problem not as a giant part of an unsurveyable tableau, but as a fraction of the composite picture to which it belonged. Philosophers, as also poets and artists, were by nature *universal* geniuses because they always saw the totality of life in its full richness, variety, and harmony without having to rely on secondhand information or to resort to superhuman efforts. Without going out of their way or making a special job of it, they could witness in a day's passing jealousy, murder, rape, magnanimity, and bliss. Their life was a constant participation in human and political passions. It was not spent in modern one-dimensional incestuous intercourse with individuals sharing one's own interests, but in daily contact with everybody ranging from peasant wenches to rulers. As a result, they could write as competently on the subtleties of political doctrines as on the nature of the universe or the tribulations of love. And the characters they created in marble or in verse were not synthetic carriers of mass issues but human beings so full, true, and earthly that their unsurpassable veracity still captivates our imagination.

4. The Testimony of History

It is for these three reasons that the overwhelming majority of the creators of our civilization were the sons and daughters of *little* states. And it is for the same reasons that, whenever productive small-state regions were united and moulded into the formidable frame of great powers, they ceased to be centres of culture.

History presents an irrefutable chain of evidence in this respect. All the great empires of antiquity, including the famous Roman Empire, have not created a fraction of the culture in all the thousands of years of their combined existence which the minuscule ever-feuding Greek city-states produced in a few decades. Having lasted so long, they did of course produce a few great minds and impressive imitators, but their chief accomplishments were technical and social, not cultural. They had administrators, strategists, road builders, and amassers of stones in giant structures whose forms could be designed by every two-year-old playing in the sand. They had great law-givers and masters of government, but so had the Huns. As far as true culture was concerned, they obtained what they did from Greeks, Jews, or other members of small, disunited, and quarrelsome tribes whom they bought on the slave markets like chattels and who lectured and mastered them like the barbarians they were. Underlining the connection between cultural productivity and the smallness of the social unit, Kathleen Freeman writes in her book on *Greek City States*:[1]

'The existence of these hundreds of small units . . . seems uneconomic nowadays . . . But certain of these small units created the beginnings of movements which transformed the world, and ultimately gave Man his present control over Nature . . . It was the small unit, the independent city-state, where everybody knew all that was going on, that produced such intellectual giants as Thucydides and Aristophanes, Heraclitus and Parmenides. If these conditions were not in part responsible, how is it that philosophy, science, political thought, and the best of the literary arts, all perish with the downfall of the city-state system in 322 B.C., leaving us with the interesting but less profound and original work of men such as Epicurus and Menander? There is only one major poet after 322: Theocritus of Cos, a lyric genius of the first rank, who nevertheless (unlike Sappho) wrote much that was second-rate also, when he was pandering to possible patrons like the rulers of Alexandria and Syracuse. The modern nation that has replaced the *polis* as the unit of government is a thousand times less intellectually creative in proportion to its size and resources; even in building and the arts and crafts it lags behind in taste, and relatively in productivity.'[2]

[1] New York: W. W. Norton and Co., 1950, p. 270.

[2] Seton Lloyd, in an article in *The Listener* of 19 April 1951, makes a similar point when he writes: 'Yet it was here in this nameless constellation of city states on the mainland east of the Aegean, even in the days before Athens had become famous, that for the first time and almost the last time in history all the major

Similarly, England produced a glittering string of eternal names, but when? When she was so small and insignificant that she had the hardest time winning a few battles against the Irish or Scots. True, she won a historic victory against Spain, but the greatness of this victory, as in the case of the wars between ancient Greece and Persia, lies precisely in the fact that it was won not by a great power but by one of the minor states of Europe over the then principal power on earth. But it was during this period of quarrelsome insignificance and with a population of about four million that she produced the principal share of her great contribution to our civilization—Shakespeare, Marlowe, Ben Jonson, Lodge, and many others who are unsurpassed in the world of literature. As she grew mightier, her talents were diverted into the fields of war, administration, colonization, and economics. If she still continued to contribute outstanding names to art and literature, it was because of tenaciously surviving small groups within her expanding empire such as the Scots and Irish. It is no coincidence that many of the most eminent and fertile contributors to modern English literature, Shaw, Joyce, Yeats, or Wilde, were Irish, members of one of the world's smallest nations.

But no two countries illustrate better the cultural productivity of small, and the sterility of large, units than Italy and Germany. Both have in relatively recent times undergone the transformation from small-state organizations to powerful unified empires. Up to 1870, both were split into countless little principalities, duchies, republics, and kingdoms. Then, under the applause of the world, and to its subsequent terror, they were unified into big, rich, and pacified countries. Though the two world wars have somewhat dampened the enthusiasm of our intellectuals with regard to the unity of Germany,

problems of human society seem to have been simultaneously solved. For a time group-life on a national scale became possible, with a full complement of those freedoms to which we in our time aspire with such limited success. To quote Dr. Keith Monsarrat, "Not only was there peace between city and city, but the men of the cities seem to have given peace to each other. They found leisure to concern themselves with the adornment of their own way of living, and in the course of this they found harmonies of relation as no men had ever done before." It is strange in these circumstances to realize that there was no sense of unity among the states themselves. Throughout the coastal provinces of Asia Minor, from Cicilia to the Plain of Troy, every valley and sheltered upland seems to have been a miniature state, contributing to the economy of a single large city. And each state had a strong individual character.' The only comment to this is that it is not at all strange that 'there was no sense of unity'. The reason of that paradisical situation was that it consisted of a harmony produced by states, neither big nor united, *because* they were neither united nor big.

they are still apt to break into raves when they hear the name of the Italian Bismarck and unifier, Garibaldi.

As long as the Italians and Germans were organized, or disorganized, in little comic-opera states, they not only gave the world the greatest masters of comic opera but, as in England during her time of Elizabethan political insignificance, an unrivalled string of immortal lyricists, authors, philosophers, painters, architects, and composers. The mess of states that were Naples, Sicily, Florence, Venice, Genoa, Ferrara, Milan, produced Dante, Michelangelo, Raphael, Titian, Tasso, and hundreds of others of whom even the least outstanding seems greater than modern Italy's greatest artist, whoever that may be. The mess of states that were Bavaria, Baden, Frankfurt, Hesse, Saxony, Nuremberg, produced Goethe, Heine, Wagner, Kant, Dürer, Holbein, Beethoven, Bach, and again hundreds of whom the least known seems to outrank even the greatest artist of unified Germany, whoever that might be.[1] Some, like Richard Strauss, have reached eminence in modern Germany, but their origin reaches back to particularism which continued to exist in Germany and Italy as it did in England and France even after their union and is responsible for a few final creative stragglers.

This is what the reactionary little states of Italy and Germany have

[1] As Bertrand Russell has pointed out: 'In the ages in which there were great poets, there were also large numbers of little poets, and when there were great painters there were large numbers of little painters. The great German composers arose in a milieu where music was valued, and where numbers of lesser men found opportunities. In those days, poetry, painting, and music were a vital part of the daily life of ordinary men, as only sport is now. The great prophets were men who stood out from a host of minor prophets. The inferiority of our age in such respects is an inevitable result of the fact that society is centralized and organized to such a degree that individual initiative is reduced to a minimum. Where art flourished in the past it has flourished as a rule amongst small communities which had rivals among their neighbours, such as the Greek City States, the little Principalities of the Italian Renaissance, and the petty Courts of German eighteenth-century rulers. . . . There is something about local rivalry that is essential in such matters. . . . But such local patriotisms do not readily flourish in a world of empires. . . . In those who might otherwise have worthy ambitions, the effect of centralization is to bring them into competition with too large a number of rivals, and into subjection to an unduly uniform standard of taste. If you wish to be a painter you will not be content to pit yourself against the men with similar desires in your own town; you will go to some school of painting in a metropolis where you will probably conclude that you are mediocre, and having come to this conclusion you may . . . take to money-making or to drink. . . . In Renaissance Italy you might have hoped to be the best painter in Siena, and this position would have been quite sufficiently honourable.' (Bertrand Russell, *Authority and the Individual*.)

given to the world—beautiful cities, cathedrals, operas, artists, princes, some enlightened, some bad, some maniacs, some geniuses, all full-blooded, and none too harmful. What have the same regions given us as impressive great powers? As unified empires, both Italy and Germany continued to boast of the monuments of a great civilization on their soil. But neither of them produced these. What they did produce were a bunch of unimaginative rulers and generals, Hitlers and Mussolinis. They, too, had artistic ambitions and wanted to embellish their capital cities but, instead of hundreds of capitals, there were now only two, Rome and Berlin, and instead of thousands of artists, there were now only two, Hitler and Mussolini. And their prime concern was not the creation of art but the construction of the pedestal on which they themselves might stand. This pedestal was war.

From the moment the small interstate strife had ceased amongst the Italian and German principalities and republics, they began to cultivate imperial ambitions. With physical and military glory within their grasp, they forgot about their great intellects and artists, and began to flush with excitement when some conqueror was resurrected from their remote history for purposes of imitation. They began to neglect Goethe in favour of Arminius, a Teutonic general who beat the Romans. They began to forget Dante in favour of Caesar, a Roman war reporter who beat the Teutons, Celts, and Britons. Having the choice between a great tradition of culture and a great tradition of aggressiveness they chose, as every great power does, the latter. The Italy and Germany of poets, painters, thinkers, lovers, and knights, became factories of boxers, wrestlers, engineers, racers, aviators, footballers, road builders, generals, and dehydrators of swamps. Instead of annoyed defenders of little sovereignties, they became the virile rapers and back-stabbers first of the countries around them and then of the entire world.

And we, of our time, so taken with the glory of mass, unity, and power, just adored it. Before our intellectuals called the dictators criminals, murderers, and maniacs, they called them geniuses. Only when the latter began to play with their own throats did they revise their estimates. So they began to vilify the dictators. But by no means did they revise their general abject submissiveness to power which they continued to glorify. Not being decently able to worship Hitler and Mussolini while the dictators won whopping victories over us, they shifted their affection from the contemporary conquerors to their predecessors. What they now praised less in Hitler, they praised all the more in Napoleon—that he wanted to unify Europe. To this day they are reluctant to realize that all our degradation as individuals is due to social unification beyond the limits required for a pleasant life.

5. *Romans or Florentines*

I have with some purpose chosen the comparison between Germany and Italy, and shown the identity of the development of both from cultural refinement to barbarian aggressiveness, from designers of cathedrals to builders of empires, from intellectual greatness combined with political weakness to political greatness combined with intellectual mongolism. The reason for this is that all too many authors still differentiate between German and Italian characteristics and cultural productivity as if one nation had special talents and the other had not. Outwardly both are assumed to have behaved equally abominably under their respective dictators. But, it is said, the Italians did not really mean it. In contrast to the Germans, they are artistic, sanguine, light-hearted, and not at all militaristic or imperialistic. Yet this darling people to which our infatuated commentators attribute such collective appreciativeness of everything artistic, has as a group cared so little about its cultural heritage that it left most of its ancient architectural glory to fall to dust. What was saved for our delighted eyes was dug back from oblivion by Prussian and English professors, not by the artistic Italian people who used the stones of Roman temples to build outhouses and, when they realized that money could be made, sold whatever they could in coins and statuettes to eager foreigners. What every Medici would have guarded with jealousy, the Garibaldis gave away for profit. And as to their anti-militarism and anti-imperialism, their whole political treachery was due to the fact that they were not given enough colonies after World War I. And hardly were they defeated in World War II, when they began to press for colonies again.

Ever since their emergence as a great power in 1871, the Italians as a people no longer wanted to be known as artists but as masters, not as peace sissies but as conquerors, not as Florentines but as Romans. Power has turned them into Prussians as it did the Prussians, and goose-stepping, which Mussolini appropriately introduced in his army, was by no means alien to Italian mentality after 1871, even as gentleness, artistry, gracefulness, and delicacy were by no means alien to the Germans before that date, when a large part of them still lived in a medley of little states. Culture is the product not of peoples but of individuals and, as we have seen, creative individuals cannot flourish in the consuming atmosphere of large powers. It makes no difference whether the people concerned are Germans, French, Italians, or English. Wherever the process of union comes to its logical conclusion, their cultural fertility withers away. As long as democracy, with its system of divisions, factions, and small-group balances, exists, or as long as the process of internal consolidation has not reached its end, even seemingly large powers may benefit from an afterglow of intellectual vitality without, however, being responsible for it. Great power and democracy, as the previous chapter has shown, are mutually exclusive in the long run, since bigness in its ultimate form cannot be maintained except by totalitarian organization.

6. The Universal State—Symbol and Cause of Cultural Decline

Toynbee, in his *A Study of History*, which is a study of the rise and decline of civilizations, has portrayed a similar relationship between political unification and intellectual decay. He refers to the 'phenomenon' that the last stage but one of every civilization is characterized by 'its forcible political unification in a universal state'.[1] He understands by this what I understand by great power, a state comprising all members of a specific civilization, not all nations of the earth. But he overlooks the all-important *causal* connection when he considers the universal state simply a symptom, a 'phenomenon', a 'token of decline', rather than the cause and ratification of cultural collapse. Apart from this, however, his analysis penetrates to the centre of the problem when he writes:

'For a Western student the classic example is the Roman Empire into which the Hellenic Society was forcibly gathered up in the penultimate chapter of its history. If we now glance at each of the living civilizations, other than our own, we notice that the main body of Orthodox Christendom has already been through a universal state in the Ottoman Empire; that the offshoot of Orthodox Christendom in Russia entered into a universal state towards the end of the fifteenth century, after the political unification of Muscovy and Novgorod; and that the Hindu Civilization has had its universal state in the Mughal Empire and its successor, the British Raj; the main body of the Far Eastern Civilization in the Mongol Empire and its resuscitation at the hands of the Manchus; and the Japanese offshoot of the Far Eastern Civilization in the shape of the Tokugawa Shogunate. As for the

[1] Arnold J. Toynbee, op. cit., p. 244.

Islamic Society, we may perhaps discern an ideological premonition of a universal state in the Pan-Islamic Movement.'[1]

To escape the 'slow and steady fire of a universal state where we shall in due course be reduced to dust and ashes',[2] Toynbee suggests the establishment, not of an all-embracing unitarian arrangement, 'but of some form of world order, akin perhaps to the Homonoia or Concord preached in vain by certain Hellenic statesmen and philosophers'.[3] But there is only one way of establishing such Homonoia or harmony, and that is by restoring the little-state world from which our individualistic Western civilization has sprung, and without which it cannot continue. For large-power development drives us inevitably into the age of control, tyranny and collectivism.

Mistaking the cause for a symptom, Toynbee has not quite reached this conclusion which his own monumental argumentation seems to force upon the reader. That is why he ends his work on a note of unjustified but characteristically modern optimism. He thinks 'that there is no known law of historical determinism' that would compel the Western world to go the same road of destruction that has been trodden by every other civilization, the road of a Western universal state, or empire, which would be the better name for it. He fails to see that this development has become inevitable from the moment states have grown beyond the Aristotelian optimum size into great-power complexes. From then on further growth meant closer ruin. Today, pushed by the United Nations and their cultural agency, UNESCO, the Western universal state has advanced far beyond the dim outlines of an 'ideological premonition'; in fact, our statesmen seem to have nothing at all on their minds *except* our unification that will preserve our existence, but doom our civilization.

Social size appears thus once more at the root of things, of the good as well as the bad; of cultural productivity and human wisdom, if it is limited, of specialized ignorance and meaningless excellence in social utilitarianism, if it is too big. And again, while historic and economic factors such as great leaders, national traditions, or the mode of production may explain a great deal, the theory of size seems to explain more.

[1] Ibid., p. 244.   [2] Ibid., p. 553.   [3] Ibid., p. 552.

Chapter Eight

THE EFFICIENCY OF THE SMALL

'Luxury here takes a turn much more towards
enjoyment than consumption.'

ARTHUR YOUNG

*Higher living standard in small states. Modern large-scale
production, a token of enslavement rather than of rising living
standards. Life in the Middle Ages. Cyclical depressions
characteristic not of capitalism but of large-scale economy.
The law of diminishing productivity. Greater efficiency of small
productive units. Aggregates—the opiate of economists. Justice
Brandeis on the limits to size. Monopolies are to economics
what great powers are to politics. Small states no bar to large
free-trade areas. International Service Unions. Customs
Unions.*

The Economic Argument

WE have found that the small-unit principle is superior to the
large-unit principle in almost all fields ranging from physics
to technology, and from politics to culture. We have also
found that practically all problems of existence result from overgrowth
and must therefore be solved through splitting the big, not through
the union of the small.

There is, however, one field in which our arguments in favour of a
return to a system of small states seem to lose their validity. This is
economics. Would not such a return mean economic chaos? Would it
not be truly reactionary to erect again the countless barriers separating
countless regions from each other, impeding traffic and trade, and undoing the gigantic economic progress which the existence of large-area
states and the resultant big-plant and mass-production facilities have
made possible? If union has sense nowhere, it certainly has in the economic sphere considering that without it our living standards would

in all likelihood still be at the low level that characterized the Middle Ages.

How can we answer these objections which, as we shall soon see, are not only of the same kind but of the same superficiality as those raised against the *political* parcellation of the great powers. Instead of giving testimony of the validity of modern theories they illustrate the sloganization of our thinking. For even in economics every single fact indicates that unification is not the solution of our problems but their very cause. As everywhere else, it is not a system that is at fault, be it capitalist or socialist, but its application to too vast a scale. If capitalism has had such stunning success in its earlier stages, it was not because of the incentive effect of private property relationships. Stalin medals produce the same results. It was because of its embodiment of the competitive principle whose most fundamental prerequisite is the side-by-side existence not of a few large but of many small facilities requiring not the waste of extensive but the economy of intensive operation. And if it developed cracks in its later stages, it was not because of its social shortcomings but because of its infection with large-scale organisms such as monopolies or unsurveyably huge market areas which, far from being responsible for economic progress, seem to be its principal obstacle.

1. *The Living-standard Argument*

Before discussing the theoretical implications of economic oversize, however, let us analyse the most convincing argument advanced in support of large-scale development—the argument that it has improved the allegedly low standards of previous small-state economies.

To deal with this principal apology for economic bigness, it is first of all necessary to know what we understand not so much by living standard but by a *rise* in living standard. Assuming that the zero level, below which no standard can decline, is expressed by the possession of those consumer goods which are necessary for survival, a *rise* in living standard would express itself by the widening margin of consumer goods available to the various groups of the economic community in excess of these essentials. In other words, a rise in living standard must be measured in terms not just of goods but of *consumer* goods, since these alone—in contrast to *producer* goods—make for the enjoyment of life. Moreover, it must be measured not just in terms of consumer goods in general, but of consumer goods *in excess* of the essentials, the luxuries. Thus, if vast-scale development has been accompanied by a rise in living standards, as its supporters assert by using such descriptive words as phenomenal, fantastic, undreamt and unheard of, it must have manifested itself in an *increasing margin* of luxuries, enabling modern man to satisfy a greater variety of material wants, or the same variety to a greater extent, than was possible before.

What actually happened under the impact of mass-production facilities and large-area markets was a phenomenal increase in the production not of non-essential but of *essential* consumer goods, accompanied by a still more phenomenal increase in the production of *producer* goods such as factories which satisfy no direct human want but have become necessary in order to enable us to meet our increasing requirements for essentials. Considering the enormous statistical weight of the production figures in these two fields, it is not too surprising that our macro-economic analysts should have lost sight of a much less pleasing fact. This is that the production of luxuries—the goods above the zero level of survival, which alone measure the degree of a country's living standard—not only failed to experience a rise along with the output of those other goods. They actually seemed to have suffered a serious decline. As a result, what statistically looked like an advance, amounted in fact not to a rising but a declining standard of living.

To realize this, we need only compare the vaunted advanced living standards of our modern great-area states, the great powers, with those of small economic entities such as present-day Switzerland or medieval Nuremberg. Since the small *medieval* states are considered to have been more retarded in their economic development than the small states of our own time, let us concentrate on them rather than their modern counterparts. For even *medieval* states will show that, in spite of all the cars, bathrooms, health and education services made possible through large-area economies, we seem worse off than those much-ridiculed little economic realms that did without these facilities not because they were poorer but richer. They could *afford* to do without them.

Let us give some examples. It is, of course, conceded that no medieval state could have produced in a century as many units of a commodity, such as shirts or shoes, as a single modern factory is able to produce in a year. But this is beside the point, for the purpose of economic activity is not the increase in production but the satisfaction of human wants. And in this the medieval small state was as efficient as the modern great power, particularly if we take into account that its goods, being produced at a slower pace and by hand, were in addition better than their modern equivalents. The fact that they were maintained in serviceable condition for generations proved not the misery of an age that could not have paid for replacements, but the excellence of manufacture which made quantity efficiency unnecessary even if it had been feasible. If chairs, tables, doors, ironwork, chests of drawers produced in the quality-efficient small workshops of former days command even today such infinitely higher prices than their mass-produced modern equivalents, it is not because they are *scarce*. No man in his senses pays for something merely because it is old and cannot be reproduced. They fetch these high prices because they are *better* than our modern products. And one should not imagine that these pieces of furniture, which give such prestige to their present owners, could formerly be found only in the homes of the rich. They were and, if not destroyed by war or the deterioration of taste that accompanied the advent of the age of mass production, still are today, hundreds of years later, found in the peasants' houses of many European countries, giving them an air of stability and prosperous stateliness for which we look in vain in the shaky frame houses of the mechanized television-owning farmers of our own day.

Thus, though mass production yields unquestionably more units of goods per individual than small-shop manufacturing, it does not indicate the achievement of a higher living standard. For the *quality* of these more numerous goods, and their ability to satisfy our wants, seem to have declined in proportion to their increased availability. We not only *have* more shirts or shoes; we also *need* more shirts and shoes merely to *maintain* past standards. As a result, the actual satisfaction of our wants cannot be said to have experienced any increase simply because *essential* goods have become more plentiful along with our increased *need* for them.

But what about such goods as cars or aeroplanes which more than anything else symbolize the achievement of an integrated modern large-scale economy? There is again no doubt that these could never have been produced in small economies, at least not in such quantities. But once more the question arises: has their increased production increased the satisfaction of our travel wants? Hardly! In a small-state world, motor-cars were not needed. The satisfaction we desire in our travels is not the spanning of distances for the sake of distance but for the sake of extracting pleasure from the variety of different experiences which each different region and habit offers us. What we want from travel is adventure, not cars. The small-*state* world, being also a small-*scale* world, gave us all the excitement of vast space travel with the difference that we could find it all near by. A journey of fifty miles surprised the voyager with an almost infinite variety of new vistas and heretofore unknown experiences. Walking along, he would meet adventures, couriers, brigands, merchants, monks, and lords, and since they could not flit by in seventy-mile speeds as they do today, he not only would meet but also get to know them. He passed smoky smithies and stately inns. He passed vineyards and tin-mines. Each different city was a new world to him, with different customs, architectures, laws, and princes. The conversation with customs officials alone gave him more information than the reading of a dozen modern travel books whose main interest incidentally is that they still guide one occasionally through the remnants of former times. On a fifty-mile trip he passed through worlds, and learned about new products and devices he had never known before. And to sally forth into the unknown space for a distance of fifty miles required neither aeroplanes nor motor-cars.

To extract similar satisfactions from a large-area world, we must now travel not fifty but thousands of miles. To do this, we indeed need cars and planes, and speeds of a hundred miles per hour or more. But what do they give us in experience? Almost nothing. If we travel three thousand miles from New York to Los Angeles, we find the same kind of city on which we have just turned our back. If we go to the village of Hudson, one of the most northern places along the Canadian National Railway hewn out of the wilderness of virgin forests, and walk into a restaurant, we find the same sort of place we have just left behind in Brooklyn. Things that might be different, we have passed by because our super highways have been smoothed and straightened to such an extent that we no longer can afford to lose time by driving slowly. We may race up and down the entire North American continent and see nothing but Main Street all over again, filled with the same kind of people, following the same kind of business, reading the same kind of funnies and columnists, sharing the same movie stars, the same thoughts, the same laws, the same morals, the same convictions. This is why, if we want to read really exciting adventure stories nowadays, we have to fall back on Homer or Stevenson who crammed into their journeys of a few hundred miles more fascinating incidents than our modern cartoonists whose spaceships, travelling with many times the speed of light, lead us to distant stars in distant galaxies only to find what? That Kilroy had already been there, leaving a copy of the Constitution and a can of the beer that made Milwaukee famous.

If in several European vast-area states such as Italy, France, or Germany, so many exciting though rapidly dwindling differences are still experienced on relatively short journeys, it is because the medieval small-state diversity has left so lasting an imprint that no unifying process has as yet been able to wipe it out. Ironically, the largest single source of income of some of these advanced big-area states is often not found in their giant industry in which they take such pride, but in the money left them by tourists coming to enjoy the old-world charms and comforts created not by them but their 'backward' little predecessors. However, soon these last refuges of former small-scale living will be swallowed up by the impending further improvements of our travel and transportation means. Being able to span distances still faster, it will become uneconomical as well as impossible to stop anywhere except at hamburger stands along the roads, and in the terminal towns of the big autostradas from which every difference will have disappeared for ever. And with it will be gone the purpose of all travel.

2. The Creation of Necessities

Cars seem thus to have brought us less satisfaction than a good old steed or a pair of sturdy shoes brought our forefathers. However, one may say, cars and other highly efficient means of modern transportation such as tubes or bus services are no longer a luxury to satisfy our travel wants. They have become a necessity to satisfy our basic needs. This is quite true. But since when is the creation of new necessities a sign of progress? Our fantastic media of communication and transportation, which we take for a token of higher living standards, are nothing but the symptom of our increasing enslavement. Without them, we would not only be reduced to a level of hopeless starvation; unlike our forefathers, who did not need them, we would be condemned to extinction. Their introduction has cost us much, but brought no gain. Previously we would reach our place of work by strolling leisurely from the second floor of our homes to the first, or across the street. Because we spent most of our time near our homes, we beautified them and thereby helped create the lovely cities of former days in which it was as joyful to live as it is now an agony. No one dreamt of *escaping* from them. Everything, the church, the taverns, the authorities, the theatres, our friends, and even the countryside, was within easy reach of everybody. Since the things that belonged together for a rich and full life were not separated into residential, theatre, business, banking, government, and factory districts, an unhurried walk of half a mile per day met all economic requirements without the dependence on 'the world's best commuter service', whose very necessity for excellence is an indication of the misery of functionalized modern large-scale living. Professor Schrödinger has well described this condition when he writes:

'But consider only the "marvellous reduction of size" of the world by the fantastic modern means of traffic. All distances have been reduced to almost nothing, when measured not in miles but in hours of *quickest* transport. But when measured in the costs of even the *cheapest* transport they have been doubled or trebled even in the last 10 or 20 years. The result is that many families and groups of close friends have been scattered over the globe as never before. In many cases they are not rich enough ever to meet again, in others they do so under terrible sacrifices for a short time ending in a heart-rending farewell. Does this make for human happiness?'[1]

All that modern large-scale development has brought about seems thus a phenomenal increase in the production, not of luxury goods, which would indeed mean a higher living standard, but of the goods we *need* to cope with the phenomenal difficulties it has created. It has showered tools on us, without adding to the value of our possessions. Having placed *un*necessary distances between friends and families or between offices and homes, it has provided us with the now *necessary* facilities to span them again but at an expense which increasingly fewer people can afford without curtailing their consumption of more pleasureful commodities. It has given us air-conditioning, not as an improvement, but as a *necessary* addition, since modern buildings have lost the magic of pleasant temperatures that clung to the thick-walled houses of former times. And along with its new cooling system it has furnished us with previously unknown techniques of catching pneumonia. It has shortened our working time, but it has lengthened our unproductive, though not less exhausting, commuting time by more than we have gained by working less. It has enabled us to keep homes in the country instead of the now hated city. But their function has declined to serving us as inconveniently distant dormitories of which we have become the tired absentee owners. It has provided us with those famous bathrooms in which our theorists must think we spend most of our waking hours, so proud are they of this particular symbol of a high living standard. But at the same time it has made us so dirty by the end of the day that we can hardly say that our daily showers have made us any cleaner. It has enabled us to drive to our offices in our own vehicles, only to cause the disruption of our wits when we try to find a parking space. This means that now we are in need not only of space, rendered scarce by the abundance of cars, but

[1] Erwin Schrödinger, *Science and Humanism*. London: Cambridge University Press, 1951, p. 3.

of psycho-analytic treatment, rendered necessary to undo the mental effects of our harassing search for space. It has lowered our death rate at birth, but the resulting population densities have produced a proportionate increase in the death rate of mid-life. A survey conducted in 1951 showed that in the United States the 'death rate as a whole is one of the world's lowest; but after the age of 45, Americans cannot expect to live as long as their contemporaries in many other countries, e.g. England, Canada, the Netherlands, and especially Denmark and Norway ... A dig into the records shows that American men have more fatal accidents and more heart disease. American women have more accidents, more diabetes.'[1] But why should there be more heart disease and accidents in the highly advanced United States (population 155,000,000) and, in descending order, in Great Britain (51,000,000), Canada (15,000,000), and the Netherlands (9,000,000), than 'especially' in Denmark (4,000,000) and Norway (2,500,000) except for the fact that the strains of integrated modern large-scale living lessen as the size of a country's population becomes smaller and its pace slower?

It is said, however, that modern life has at least taught us all to read and write. Which is true. But it seems to have failed to raise our educational standards. So that the modern literate person can grasp anything at all, he must have everything pre-chewed, condensed, and broken down into cartoon language. Marx's *Communist Manifesto*, a brilliant essay that a hundred years ago could be understood by the workers of the world to whom it was addressed, has outgrown the reach of the average mass-educated college student of the twentieth century. His vaunted literacy seems to have given him no other ability than that of answering *yes* or *no* to questions if they are properly put, and of filling in forms entitling him to intellectual senility pensions from the age of twenty onward. Our ancestors, unable either to read or write, seem to have had more education in the tips of their fingers than we have in our heads. When the brothers Grimm wrote down their fairy tales, which they had collected by listening to illiterates, they brought forth one of the masterpieces of literature. In antiquity, not only people were unable to read or write but, as in Greece, even some of their greatest poets. So they *sang* their epics! And what epics these were! And what audiences they had! Never again will it be possible for a poet to capture in the melody of his lines the sound of the sea, or of leaves rustling softly in a breeze, since our advanced technology has enabled us to do all this much more realistically and fashionably by crushing ice cubes in a champagne bucket.

[1] *Time*, 3 December 1951.

While it is thus true that smaller economies did produce fewer goods, these were both more lasting than ours and more satisfying in meeting the demands of a society adjusted to the pleasures and leisures of a slower pace. Life, there, was like walking on a belt moving under one's feet in opposite direction. But since the belt's movement was slow, it needed only a leisurely effort to counterbalance its speed. Few shoes were worn out and little energy was consumed by the tasks of existence.[1] Large-scale living, on the other hand, has increased the speed of the belt tremendously, with the result that the successful individual now no longer can afford to walk. He must run. And our production and living standard experts point to the runner with pride and say: 'Look at his health, his physique, his muscles, his chest, and take note of the food, vitamin, shoe, and bath-water supply which modern science provides for him.' All of which overwhelms us. But what we fail to see is that he *needs* all this desperately, and to accomplish what? the same thing the small-state stroller accomplished in leisure and pleasure—to keep up with the belt's speed. Nothing more and, perhaps, not even that, because, the greater the belt's speed, the more likely is it that even the best runner will fall behind. And this is, indeed, what historic evidence seems to prove: that vast-scale economic expansion has caused not an advance but a back-sliding of living standards and that what we confront in the fantastic increase in production is nothing other than a form of inflation. More of the new goods seem to give us less satisfaction than fewer of the old ones.[2]

[1] That this did not mean a low standard of living was well illustrated by an eighteenth-century traveller through Italy and France. When comparing the seemingly poorer life of Venice with that of his native England which was already harvesting the first fruits of the Industrial Revolution, he noted: 'Luxury here takes a turn much more towards enjoyment than consumption; the sobriety of the people does much, the nature of their food more; pastes, macaroni, and vegetables are much easier provided than beef and mutton. Cookery, as in France, enables them to spread a table for half the expense of an English one.' (Arthur Young, *Travels in France and Italy*. Everyman's Library, No. 720, pp. 254–5.)

[2] As a monetary inflation, according to Professor Anatol Murad of Rutgers University, is characterized not by an abundance but a shortage of currency which banks must try to meet by issuing increasing quantities in response to the rising demand of people who now need *more* currency simply to buy the *same* amount of goods, so a production inflation may be said to be characterized not by an abundance but a shortage of *producer* and *essential* consumer goods which is met by manufacturers producing more and more of these new goods simply to obtain the same degree of satisfaction it obtained previously from fewer units of the old ones.

3. From Princes to Paupers

So far, the comparison of living standards has run perhaps on lines too general to be entirely believable. In order to obtain a more realistic picture it will, therefore, be of help to test the relative effect of small- and large-area economic development on the style of living of some specific professions, from kings down to workers. This will show that, from whatever angle we approach the subject, the result is always the same, indicating not a rise but a decline along the entire line.

To begin with the *rulers*, there can be no doubt that the sovereigns of little states lived in far greater material splendour than their large-power successors of modern times. Could the Queen of England afford today what every petty prince could afford formerly? Build a riding school, a theatre, an art gallery? What she still has in regal trimmings such as palaces and castles has been provided for her not by the rich present but the poor past. If the President of the United States were to build a swimming pool for his horses, he would be investigated and possibly impeached for reckless spending. Even if he could afford the extravagance of our ancestors, our socially conscious age would not permit him to display it in deference, obviously, not to the superior but the inferior standards of the masses. However prosperous our century may be, our rulers can hardly be said to have benefited by it. Nor have the rich. In fact, nowhere has the decline in living standards been experienced more drastically than amongst the rich and the heads of those states whose economies are said to have advanced most conspicuously.

But what about other professions such as *scholars?* University professors of Bologna or Prague of former days, or of contemporary Denmark or Switzerland, lived in a style that is scarcely within the reach of American bank directors of the 1950s. They owned stately houses, had coachmen and maids, gave two or three lectures a week, entertained scholars of near and distant lands, and set a table for their guests whose culinary excellence rivalled that of the best inns. Their present-day counterparts in the world's richest countries, preaching in their classrooms the improvements of modern living, teach twelve to fifteen hours a week, live in small cottages with cubby-hole rooms if they are prosperous or, if not, in trailers mounted on cement, supplement their incomes by taking on extra jobs and, if they give a cocktail party for their colleagues more than once a year, are pushed to the border of financial ruin.

College students in the 'low-living-standard' countries of former times used their summer vacations for reading, musing, travelling abroad, or generally doing little except absorb the fruit of a year's learning. Students of today, on the other hand, again full of pride in the rise of a living standard which is praised by all and experienced by none, have to work through all of their vacations as dishwashers, postal clerks, or lorry drivers to get enough cash by autumn to finish an education from which they cannot profit because modern 'wealth' does not give them enough leisure to digest it. In fairness to the argument I should, however, point out that students of earlier times did not always have the luxurious ease just pictured. They, too, had to work occasionally. Thus, Professor G. G. Coulton, in order to awaken the sentimentalist lovers of the Middle Ages to the facts of life, writes of the end of the fifteenth century that 'if we ourselves were Cambridge University men of that day, we might very well recognize several undergraduates among the harvesters; the Long Vacation, such as it was, would include both hay and corn harvest, and some students, like their brethren of America today, must have been able to do manual work in part payment of their expenses'.[1] This was undoubtedly the case. But it must be kept in mind that, in the first place, fifteenth-century England, though small, had, unlike Bologna or Florence, as yet not reached a state of economic maturity and can consequently not be compared with *mature* large-area economies. And secondly, in spite of its admitted stage of retarded development, the worst Professor Coulton could say in an apparent attempt to prove the lower living standard of the Middle Ages was that 'some' students of that period did what a vast number of 'their brethren' still have to do today in the fully developed rich America—work in part payment of their expenses. Whatever this proves, it does not exactly seem to prove any advance in a student's style of living.

And so we could run through nearly all professions and still come to the same conclusion. *Shoemakers* or *tailors* from the city-state of Nuremberg, to judge from contemporary descriptions and the evidence of pictorial illustrations, lived in a patrician style such as few prosperous modern merchants can afford. *Journeymen* were able to lead a life now enjoyed, perhaps, by the higher ranks of university professors in the United States. *Workers* had the material comforts and goods which their modern equivalents may have also, with the difference, however, that the latter seem no longer able to enjoy them as much in this age of haste, superficiality, and separated functions.

And *housewives?* Well housewives had maids, those most pleasant

[1] G. G. Coulton, *Medieval Panorama*. Cambridge University Press, 1938; New York: Macmillan, 1945, pp. 69–70.

symbols of high living standards whom almost no one in the 'high-living-standard' countries of the world seems to be able to afford any longer. And the few who still can, have found out that they must humour them to such an extent that it is no longer worth having them in the first place. In England, for instance, in order to ensure their return in the morning, housewives must do the dishes of the preceding evening meal themselves. For a maid will no longer condescend to start work except in an atmosphere indicating that most of it has already been done by the mistress. Which again cannot exactly be called an improvement in the latter's position. The only profession that seems to have experienced a genuine improvement is that of the maids themselves. And this, ironically, is the only profession which its own rising living standard is rapidly driving out of existence.

However, it is said, the disappearance of maids is precisely one of the most convincing proofs of the advance in living standards. For those who formerly were servants are now housewives, secretaries, or business women. But in this case they must, of course, be compared not with maids of former times but with the former occupants of the jobs they hold now—with housewives, secretaries, or business women. And these, as we have seen, could afford the maids which their successors of today no longer can. That there are now more individuals in a higher profession than there were previously does not in itself indicate that the standards of that profession have risen. On the contrary! As the laws of diminishing marginal productivity tell us, an increase in the numbers of a professional group will eventually not raise but depress individual standards. This is exactly what has taken place. Thus, all that the disappearance of maids shows is not an improvement of their condition, which has become meaningless since their species is dying out and the dead cannot have any standards; but a lowering of the level of those professions whose ranks they swelled in the expectation of greater benefits only to find that their very act of joining whittled them away. When they broke into the ranks of housewives in those 'unprecedented numbers' which are for ever presented to us as the infallible sign of progress while they indicate merely an inflationary washing-down process, they hoped to have maids themselves now. But what did they discover? That their 'rising' living standard had successfully eliminated the quaint amenities of a 'retarded' past. Instead of turning every maid into a housewife, progress has turned every housewife into a maid.[1]

[1] Jane Whitbread and Vivian Cadden (*The Intelligent Man's Guide to Women.* New York: Schuman, 1951) have well described the blessings of progress when

What is true of individual professions is equally true of classes and communities. Naturally, small states also had their share of poverty but, since their inhabitants were few, their poor were fewer still. And these did not constitute a fraction of the social problem reflected in the scandalous unemployment figures of the rich great powers of our time. In addition, it must be noted that the 'unemployed' of former times, the beggars, were not frustrated proletarians but members of an ancient and honourable caste who abstained from the hardships of work not as a result of the insensible forces of depression but, like kings, in pursuit of a dignified and happy way of life. Had a reformer offered them relief, he would in all likelihood have met with the same objections as were raised in 1951 by the beggars of Lhasa when the Chinese communist invaders of Tibet tried to 'rehabilitate' them, free them from 'oppression', and improve their economic status by providing them with work. Instead of showing gratitude they firmly rejected the very idea of employment by pointing out that 'they followed their "traditional profession" as a result of "sins in previous life" and not because of "oppression".' How greatly they must have enjoyed suffering for their previous sins may be deduced from the assertion of one of their spokesmen to the effect that 'we are happy begging, and furthermore we are not used to work'.[1]

We frequently bewail the poverty of the Middle Ages, and in the next breath castigate the profligacy of their princes for staging festivals for their subjects lasting weeks, and the economic madness of their bishops for declaring half a dozen saint's days every month. Thus, Professor Pasquale Villari writes in his work on Savonarola that Lorenzo the Magnificent

'. . . encouraged all the worst tendencies of the age and multiplied its corruption. Abandoned to pleasure himself, he urged the people to lower depths of abandonment in order to plunge them into the

---

they write that 'every laboursaving device of the past century has added to women's work. . . . A man invents a vacuum cleaner and . . . a co-conspirator popularizes Venetian blinds, so there will be something else for the vacuum cleaner to do in a jiffy. A man turns out a simple little mechanism to make melon balls, and it's no longer *comme il faut* to toss a plain hunk of melon into a fruit salad. . . . In the period when beer came in kegs, the man of the house hauled it himself. Now that it comes in handy little cans, even a woman can lug a dozen from the delicatessen. The man who speeds by a woman, stopped by a flat tire, can't be accused of lack of chivalry. He knows that the way they make jacks these days, even a woman can change a tire.'

[1] *New York Times*, 11 November 1951.

lethargy of intoxication. In fact, during his reign Florence was a continuous scene of revelry and dissipation.'[1]

We know from many other sources that this picture of princely *and*
popular revelry and dissipation is neither exaggerated nor unique. It
prevailed in many other little states. But surely, if they could afford
this extravagance in work-free holidays and the 'lethargy of intoxication' which even the most ambitious labour leader of our day would not
dare to claim for his wards, their living standard must have been considerably higher than we imagine, and the last beggar must have had a
jollier time than a car- and bathtub-owning member of John L. Lewis's
powerful mineworkers' union. This is all the more striking as, unlike
the sterile extravagance of modern periods of prosperity, these earlier
periods produced not only material but also intellectual abundance. In
the midst of this revelry and dissipation, slumless cities grew of unmatched beauty, books were written of unmatched depth, and paintings
were created of unmatched charm.

4. The Size Theory of Business Cycles

If we could overcome the preposterous conceit of considering ourselves the most advanced of all generations, though no other generation has proved itself so utterly incapable of solving its problems as
ours, we might at last surrender to the evidence of facts and realize
that the small-state world was economically as happy and satisfying as
any world inhabited by man could be. It certainly seems to have been
more satisfying than the big-scale arrangement that followed it. But
why should this have been so? Up to this point we argued with comparisons. Now we must furnish a reason. And the reason for the
deterioration of modern economic development is again, as in the case
of all other problems of the universe, that something has become too
big. And the thing that seems to have become too big is not only the
individual production *unit* which is discussed later, but the production
area, the market, the integrated economic territory of modern large
powers.

As has already been indicated, it is not any particular economic
system that seems at fault, but economic *size*. Whatever outgrows certain limits begins to suffer from the irrepressible problem of unmanageable proportions. When this happens to a community, its problems will

[1] Pasquale Villari, *Life and Times of Savonarola*. New York: Charles Scribner's
Sons, 1896, p. 45.

not only increase faster than its growth; they will be of a new order, arising no longer from the business of living but from the business of growing. Instead of growth serving life, life must now serve growth, perverting the very purpose of existence. Economically speaking this means that once a society outgrows its proper size, a size determined by its function of providing the individual with the greatest possible benefits, an ever-increasing portion of its increasing product and productivity must be used to raise not the personal standard of its members but the social standard of the community as such. Up to a point the two are complementary and can be raised simultaneously; but beyond it they become mutually exclusive, the perfected tool turning into a self-seeking master, and the swollen means into its self-serving end. From then on, the more powerful a society becomes, the more of its increasing product, instead of increasing individual consumption, is devoured by the task of coping with the problems caused by the rise of its very power. The more it gains in density, the more is devoured by the process of meeting the problems caused by its increasing density. And the more it advances, the more is devoured by the problems resulting from its very advance.

Examples of the first category of such 'growth' products which enhance the standard of society without adding to the material welfare of its members are what might be called *power commodities* such as tanks, bombs, or the increase in government services required to administer increased power. In the United States, the production increase in this field between 1950 and 1951, as expressed by the increase in government expenditures, amounted to no less than 18 billion dollars, or 72 per cent of the much-hailed 25-billion dollar increase of our total gross national product.[1] Growth products of the second category, or *density commodities*, rendered necessary as a result of population increases but no more capable of adding to an individual's happiness than bombs, are goods such as traffic lights, first-aid equipment, tube services, or replacement goods for losses which would never have occurred in less harassed smaller societies. In 1950, such replacements necessary as a result of fire losses in the United States amounted

[1] As to the objection that the period 1950–51 represents an exceptional rise in government expenditures due to exceptional defence outlays, it must be pointed out that in the future high and increasing defence expenditures will not be exceptional but normal, considering that the danger of war is not the exceptional but normal by-product of the uneasy balance of our two-power world. Exceptional was the pre-1950 illusion, inducing a *temporary* reduction in government expenditures between 1945 and 1950, that defence expenditures could ever be reduced again.

to almost $700,000,000,[1] and those caused by the 9 million casualties of the same year—of which 35,000 were fatal *car* accidents, more than the loss of life incurred in many a major war—to $7,700,000,000.[2] Growth products of the third category, which one might call *progress commodities*, are (*a*) improvements rendered necessary by improvements such as the improved anti-aircraft guns whose costs rose between 1945 and 1950 from $10,000 to $275,000, or more than twenty-seven times, so that they could match the improvements achieved during the same period by aircraft which, in turn, had to be further improved to match the increased deadliness of the improved anti-aircraft guns; and (*b*) those *unwanted* tie-in products we must acquire along with the *desired* fruit of progress such as licence plates or parking space with cars, repair work with television sets, idle standby orchestras with gramophone records, or *bogus* printer's type along with the real. The bulk of the vaunted production and productivity increase experienced by to-day's great powers goes into these personally sterile but socially necessary growth commodities. It raises not our real but our bogus standard of living by giving us the illusion of increasing wealth while, like currency in inflation, it amounts to nothing but an enormous increase in the price and effort an expanding society imposes on us for giving us the goods we really desire.[3]

But even if we allow ourselves to be swept for a moment off our feet by the stunning production figures of large-scale economies; and even if we concede that in modern times production can reach such staggering totals that it may lift not only the margin of essentials but of luxuries as well; we cannot ignore the fact that along with vast-scale economies developed the phenomenon of *business cycles* which, as Penelope did with her cloth, undo in the nights of depression whatever they may have accomplished in the days of prosperity. And business cycles are no longer just inherent in the *capitalist* system, as is maintained by capitalist and socialist theorists alike. That is why both advocate some form of a *controlled* economy as a solution to our present economic difficulties. With their modern connotation of destructiveness, they are inherent in *large-scale* systems. They arise from over-

---

[1] *Facts and Trends.* National Board of Fire Underwriters, Vol. VIII, No. 4.

[2] National Safety Council, 1950.

[3] The price of society (price of government plus price of security plus price of producer goods necessary to provide us with consumer goods) has risen in the growing United States from 27% of our total gross national product in 1939 to 37% in 1951. Though the latter figure represents a decline from the 51% of the peak war year of 1945, the trend of the cost of society to increase more than proportionately with its increasing power has established itself firmly since 1947.

growth. A better name for them would therefore be *growth cycles*, since their destructive nature and scale depend not on business but on *growing* business, and not only on growing *business* but on growing *industrialization* and *integration*.[1]

Nothing proves this better than a glance at Russia where communism has been introduced on the assumption that this would eliminate once and for all the wasteful misery of cyclical fluctuations. Yet, in

---

[1] Business cycles, in so far as they are defined as periodically recurring fluctuations of economic activities, adhere to all economic systems that live, whether they are small or large. They are a sign of life. As such they constitute neither a problem, nor can they be avoided. But while all have as their general cause the dynamics of existence, a number of special causes may have multiplying effects on either specific or all economic systems. And it is the multiplier that constitutes the problem, not the fluctuation, just as in man it is not the heartbeat but the excessive heartbeat that causes concern. Before capitalism, cyclical fluctuations in economic activities were magnified by the cyclical fluctuations of non-economic forces such as weather, disease, or war. With the advent of capitalism, the external non-economic causes were augmented by internal economic causes, magnifying the natural fluctuations as a result of the working of the economic system itself. Modern business cycle theorists are therefore quite correct when they maintain that certain cycles, business cycles in the narrower sense, are inherent in the profit-seeking business system of capitalism. The accumulation of profit or, as Marx says, of surplus value, must periodically lead to the impossibility of selling the full output since those retaining the money profit from production do not want to buy their own surplus product, while those willing to buy it, the workers, have no surplus money left with which they *could* buy it. Hence, curtailment of production, unemployment, and the idea that capitalist business cycles might be checked through the introduction of a planned economy. Up to a given development stage, the traditional interpretation as well as the idea of an effective cure by control was perfectly valid. However, with the large-scale integration of modern economies resulting on the one hand from the growth of capitalist business and, on the other hand, from the political integration of increasingly large population complexes, the peculiarly capitalist cause of cyclical fluctuations has lost most of its significance. For even under capitalism, the true problem of cyclical fluctuations has never been one of origin or nature but of scale, just as the problem of waves in the sea is not whether they are caused by winds or the inner agitation of water, but whether they are large or little. And the scale of fluctuations, depending in its magnitude not on the system but on the size of the integrated social complex through which the wave of economic activities transmits itself, has become such as a result of recent unification processes that a controlled economy is as unable to offer checks as an uncontrolled one. For even the effectiveness of control depends on limited social size. Thus while it is true that certain kinds of cycles are in their origin peculiar to capitalism, they have long ceased to be a problem plaguing the world. The modern problem in economics, as in most other fields, has become one of scale, making the distinction among systems obsolete. It is in the sense of the scale, growth, or size cycle, that the term business cycle is used in this chapter.

spite of the most rigid control measures, depressions occur in Russia as regularly as in any other large-area state. The only difference is that, there, they are neither called nor recognized as such. Unable to comprehend why a typically capitalist phenomenon, attributed to the business man's effort to increase his profit, could play havoc also with the heartland of communism where profit is no motive and everything is supposed to be under control, Soviet authorities have solved the dilemma by ascribing the mysteriously recurring dislocations of their economy to either incompetence or the criminal negligence of 'the enemies of the people, the Trotskyite-Bukharin and bourgeois nationalistic diversionaries and spies'.[1] As a result, Russian depressions have produced the peculiarity of being frequently accompanied by waves of managerial purges, giving rise to the irreverent but highly descriptive term *liquidation cycle*. Otherwise, however, they show all the traditional hallmarks of old-fashioned cyclical disruptions such as misdirected production, unemployed resources, and the uncanny inability to distribute stocks piling up in regions where they are not needed. Thus, Harry Schwartz quotes in his book on *Russia's Soviet Economy* a Soviet writer as declaring in 1933 that 'mines, steel works and plants in the light and food industries were choked up with unshipped output . . . The railroads could not even deal with shipments of rails, fastenings, or pipe, the needs of transport itself.' By the end of 1934, the situation had deteriorated to a point that 'there were more than 3 million tons of timber awaiting rail shipment, along with 2 million tons of coal and almost 1 million tons of ore. A total of 15 million tons of cargo, altogether, awaited shipment at that time. Heavy industry alone had 650,000 freight cars piled up awaiting transportation.'[2] All this in a *controlled* economy.

What caused this? Communism? Of course not, since the same things happen in capitalist depressions. Mismanagement? This was still less likely, since the Soviet manager knows that his failure, unlike in capitalist countries, means not only the loss of his job and wealth, but of his freedom and perhaps even his head. Absence of experience and technical knowhow? This can again not be the reason, since their uncontested possession in capitalist countries could not prevent *their* depressions either. It is inability, the plain sheer unadulterated inability of man to cope with the problems of societies that have grown too large. What Thomas Malthus said of the relationship between food and population—that the population must outrun its food supply because

[1] Harry Schwartz, *Russia's Soviet Economy*. New York: Prentice-Hall, 1950, p. 210. [2] Ibid., p. 337.

of its tendency to multiply at a geometric ratio while the latter increases only at an arithmetic ratio—is true also of the relation between human talent and the problems of size. While the latter multiply at a geometric ratio once an organism begins to outgrow its optimum limits, the human ability to cope with them seems to increase only at an arithmetic ratio, and even that only up to a certain point. No degree or training, university education, or organization can compensate for the pace with which the problems of size outdistance our effort to catch up with them.

This is why no measure of human control, whether suggested by Karl Marx or Lord Keynes, can present a solution to problems which have arisen precisely because an organism has outgrown all human control. The cause of modern business cycle problems can therefore not be found in the *natural* functioning of capitalism, nor in the *mismanaged* or *immature* functioning of communism. It is found in the *vast scale* of modern economies. It is found in what some lucid Soviet writer was able to sneak into the text of a decree of 26 February 1938, when he wrote in involuntary deviationism from strictly Marxist doctrines that 'the biggest shortcoming in planning and construction is gigantomania'.[1] And gigantomania is the natural concomitant not of capitalism but of large-scale development.

The idea that cyclical fluctuations, in so far as they do constitute a major problem, are phenomena of size and not of capitalism seems also verified by the fact that, while they have made their appearance in communist Russia, which is large, they have failed to give evidence of their destructive nature in capitalist countries which have remained small politically as well as economically.[2] No one has ever heard of a depression problem in capitalist Liechtenstein or Andorra (or, for that matter, in any country during the early stage of capitalist development, which is always characterized by its competitive *small*-unit pattern or in largely agricultural countries whose lacework of self-sufficient farms and regions splits their economic unity). Their boundaries have the effect of piers and sea walls, breaking the violence of the storms tormenting the open oceans, and admitting them into the sheltered smallness of the harbour only as harmless ripples. Switzerland, Denmark,

---

[1] Ibid., p. 209.

[2] The two are not necessarily always the same. Luxembourg is politically a miniature state but through its giant steel industry it is economically a vast-scale economy. Because of this we find cyclical fluctuations of considerable degree in spite of the fact that the country is small, since it is small only politically, not economically.

Norway, or Sweden, having a number of industries which have broken through the limiting boundaries of their states, are somewhat more vulnerable but, being small none the less, the problems of business cycles have never as yet outgrown the natural ability of their sturdy leaders. One may say that, as in the case of Denmark, Norway, or Sweden, this is due to the fact that capitalism has been tempered by a measure of socialist direction, and that it is because of *this* that the Scandinavian countries could check the germ of depression more successfully than others. True, they did check it, but not because of socialist direction. All they proved was merely that *everything* works on the small scale, capitalism *as well as* socialism. In small states only nature can exert a depressing influence, and with this man's ingenuity can cope. In large states, on the other hand, it is not nature which leads to depressions but man's inability to deal with monstrous proportions. As a result, only there do we find 'poverty in the midst of plenty', except in Russia, where we find poverty in the midst of poverty. Only there do we find factories ready for use, workers willing to work, employers eager to produce, side by side with a total and allegedly inexplicable inability to do anything whatsoever.

The consequence of bigness is thus always the same: the inability to cope with the problems it creates. Whatever large-scale economies may have accomplished in the way of production increase in the only field that counts from the point of view of rising living standards, the field of luxuries, has been devoured in cyclical destruction. And what has not been devoured in destruction has been whittled away by the necessity of dividing the greater product amongst a greater number of people to meet greater needs, or of putting it aside as an idle reserve against uncertain disaster.

It is therefore only when dealing with overall aggregates and *national* income figures—which, to paraphrase Marx, are the opiate of all those who delight in the soothing macro-economic approach that has become the unfortunate necessity of macro-social living—that modern times do indeed show impressive increases in *total* income and *total* wealth. But we do not live in macro-economic aggregates, as the youth indicated who complained: 'According to statistical evidence, there are two and a half women to every man—and I have none.' So long as society has not become a levelled-off honey-producing bee cooperative, we shall live as micro-economic individuals, at the margin of reality, not in consoling averages. This is the only level that matters. It is there that we realize what we would never guess by reading our textbooks—that our vaunted modern vast-scale development seems to be nothing but a backsliding device. It runs in vain against the iron laws of economics which, like those of the universe in general, put a limit to every expansion and accumulation. The totals may increase, yet the margins may decline. But it is at the margins where living standards are determined and where we see that, with every new promulgation of record figures praising progress and unification, streets which were previously clean become dirty; and that, with every new economic concentration at the centre, a new slum arises at the widening fringes of the periphery, dissolving its social fabric, and breeding miseries such as no small-scale economy ever knew. For on a small scale, ends never fringe.

Oblivious of their own inconsistency, some of our modernists point out that small states had an easier time of it, being so insignificant in size and population. But this is exactly it! Because they were small, they could not only solve their problems better than their large counterparts; they could do so without the assistance of such brilliant minds as Marx, Schacht, Cripps, or Keynes. They did not need to deal with aggregates which, in large countries, even statisticians can only guess, and whose meaning even experts do not always understand. They could at all times see their economy at their feet—open, surveyable, manageable. They did not need to operate on assumptions which no one on earth can prove, however great his learning and many his degrees. Even a Minister of Finance could understand what was going on, and could direct economic activities with lucidity instead of daring. And every elementary-school teacher could be Minister of Finance.

What our macro-economists might do, therefore, is not to complain that small states had no great problems because they were so small, and then blissfully suggest their elimination in the interest of economic progress. They might advocate the elimination of the condition that requires a macro-economic approach in the first place. If gigantomania seems our chief economic problem, as it seems also our chief political problem, the solution is of course not further unification but the restoration of a small-cell economic system in which all problems are reduced to proportions in which they can be solved by everybody, not only by a genius, who may not always be forthcoming. A small-*cell* pattern does not necessarily mean a small-*state* pattern. But it is so obviously the cure that even Russia has come to the conclusion that she must abandon her original dream of turning the entire country into a single factory. Rather, as becomes increasingly evident, she is developing a pattern of small self-sufficient economic regions. Instead of erasing economic boundaries, she has begun to recreate them, not as tariff

barriers but as invisible walls behind which innumerable local economies can be developed within ranges that can again be mastered by
normal human beings.[1] The same tendency has manifested itself also
in capitalist countries in the form of the *co-operative* movement. The
principal device of the latter for eliminating the terrors of violent economic fluctuations is the creation of production and market units of so
small a size that their activities can at all times be surveyed and antici-
pated. Since the consequences of economic behaviour can be foreseen
only in units that are small, the smallness of the economic complex is
not an accidental but the most fundamental characteristic of co-
operative concepts. It excludes gigantomania by constitution, as early
capitalism excluded it by competition.

The productive superiority of small *economies*, based in addition on relatively small economic *units*, was shown in a United States Senate Report
of 1946, of which David Cushman Coyle gives the following summary:

'A Senate report in 1946 compared the life of various middle-sized
cities which are dependent on either big or little business but otherwise
closely alike. In cities A and C about 95 per cent of the factory workers
were employed by big absentee companies; in cities B and D only 13
to 15 per cent were so employed. Wages were higher in the big-business
towns A and C, but unemployment was worse during the depression.
In A and C the stores were poor because of the heavy risk of unemployment, and many people went to other towns.

'Naturally the small-business cities, B and D, had many more business owners and officers, and there were several times as many $10,000
incomes and 50 to 100 per cent more income-tax payers. That is, there
was a larger middle and upper class, with loyalties that were mainly
local. Accordingly, these small-business cities had more civic enterprises, better co-operation with labour in civic affairs, and a better city
to live in. Statistics were there to prove the point. The small-business
cities had less than half the slums and a much lower infant death. They
had more magazine subscribers, more private telephones and electric
meters, more church members, and bigger libraries and parks.'[2]

5. *The Reason for the Illusion of Progress*

From whatever point we may look at it, the idea of a rising living
standard produced by modern large-scale economic development seems

[1] See Harry Schwartz, op. cit.
[2] David Cushman Coyle, *Day of Judgement*. New York: Harper and Brothers,
1949, p. 116.

little more than a myth magnified by repetition to a degree that it has taken on the appearance of unchallengeable truth. But how could this have come about, particularly in an age whose scientific pretensions demand that everything must be proved by facts and figures? The explanation is not too difficult.

In the first place, in spite of the mass of figures at their disposal, our analysts are frequently too timid to give them interpretations contradicting accepted prejudices. They do what that acolyte opinion pollster of Denver, Colorado, did before the presidential elections of 1948, when all his figures indicated a victory for President Truman. But because the renowned prince-archbishops of polling proclaimed *ex cathedra* that the President did not have a chance, he mistrusted the result of his own research and, by his own admission, changed his figures for fear the correct ones would not be believed.

In the second place, even where analysts do not inflict violence on their material, they often convey wrong impressions by comparing the wrong things. Instead of comparing *mature* large economies such as the United States with *mature* small ones such as modern Switzerland or medieval Florence at the peak of their development, they compare them with *immature* small ones such as modern Haiti or medieval England. The reason for the latter is in part because England is the one country with whose medieval history most of us are really familiar. But it is unfortunately also one of those countries whose medieval development was amongst the most retarded. Naturally, by having medieval England instead of medieval Florence, Venice, or Nuremberg in mind, we are able to construe an illusion of our own progress that has nothing to do with reality. The same illusion can be obtained if we compare our farmers' houses with those of modern Haiti which, in spite of being small, is also retarded. To get a proper picture we have to compare them with the peasant houses of small *mature* states such as Liechtenstein or Switzerland. Then we shall find that it is safer to advertise the progress of modern times in Haiti rather than in the valleys of the Alps.

The most important error, however, has been made with regard not to countries but to periods. Because of the wealth of sources made available through the work of great economic writers, we have fallen into the habit of comparing the well-documented twentieth with the well-documented nineteenth century. Both of these are characterized by the same vast-scale development. Within *this* period we may indeed say that we have economically advanced. But this is not surprising considering that the first result of economic unification and large-area development was not only an increase in wealth but also in misery. Marx has formulated this phenomenon in his *law of capitalist accumulation* whose only error is that it attributes to the system of capitalism what was solely due to the *overgrowth* of its institutions.[1] Before capitalism outgrew its competitive small-unit pattern, it suffered little of the subsequent miseries of accumulation. For as long as its cells were small, it provided automatically what our time tries so desperately to accomplish through the use of government direction—a harmonious distribution that prevented the accumulation of either excessive wealth or excessive misery in the first place.[2]

It was *this* period then, symbolized by the advent not of capitalism but of vast-scale economic unification made possible through the industrial revolution, which characteristically furnished as the first sign of its 'stupendous improvement' descriptions of poverty and child labour abuses such as no retarded medieval state could ever have provided. And it was *this* period which, also characteristically, produced the world's greatest social reform movements. But an increase in social reform movements is a sign of worsening, not of improving, conditions. If social reformers were rare in former ages, it could only have been so because these were better off than ours. After all, man was not less courageous and eager for happiness in the fourteenth century than in the twentieth. All that can therefore be said in favour of the idea that we have advanced is that the living standard of the earlier small-state period had so declined under the first impact of the industrial

---

[1] It is strange that Marx should have failed to link misery to the *scale* rather than the *system* of economic activities, for no one has shown better than he himself that the weaknesses of capitalism come into existence only when things outgrow certain limits. In his *Capitalist Contradictions*, as has been mentioned in an earlier chapter, he pictures the decline of capitalism as due to the fact that *increasing* surplus value will result in declining profit; *increasing* exploitation in the strengthening of the proletariat; *increasing* production in declining sales possibilities; *increasing* competition in the elimination of competition; *increasing* colonialism in the freedom of the colonies. In each case, the element of destruction is the fact that something *increases* in magnitude, that growth is driven beyond the point where it is beneficial. Had Marx drawn the logical conclusion from his own diagnosis, he would have suggested the prevention of overgrowth, not the elimination of capitalism and its replacement by socialism which, far from preventing overgrowth, is based on it from its very beginning.

[2] There were, of course, great accumulations of wealth in the hands of princes and lords, but these arose not from their economic but their political functions as heads of their principalities. As it would be foolish to accuse the mayor of a city for having at his disposal large accumulations, it would be equally foolish to accuse a former lord on this account.

revolution with its crushing large-scale consequences that the subsequent improvement means only that our present living standard is higher than that of the *nineteenth* century, but not necessarily of the *preceding* periods. Nor does it mean that it is higher than that still found today in mature small countries such as Switzerland or Sweden.

Far from solving the insignificant problems of small economies, the solidified large-area states have magnified them to the point where they defy any solution whatever. Were it not so, how could one explain the abject dependence on American aid of such great powers as Italy, France, or Germany? How could one explain why Great Britain, struggling heroically to do without this aid, can give her inhabitants no more than varying degrees of an unvarying austerity? or why mighty Russia, deprived of American aid altogether, can grant none of the amenities of life to her tried populations and depends in addition on the small economies of her satellites to such an extent that she could not permit them to leave her orbit on this ground alone? Or how could one explain why the very birth of another great power, India, was accompanied not by economic independence but by her prompt addition to the list of applicants for American aid? One might say that at least the United States represents an example of the success of large-scale development. But where would the United States be if the other large powers did not need her so badly? We are as dependent on them as they are on us, and the more dependent they are on us, the worse off we become ourselves.

On the other hand, while the gun-doting, grandiloquent great powers of the world seem to show nothing to their account except their inability to support themselves, coupled with a pitiful efficiency in sending one backmailing mission after another to Washington in the hope of maintaining what is still left of their dilapidated greatness, the small states—whom they are so eager to reason off the surface of the earth on the ground that they are economic anachronisms—continue to blossom by their own resources. There is no record of help-seeking missions from Switzerland, Sweden, Liechtenstein, or such remote Himalayan states as Nepal, Sikkim, Bhutan, and many another from whom one has never heard because they have never asked anything and are able, in many respects, to provide their citizens with higher living standards without American aid than their powerful neighbours are able to afford with it. If their representatives do once in a while put in an appearance in Washington it is to convey greetings to the President, not to ask gifts. This sounds so incredible that the Washington press corps could hardly believe its ears when Prime

Minister Sidney G. Holland of New Zealand told them during his visit in February 1951:

'I'm on my way back home, you know, and I came to pay my respects. And I told the President we are making no requests of any kind. There is nothing we need that we can't pay for out of our own resources. I just happened to say we are not seeking any gifts or loans of any kind.'[1]

Which representative of the vast economic realms of France, Great Britain, Italy, India, China, or Russia could nowadays make a statement of this kind? None! If also small countries are occasionally found in the boat of economic distress, it is only because their problems, as in the case of the giant Marshall Plan area, have been fused with those of their neighbours. But even there they proved to be the healthier of the partners in need, as can be seen from the fact that by far the fastest recovery from the dislocations of World War II has been experienced by the smaller states of Europe such as Belgium, Denmark, Luxembourg, or the Netherlands, and not by the great powers.

6. The Law of Diminishing Productivity

The principal argument against the fetishism of large-scale economies, however, is not derived from the comparison of economic development in large and small states, but from economic law. Every student of economics must acquaint himself in one of his first lessons with the *law of diminishing productivity* as the most basic of all economic principles. This, however, is again nothing other than the economic version of the small-unit principle which, as we have found, permeates all creation.

The law of diminishing productivity states that, if we add *variable* units of any factor of production to a *fixed* quantity of another, a point will be reached beyond which each additional unit of the variable factor adds *less* to the total product than the preceding one.

What does this mean? Economists distinguish amongst four factors of production, land, labour, capital, and the entrepreneur. Let us assume that the *variable* factor is labour, and that we add it in varying units to a *fixed* quantity of land. The yield of this fixed unit of land, if worked by a single labourer, is, let us assume, 10 bushels of wheat. Two labourers may boost this to 22 bushels, three to 27, and four to 28. If we add a fifth labourer, the total may actually decline because each

[1] *New York Times*, 8 February 1951.

may now be in the other's way and impede instead of assist work. What we see from this example is that, up to the fourth labourer, each additional worker is able to increase the *total* output, but that already after the third each increase per man is effected at a *diminishing* rate. Expressed in figures this means that if we employ only two workers, their total product will be 22 bushels, and the product per man 11. If we decide to employ four workers, however, we shall increase their total by only six additional bushels to 28. This means that, though we employ more, the output per man is now much less in terms of wheat, having declined from 11 to 6 bushels.

The application of too much power to a fixed production unit has thus the overall effect of decreasing instead of increasing individual efficiency, though this is hidden for a time by the continued rise in aggregates. In the case of our example, it would thus obviously be more profitable—provided that land is available in sufficient quantities and could therefore be made variable also—to apply the other two workers to a *second* unit of land. In this way, having made both factors variable, the yield per unit of land would decline from 28 to 22 bushels, but the product per man would go up from 7 to 11, and the combined product from 28 to 44. By making other factors variable also and expanding on a small-unit pattern instead of turning a single fixed cell into a compact production concentrate, it is possible to increase general efficiency through expansion and bypass *for a time* the inexorable law of diminishing productivity.

But, one may say, is this not an argument for larger rather than smaller units? Up to a point, yes, as is indicated by the law of diminishing productivity itself, according to which decline sets in only after a certain expansion has been accomplished. It is therefore not only reasonable but also economical to add *fields* until they reach the optimum size in the form of a *farm*. Beyond that, however, efficiency decline can no longer be bypassed by utilizing the variability of factors, since one of the essential factors of production, to which the law applies also, is by its very nature not subject to variation. This is the entrepreneur or, in the case of our example, the farmer. Entrepreneurial ability, being limited and unexpandable once it has reached full maturity, can cope only with the problems of a *limited* enterprise, an enterprise whose activities do not become dimmed at the horizon. It is for this reason that the law of diminishing productivity is not an argument for unlimited expansion but for limitation, a limitation adjusted to man's unexpandable small intellectual stature.

Every producer knows and follows this basic economic law whether he is familiar with its name or not. And every consumer follows a different version of it under the name of the *law of diminishing utility* in which the production concerned is not the creation of goods but of satisfactions. We could satisfy our hunger with nothing but a ten-unit chunk of bread. Yet, if we have a chance, we shall prefer to eat only one unit of bread, and one unit of something else such as meat, one other unit of milk, and one other unit of dessert. By taking only first units of different goods instead of a big multiple-unit chunk of a single good, we avoid the deplorable decline of satisfactions which each additional unit of the *same* good would cause. In this way we are able to increase the total utility of our meals by breaking them down into a succession of small items.

In other words, increase in quantity, mass, size, power, or whatever physical element we may use, does not produce a corresponding increase in productivity or satisfactions. Up to a certain point, yes! But beyond a certain point, no! There is a limit. And the ideal limit is always relatively narrow! It is again Aristotle who has expressed the significance of oversize so succinctly in his *Politics* when he writes:

'To the size of states there is a limit, as there is to other things, plants, animals, implements; for none of these retain their natural power when they are too large or too small, but they either wholly lose their nature, or are spoiled.'[1]

We experience this spoilage in our typically modern prize-winning attempts at growing fruit or vegetables of monster proportions. They look extraordinary to the eye, but they are not only spoiled, they have also lost their nature. It is like giving a premium for obesity which, as we all know, does not add to, but detracts from, performance. What pleasure do we gain from eating strawberries that are huge but taste like half-brewed beer, or from tomatoes that have the size of grapefruit but taste like soiled water? It is taste that attracts us in food, not bulk. And taste, like vitality, vigour, efficiency, does not increase with size. What does increase, of course, if we add units of effort to fixed quantities, is the *aggregate* product which keeps growing long beyond the point of diminishing productivity. But although this is not more praiseworthy than the gain of additional weight in a woman after she has reached her optimum figure, we are for ever stunned and impressed by it in the field of economics, forgetting our fundamental aim which is not quantity but quality, not the bulk of *aggregates* but the flavour of the *unit*, and not *total* output but output *per man*. Four workers do

[1] Aristotle, op. cit., 1326 a.

produce more wheat than two, but if four are at work on the same plot, the individual output is much less than that of two. This is what matters. As life becomes more crowded, we cannot avoid the unit decline of productivity. But this is no excuse for diverting our attention from the iron reality of *falling individual* incomes, and for seeking irrational consolation in the meaningless things that continue to *rise* such as the aggregates of *national* incomes.

7. *Small versus Big Business Units*

As land yields less per unit of added effort after a certain point, so does the firm. According to the same law of diminishing productivity, the performance of an enterprise, after it has reached a certain size, begins to decline in relation to the amount of resources put into it, in spite of the deluding fact that, as always, its absolute performance continues to increase. This is such an elementary fact that Justice Brandeis could properly state that:

'A large part of our people have also learned that efficiency in business does not grow indefinitely with the size of the business. Very often a business grows in efficiency as it grows from a small business to a large business; but there is a unit of greatest efficiency in every business at any time, and a business may be too large to be efficient, as well as too small.'[1]

As a result, a wise business man will not extend his production to *maximum* capacity but to *optimum* capacity. Whatever that may be, it is at all times considerably lower than the maximum. It will never be a giant whose forces cannot be fully utilized. Squeezing out of his plant the last possible drops means to get these additional drops of product at a disproportionately heavy expense, so that it is far more profitable to go without these drops. Instead, if he desires to extend his production, the producer will build a new and mechanically independent plant, and begin the battle of diminishing productivity all over again, but with fresh forces, by fanning out on a *small*-cell pattern. When the optimum size is reached in the second plant, he will build a third plant, or, what is better still, plants II and III will be built by others to make them not only mechanically but also financially independent, and to add not only fresh forces, but new vitality and genius. This is the basis of a healthy capitalism and its most essential secret of success,

[1] Louis D. Brandeis, *The Curse of Bigness*. New York: The Viking Press, 1935, p. 109.

competition. And since competition means the coexistence of a *great* number of individual firms, it also means that each individual producing unit must by necessity be relatively small.

Thus a sound capitalist economy, far from thriving on large-scale concepts, is more than any other system dependent on individual diversity and its concomitant, the small firm.[1] It is this that has given us our greatest benefits and the firms their greatest efficiency, as we can easily perceive if we compare a few personal experiences and a few impersonal facts.

Everybody knows what it means to buy something in one of our vast department stores. True, we can buy everything in a single building, but is this more efficient? Being located in a large city, it takes us in the first place up to an hour to reach the place. Then we are spewed into an overcrowded interior where we are assisted by snappy information services, watched by discreet detectives, and hurled about until we arrive at our counter. There we line up in a queue and wait docilely for being processed without the benefit of old-fashioned individualized service or courtesies. Instead, neon signs on balconies or inscriptions on the bosoms of overworked sales girls flash the cheerful news abroad that *This Store Gives You Friendly Service*, or that *Our Password Is Politeness*. That takes care of that. It is the collective advance apology for any subsequent individual atrocity that may be committed on the customer. But it is useless to complain since rudeness, like any other social vice, is directly proportionate to the size of the social unit within which we move.

At lunch we sit down at another counter whose idea of efficiency is to cascade upon us within sixty seconds all the implements of eating plus sandwich, coffee, and check, so that we are through with the task of replenishing our strength in less than five minutes. Finally, we are caught in a high-speed ejector stream that tears the buttons off our overcoats, and thrust back into another subway. By the time we arrive home we need a steam bath and brandy to revive ourselves. But we acquired a tie at a saving of ten cents and enjoyed otherwise the comforts of having everything under a single roof. In a small town unable to afford either subways or department stores, we get the same

[1] By the term 'small' firm, as by a 'small' country, is understood in this study an establishment of optimum size. The use of the term 'small' rather than 'medium' or 'middle-sized' which it is meant to embrace, should emphasize the relatively low ceiling limiting development upwards. There is no such narrow limit in the opposite direction. Liechtenstein is a small country, and so is Switzerland. In spite of their vast difference in size, it would be misleading to apply the term *medium* power to Switzerland.

thing perhaps at slightly higher prices, but at an enormous saving of time and energy. We are not processed but served. We are not fed, we eat. Each effort yields infinitely more satisfactions which, translated into economic terms, means greater efficiency. Slowing down the record of life to its proper speed, it takes longer to play but it echoes at last the beautiful melodies which the fast-running gramophone of vast-scale living has turned into unbearable shrieks.

What this personal experience illustrates from the point of view of the consumer who exhausts his energy by patronizing super stores in super cities under the illusion of gaining something, a few impersonal facts and data will prove with regard to the producer. When a great combine is organized through the fusion of a number of small producing units into a single large enterprise, we are usually impressed by the unprecedented new output figures. What we overlook in our hypnotic preoccupation with totals and aggregates is that the now amalgamated empire will in most instances produce less than the combined equivalent of the previously independent units unless it maintains these units in physically separate operation. But even then, the addition of new factories cannot stave off the relentless working of the law of diminishing productivity. To quote Justice Brandeis once more:

'Man's work often outruns the capacity of the individual man; and no matter what the organization, the capacity of an individual man usually determines the success or failure of a particular enterprise, not only financially to the owners, but in service to the community. Organization can do much to make concerns more efficient. Organization can do much to make larger units possible and profitable. But the efficiency even of organization has its bounds; and organization can never supply the combined judgement, initiative, enterprise, and authority which must come from the chief executive officers. Nature sets a limit to their possible accomplishment. As the Germans say, "Care is taken that the trees do not scrape the skies".'[1]

A number of recent studies have made it abundantly clear that the idea of the greater efficiency, productivity, or profitability of large producing units seems largely a myth. The *Twentieth Century Fund* found on the basis of an analysis of income statistics for 1919, 'that the larger corporations earned less than the average of all corporations; that those with an investment of more than $50,000,000 earned the least; while those with an investment of less than $50,000 earned the most; and the earnings declined almost uninterruptedly, with increasing

[1] Louis D. Brandeis, op. cit., p. 117.

size'.[1] Another study, examining the industrial profits in the United States, found after analysing the data of 2,046 manufacturing corporations from 1919 to 1928, 'that those with an investment under $500,000 enjoyed a higher return than those with more than $5,000,000 and twice as high a return than those with more than $50,000,000'.[2] So consistent is this picture that a study of the *Federal Trade Commission* undertaken for the *Temporary National Economic Committee* came to the following conclusion:

'The results of the total tests reveal that the largest companies made, on the whole, a very poor showing . . . Furthermore, in the tests of group efficiency, the corporations grouped as medium sized or small sized had preponderantly lower average costs of production or higher rates of return on invested capital than the groups of large-sized corporations with which they were compared.'[3]

The most surprising fact, however, is that, apart from those few enterprises which, such as the railroad or steel industry, are intrinsically dependent on large-scale equipment and organization, not even *mass* production seems best served by plants of large size. For, as experience has shown, 'the economy of mass production in its proper sense . . . is more a matter of the degree of specialization attainable within a single factory than a matter of the size of the plant as a whole'.[4]

[1] Temporary National Economic Committee, *Competition and Monopoly in American Industry*, Monograph No. 21. Washington: Government Printing Office, 1940, p. 311.　　　　　　　　　　[2] Ibid., p. 311.

[3] Temporary National Economic Committee, *Relative Efficiency of Large, Medium-sized, and Small Business*, Monograph No. 13. Washington: Government Printing Office, 1941, p. 10. In fairness to this quotation, I must fill in the words represented by the three dots which show again the annoying timidity of authors whose figures point so obviously in the opposite direction from acceptable results that they do not venture to draw their own conclusions or, if so, contradict them in such a way as to render them almost meaningless. Thus, after saying that the tests revealed a poor showing on the part of the largest companies, the report continues: 'This should not be taken that in every test all medium-sized or small companies had lower costs or better rates of return than the largest companies. Indeed most cases of highest costs were those of very small companies; this in turn should not be taken to mean that the average costs of large-sized businesses were necessarily lower than the average costs of medium-sized or small businesses.' In the text above I used only the first sentence of this extraordinary sequence because either the largest companies did make a poor showing or they did not. According to the report they did, irrespective of the water the authors poured into their own wine.

[4] Professor Frank A. Fetter in his testimony before the Federal Trade Commission (Ibid., pp. 404-5).

Nor does it seem that large-scale enterprise contributed significantly in another area in which myth ascribes to it more success than the facts appear to justify—in research. Using the electric-appliance industry as an illustration of the inventive barrenness of modern laboratories maintained at enormous expense by big business, Mr. T. K. Quinn, himself a big business man as former vice-president of the General Electric Company, chairman of the board of the General Electric Finance Company, and president of the Monitor Equipment Corporation, points to the fact 'that not a single distinctively new electric home appliance has ever been created by one of the giant concerns—not the first washing machine, electric range, dryer, iron or ironer, electric lamp, refrigerator, radio, toaster, fan, heating pad, razor, lawn mower, freezer, air conditioner, vacuum cleaner, dishwasher, or grill. The record of the giants is one of moving in, buying out, and absorbing after the fact.'[1]

For all these reasons it is precisely the economists who are rediscovering the value of the small-unit principle and who suggest that a multicellular arrangement with as many independent entrepreneurs as are economically supportable would be more wholesome, productive, efficient, and profitable than a world composed of giant concerns spilling across the surface of the globe, unimpeded by limiting boundaries. They are rediscovering that the law of diminishing productivity is more than a mere formulation to be discussed in an elementary economics class. It is elementary. Up to a certain point, the addition of units of productive factors, as additional food in the human body, builds up creative energy; beyond it, sterile fat. Before the optimum size of organization is reached, be it in companies or in labour unions, such additions are used in the fulfilment of their *economic* functions; after it has been reached, they are squandered in *personal* or *political* dissipation, in unwarranted speculations, in unwarranted political pets, in unwarranted displays of power, or in that most wasteful of economic activities: the construction of an idling financial security belt with which overgrown enterprises must surround themselves to withstand disasters that may never occur or, if they do, may not be worth surviving.

[1] T. K. Quinn, 'Too Big', *The Nation*, 7 March 1953, p. 211. Explaining the relative sterility of large laboratories, Mr. Quinn continues his argument against economic bigness by quoting the following from Dr. Clarence Cook Little, former president of the Universities of Michigan and Maine: 'Scientific research is an intensely personal effort . . . like the artist, the creative scientist must be permitted to pursue his own ideas unhampered by restrictions of organized groups. The large groups have made extremely important contributions only when an original discovery, made by a single individual, is already available for further technical development.'

Capitalist theorists and even capitalist business men have therefore come to the point where they oppose rather than favour economic concentration,[1] and many have made a vicious spectre of concentration driven to its extreme—monopoly. But what is monopoly in the economic world? Nothing other than what great power is in the political world. It restricts material production and forces on us undifferentiated standardized goods, even as great power restricts our intellectual production, forcing on us standardized platitudes. But the problem of power manifests itself always in the same way, whether it is in the physical, the economic, or the political field. As Professor Henry Simons put it:

'No one and no group can be trusted with much power; and it is merely silly to complain because groups exercise power selfishly. The mistake is simply in permitting them to have it. Monopoly power must be abused. It has no use save abuse.'[2]

So we are once again back at the problem of power, and once again the conclusion forces itself on us that the way to deal with it is not by attempting to control what is by nature uncontrollable, but by cutting down what has become too big. Our macro-economists suggest cutting too, but at the wrong end. They try to solve the dislocation problems produced by the uneven accumulation of wealth and misery by attacking the consequences instead of the cause. They are always full of ideas of parcelling, redividing, redistributing the income which has been diverted from the swift stream of production into stagnant by-waters. But what should be done is, not to redivide the *income* from production but the *size* of the productive unit. For in small firms, little could be spared to accumulate in stagnant pools in the first place. All that would be needed is, therefore, to render the unitarian overgrown enterprises smaller, mobile, and multiple again. In this way, the proper distribution of income—which is quite correctly thought to be one of the most essential prerequisites of a healthy economy and of a sound policy of protection against unduly severe cyclical fluctuations—would not need to occupy the time of a single reform economist. For it would

[1] Note the present vogue by which business grows in the biological way, by multiplying and splitting, rather than the political way, by uniting and centralizing. Instead of enlarging existing factories, new ones are built on a smaller scale, and instead of keeping them together, they are distributed over many geographic regions. Another example is the trend of department stores to break down the unity of floor space by creating what Macy's in New York calls the 'thrilling new experience' of 'little shops'.

[2] Henry Simons, op.cit., p. 129.

automatically result from a proper and well-balanced distribution of productive units. A small-cell arrangement always and everywhere has this one great virtue: it solves the problems, which no degree of planning can handle if they occur on the large scale, by reducing them to proportions in which they solve themselves.

8. Economic Union

We thus see that there is nothing in either economic experience or economic theory indicating that large unified territorial entities are essential to a healthy development. If the most productive form of enterprise in most fields is the smaller business unit, there is obviously no necessity for surrounding it with a giant unified economic hinterland. As a result, a sound small-*scale* economy, while it does not exactly demand a small-*state* arrangement, is certainly not damaged by it. In fact, it represents the same thing economically as the small state represents politically, and its health is due to the same reasons. It is therefore a queer paradox that many of those who, having discovered the weakness of huge economic size, are now all out to smash big business and trusts in favour of the resurrection of a small-business world, advocate exactly the opposite in the world of politics. There the unitarian idea of concentration has taken such possession of them that nothing could delight them more than the vision of the monster holding company of a world state. Economically, more than from any other point of view, it would be more consistent with our ideals if we were to have thousands of small states rather than a single big one. That is, if our ideals are individualistic. For a collectivist, it might be different. But even collectivists and totalitarians seem no longer to preclude the development of small, self-sufficient regional economies in preference to an uncontrollable huge-area centralism, as the more recent experiments of Soviet Russia have shown.

All this should indicate that economics, which was supposed to provide the main argument for the unification of mankind into large-area establishments and even a world state, actually furnishes in the law of diminishing productivity the most telling argument in favour of small-cell sovereignty. Instead of centralized integration it suggests once more as a principle not of reaction but of advance the division of all those organisms which, such as trusts, cartels, market areas, or great powers, have become afflicted by the cancer of oversize.

Yet the abandonment of the present large unified-area system of the great powers in favour of a small-state world would not necessarily mean the destruction of all existing kinds of economic unity, even as the abandonment of centralized dictatorship in favour of *individual* self-determination does not mean the destruction of all previously existing *social* ties. In other words, *political* particularism does not automatically entail *economic* particularism, as we can well see in the United States or in the economic union of the otherwise fully independent Benelux countries. It does above all not entail the recreation of any form of *artificial* economic obstacles such as customs and traffic barriers running along the political boundaries of small states.

It is this spectre of the restoration of boundaries which seems to hold such terrors to our unification theorists, but only because they cannot visualize that boundaries do not necessarily mean barriers and that, without the connotation of barrier, they are the source of our happiness, not of our misery. This is why all our instincts drive us constantly to *create* boundaries, not to *tear them down*. We draw them around our gardens in the form of fences, and within our houses in the form of walls separating our rooms. In harbours, we erect piers to keep out the storms. Boundaries are shelters, and for that reason they must be close to us, and narrow. To tear them from human societies would be like tearing away the shell from the body of a tortoise or the shore from the ocean. But boundaries are no barriers. What we want to keep from the harbour is the storm, not the sea. Making a barrier out of a sheltering boundary would mean to seal off the ocean along with the storms, rendering its very purpose meaningless.

It is the barriers, then, which are detrimental to human development, not the protecting boundaries whose function is to keep things within healthy limits. And barriers, which one might define as unnatural boundaries, would paradoxically become meaningless in the ideal state of competitive capitalism where every business unit casts its own boundaries until it is automatically checked by the forces of competition. The ideal economic portrait of a small-state world would thus be an area full of breathing, changing and self-controlling business boundaries, but free of all obstructing unnatural obstacles such as customs and traffic barriers.

Surprisingly, then, the result of an economic small-unit arrangement would be the disintegration for lack of purpose of the true impediments to economic intercourse, the barriers of traffic and trade, without disintegrating at the same time the continued existence of political or other natural boundaries. The new economic map of Europe, for example, would thus show no barrier at all. It might, in fact, be what economists call a *customs union*, a territory presenting no obstacle to the flow of goods whatever. It would be a single region but not a unified region. It would consist of a finely woven pattern of overlapping circles, some smaller some larger, indicating the economic territories of the various individual firms. Economically, each firm would thus constitute its own business nation. Local retailers would have, as they do anyway, a boundary of a few miles; their wholesalers, being held down to optimum size by the mechanism of competition, of a few hundred miles. Their reach may already spill across political boundaries. Some firms, producing special or rare products such as gold or steel, would have territories of perhaps a thousand miles in diameter. Finally, those few serving by their very nature whole continents or the entire world, such as certain communication and transportation enterprises, would have their continents or the globe as their commercial domain. In this way, a meshwork of economic realms, each fitting in size its special purpose, could develop without encroachments set up by political authorities.

This has brought us in a roundabout way for once to a kind of unity that is acceptable since it does not represent organizational unity that builds up power with all its inherent dangers, but the physical unity of contiguous territories and market areas. Here unity has sense for two reasons. First, it exists anyway, boundaries or not. Secondly, being a physical reality, it must be served, and thus creates almost automatically its own system of service transcending all man-made boundaries. Such international *service* unions, in contrast to power unions, are for example the International Dining and Sleeping Car Company, the International Postal Union, or the recently inaugurated European steel and coal union. They resemble the *natural* monopolies[1] of domestic economies and as such are the only production units for which large-area development is justified. Their function, however, is not to unify productive or political entities but, on the contrary, to provide them with the facilities that enable them to remain separate and small. They are here to link, not to fuse, to adjust, not to unite—as roads passing through a patchwork of fields are here not for the sake of facilitating their absorption in a single large estate but for securing their continued independence of ownership and operation.

.   .   .

[1] Natural monopolies are those enterprises which, such as public utilities, are best organized monopolistically rather than competitively even in an otherwise competitive system. It is the one field in which competition is detrimental. If several telephone companies were to service a city instead of one, each user would have to subscribe to all of them to reach all his friends and associates who might be subscribers to a different system.

Summarizing, we may thus say that even economics refuses to yield arguments against a small-state world. For, even in the field of economics, the only problem of significance seems to be the problem of excessive size, suggesting as its solution not growth but the stopping of growth, not union but division. We have found that high living standards in large states seem a macro-economic illusion while they appear to be a micro-economic reality in mature small ones. We have found that, as the size of the productive unit grows, its productivity ultimately begins to decline until, instead of giving off energy, it puts on fat. We have found that the reason for this is the law of diminishing productivity which puts limits to the size of everything. And lastly we seem to have discovered the one economic area in which union of some sort may have sense: international customs and service unions. Yet, even in their case, we have seen that their purpose seems not to do away with the allegedly outmoded, diversified, small-state sovereignties with their inspiring boundaries of habits, tastes, education, art, music, philosophy, literature, and cuisine—but, on the contrary, to serve them and preserve them.

Chapter Nine

UNION THROUGH DIVISION

'These monsters of nationalism and mercantilism
must be dismantled.'

HENRY C. SIMONS

*Smallness the source of bliss. The most enchanting picture of
God—a baby in Mary's arms. The small-cell principle as the
principle of federal union. Successful federations: United States,
Switzerland, Holy Roman Empire. Unsuccessful federations:
League of Nations, pre-Bismarck German federation, United
Nations, United States of Indonesia. The cause of their failure
—cancer. The small-cell principle as the principle of all government. Its application in centralized states: Great Britain,
France, Hitler Germany. Its application in cities. The need of
the dismemberment of great powers if the United Nations are to
survive.*

The Administrative Argument

U P to this point our effort has been directed towards establishing
the principle of the small cell as the fundamental principle of
health, and the principle of division as the fundamental principle
of cure. Having traced both through their most significant manifestations we have seen that nearly all problems dissolve into non-prob-
lematic proportions if the organism of which they form part is reduced
in size. This is why, within our smallest social units such as families,
villages, counties, or provinces, we can nearly always be happy even if
we are not endowed with great wisdom. In fact, these are the only
entities within which we can be happy at all. For no problem can arise
there which could not be brought under control as easily as a chain
reaction within the cantonized structure of an atomic pile.

But once we broaden our scope to regions beyond the horizon, and
extend our affections to vast multitudes such as nations or humanity,

everything begins to elude our grasp. What was ours in our ponds has been lost in the oceans, and our previously undisturbed emotions are now forever subject to the disturbances occurring on these vaster scales at every moment. In our villages, there may be an upsetting murder once in a decade. The rest of the time we live in unruffled peace. In a large community, on the other hand, there is murder, rape, and robbery every hour in some distant corner. But since we are linked with every distant corner, every local incident turns into an issue, a cause, a national calamity clouding our skies not once in a decade but all the time. From our local newspapers we learn that none of the massive misfortunes depressing the world ever happens in our own town. Yet, we must suffer because our unifiers have forced us to participate in millions of destinies that are not ours. This is the price of modern vast-scale living. Having drawn the entire human race to our anxious bosom, we have to share in all its miseries.

Largeness, then, seems the real cause of our misfortune, and smallness the source of our bliss. This is why we visualize God not as a giant infinity which we cannot grasp, but as an individual. Indeed our most captivating picture of Him is that of a child, a mere baby in Mary's arms. To hold Him in the smallness of our person, we must think of Him as a person too. As He created us in His image, we have created Him in ours. The supreme concept of might, wisdom, justice, and love, we thus do not attach to something existing as a group or a nation, of which so many of our politicians say that it is greater than the citizen, but to someone existing as a sharply circumscribed individual. Only the collectivist differs in this. His god is as impersonal as the aggregates he worships—party, people, nation, or mankind.

All this insistence on littleness offends our global unifiers to whom everything bigger is greater. But since the road of bigness has no end, and since the unifiers can never find a greatest element beyond which mass ceases to accumulate, they cannot arrive anywhere except in the asylum of the infinite. There, they become the great worriers on behalf of mankind, never stopping to wail since there is cause of worry somewhere all the time. Unable to enjoy a moment's peace, they are for ever driven to project their present trouble into the future and then to anticipate the future miseries to make their present doubly sour, conjuring dangers as yet unborn, but suffering from their vision already now. They try to solve the problems of all future generations while dying from their inability to solve their own. Like the unfortunate inhabitants of Laputa, 'they are so perpetually alarmed with the Apprehensions of these and like impending Dangers, that they can neither sleep quietly in their Beds, nor have any Relish for the common Pleasures or Amusements of Life'.[1]

But now we have manœuvred ourselves into a peculiar position. Having deprecated the aims of unionists and unifiers, and having put the small on the pedestal from which we have tried to pull the big, we have arrived at a point where the world unifiers may bless us yet. For the principles of smallness and division, solving so many other problems, solve also the problem of union. They are, in fact, the most fundamental principles underlying all *successful* regional or continental unions, international federations, or world states. Only *small* states can be united into healthier larger organisms. Only *small* states are federable. Wherever a large state participates in a federal union, the federation cannot last. In due course, it will either become a centralized state operating in the interest of its largest participant, or it will break into its component parts once the immediate reason for its creation, such as fear of a common enemy, has disappeared. If survival is desired none the less in such a case, it can be accomplished only by applying the principle of division to all disproportionately large members who are to a federation what cancer is to the human body. This may be impossible. But if large member states such as participate in the United Nations, the North Atlantic Treaty Organization, or the European Council, cannot be divided, their union cannot last even if it is technically possible to bring it into existence. The only thing that can ensure continued union is a cancer-free small-cell pattern.

1. *Successful Federal Experiments*

To understand this better, let us examine first a few successful and then a few unsuccessful federations. The two outstanding examples of the former are the United States and Switzerland whose governments, except in times of crisis, are so weak that the mystery of their cohesiveness has puzzled many a political theorist in search of a formula of union. Functioning seemingly almost on their own momentum without the requirement of strong governmental cement to hold them together, it was decided that the secret of their success was the good will of their citizens and the common cultural background of their peoples. As a result, the first aim of every world unifier is the creation of good will on earth and the production of a common culture 'irrespective of race, colour and sex' through such instruments as UNESCO

[1] Jonathan Swift, op. cit., p. 186.

whose zealous exponents of the gospel of uniformity a witty Frenchman called with appropriate disgust '*ces gens sans race, sans couleur, sans sexe*'.

Yet, neither the United States nor Switzerland is built on good will or common cultural concepts. If they were, they would not only have broken down long ago; they would never have come into existence in the first place. Why should the peoples of Switzerland have entered into a union with strangers rather than their German, French, and Italian blood relatives? And why should America have struggled away from an England with whom she is even today united in a common culture? So irrelevant are cultural bonds to political union that Bernard Shaw quite justly attributed the undercurrent of hostility separating the English and Americans to the fact that they spoke not a different but a common language, and that they competed not for opposite but for the same ideals.

The great lesson of the Swiss and American unions is not that good will and common culture led them to success, but that both succeeded in spite of severe eruptions of *ill* will and, as in Switzerland, even in the absence of a common culture. Neither of them is a fair-weather institution relying on a perpetually saintly disposition and unearthly political wisdom of its citizens. On the contrary! Their foundation is of such inherent strength that—unlike the United Nations which threatens to break apart at the slightest difficulty though boasting of the most concentrated gathering of the world's diplomatic talent—they seem able to withstand almost any degree of strain or political imbecility without any harmful effect whatever.

As already indicated, the reason for their success is very simple. Not that their member units are lacking in *desire* to break away from their union. They do not, as we can see from the numerous secessionist sentiments expressed with undisguised relish in regions such as Colonel McCormick's Midwest or Texas. They lack in the *power* to break away. And they lack in the power because their unions are built on a pattern free of political cancer. Neither the United States nor Switzerland, one of the largest and one of the smallest countries on earth, contains within its frame a member unit so strong that it could effectively challenge the federal authority. For deliberately or accidentally, both have incorporated in their structure the health-preserving principle of the small cell. And it is this, not wisdom, will, or culture, that accounts for their success. Why?

The basic problem of every federal government is the possession of sufficient executive power to enforce its laws on all its members. In order to succeed, it must be slightly stronger than its strongest member state. This is not political theory but administrative arithmetic. In a small-cell organization, superiority of federal power over its strongest unit is easily accomplished because even the strongest unit is weak. In a *large*-power arrangement, on the other hand, this is all but impossible. In the first place, the costs of the necessary police force would be prohibitive. In the second place, none of the powerful members would be willing to contribute the funds for an executive organ capable of overshadowing its own position. And the small member states could not conceivably make up for the deficiency of the big. Hence the pathetic emphasis of large-power unions such as the United Nations or the European Council on good will. But good will has no executive authority, and without executive authority no political organism can exist. As a result, large-power unions are able to live only by the grace of their large members who can, and do, veto them out of existence at will.

How essential the small-cell principle is to the success of federal union we can discern if we visualize what would happen if the United States, for example, now a patchwork of forty-eight small states, were to consider adopting the large-cell principle instead. We would then argue in this manner: 'Let us do away with the heap of disunited political entities and their wasteful duplication of local governments, legislatures, courts, and laws. Let us simplify their set-up by reducing their number into four or five regionally integrated units. This would be all the more reasonable as, *economically*, the United States divides not into forty-eight but into only four or five regions in the first place.'

What would be the result of such an arrangement which, as we immediately perceive, approximates the pattern suggested by the world unifiers on a still larger scale? They, too, advocate the establishment first of regional unions through the elimination of existing state units, and then their ultimate fusion into a super union. Applied to the United States, it would mean the end of the United States. Emotions of dissidence and secession, characteristic of every states-rightist or provincial but utterly harmless in small political units, would in larger aggregations swell to such formidable proportions that they could no longer be kept in check. While all the world laughed when the late Colonel McCormick of Illinois, an important figure in an unimportant state, referred to the members of the national government in Washington as 'those foreigners', the same world would have been seized with panic if the same Colonel had said the same thing as an important figure of an *important* unified and large Midwestern state. His pronouncement might then actually have turned the members of the Washington government into foreigners. Similarly, while a Huey Long or Herman Talmadge are able to cause only minor trouble to even a weak federal government as long as they are confined to Louisiana or Georgia, as governors of a great Southern state, which fortunately does not exist, they would be fearful Hitlers whom even a powerful federal government would be unable to control.

To enforce its laws, Washington, as the capital of a *small*-state federation, needs only to be stronger than New York, a state that seems a giant compared with tiny Rhode Island but which is none the less insignificant in relation to the whole of the union. As the capital of a *large*-power federation, on the other hand, composed of four or five members including, let us say, a Midwestern state of 50 million inhabitants, it would find it impossible to marshal the enforcement power necessary to keep such monsters together. Like the United Nations, it could function only with the consent of its Big Four or Five who would not only claim the right to veto any and all federal decisions but, if denied, exercise it anyway. For veto power is not the result of right but of might—a condition beyond the regulatory authority of even the strongest federal government.

A simplified large-state organization on the soil of the present United States would thus not foster a more efficient union, as many seem to believe, but disrupt the existing one by rendering the purely mathematical problem of federal law enforcement insoluble. Instead of securing smoother operation it would lead to a duplication of the European experience of uninterrupted strife and warfare. Indeed, when the American union at the beginning of its existence was composed of so few members that some of them ranked as quasi-great powers in relation to the others, sentiments of hostility amongst the states were at times as violent as those felt against England, and war threats and secession movements were as commonplace as they are now rare. If all this is unthinkable today, it is not because we have become wiser but because the power behind regional ambitions has become smaller under the impact of our present tightly sealed compartmentalized little-state pattern. But when in the midst of our growth a number of states, previously linked with each other only through Washington, suddenly began to coalesce on a cancerous regional pattern, the federal union not only threatened to break asunder; the simplified North-South division presented the world with one of its great catastrophes, the American Civil War of 1861. Common education, common language, common history, common heroes, good will—they all proved meaningless assets in meeting the administrative problems arising not from the short-comings of human nature or local disaffections but from the volume given them by the overgrown size of their integrated provinces.[1]

A similar picture unfolds itself if we look at the superbly functioning Swiss federation which so many of our political experts have the habit of praising for the wrong thing. They hold it up to the world as an example of the peaceful living together of some of the most diverse nations on earth. Actually, nothing is further from the truth. The percentages of Switzerland's three national groups (not speaking of the Romansch, her minute fourth nationality) are roughly: 70 per cent for her German, 20 per cent for her French, and 10 per cent for her Italian speaking population. If these were the basis of her famed union, the inevitable result would be the exercise of dominion of the large German-speaking block over the other two nationalities which would be degraded to the logical status of minorities representing, as they do, no more than 30 per cent of the total population. The rules of democracy would not impede but favour such a development, and the reason for the French- and Italian-speaking communities to remain in a chiefly German enterprise would be gone. A union of this kind would have met with no greater success than a union of the nation-states of Germany, France, and Italy as a whole.

However, the basis of the success of Switzerland is not that she is a federation of three nationalities, but a federation of twenty-two states, the *cantons* which, far from uniting her unequal national blocks, have *divided* them into so many small pieces that no single federal unit has a sizeable preponderance over any other. By this the essential precondition of every well-functioning federation was created: a pattern which furnishes harmony and manageability by ensuring the physical and numerical balance of all participants on a small enough scale to enable even a weak central authority to execute its decisions.

[1] What a contrast to the ease with which thirty years earlier President Jackson solved an almost identical secession problem when South Carolina tried to invalidate a federal tariff law and, indeed, the whole purpose of the union by her famous Ordinance of Nullification of 1832. Though she went so far as to call for a volunteer army, the then prevailing small-state pattern enabled Jackson to accomplish with the determined waggling of his presidential finger what Lincoln almost failed to accomplish with the help of a huge army and by means of a ruinous war. This shows how essential the small-state pattern is to the success of federal union. It also shows the potential danger of the as yet unimportant beginnings of regional consolidation as manifested in the occasional regional governors' conferences. If states should go further on this treacherous road of *regional* union, it would spell the end of the *national* federation.

The greatness of the Swiss idea is thus the smallness of the cells from which it derives its guarantees. The Swiss from Geneva does not confront the Swiss from Zurich as a German to a French confederate, but as a confederate from the Republic of Geneva to a confederate from the Republic of Zurich. The citizen of German-speaking Uri is as much a foreigner to the citizen of German-speaking Unterwalden as he is to the citizen of Italian-speaking Ticino. Just as there is no intermediary Prairie government between Wisconsin and Washington, so there is no intermediary organization between the canton of St. Gallen and the Swiss federation in the form of a German-speaking sub-federation. The power delegated to Berne derives from the small member republic and not from the nationality. For Switzerland is a union of *states*, not of *nations*.

This is why it is important to realize that in Switzerland there live (in rough numbers) 700,000 Bernese, 650,000 Zurichois, 160,000 Genevese, etc., and not 2,500,000 Germans, 1,000,000 French, and 500,000 Italians. The great number of proud, democratic, and almost sovereign cantons, and the small number of the individual cantonal populations, eliminate all possible imperialist ambitions on the part of any one canton, because it would always be outnumbered by even a very small combination of others which at all times would be at the disposal of the federal government. If ever, as a result of our modern unification and simplification manias, an attempt to reorganize Switzerland on the basis of her nationalities should succeed, the twenty-two 'superfluous' states with all their separate parliaments and governments would become three provinces—not of Switzerland, however, but of Germany, Italy, and France.

2. *Other Successful Federations*

The small-state device, which alone accounts for the success of the American and Swiss federations because it alone solves the all-important problem of enforceable executive authority, is also responsible for all other successful experiments of international union. It prevails in the federations of Argentina, Brazil, Mexico, and Venezuela. It prevails in Australia and Canada. If it is somewhat less effective in the last-mentioned country where national frictions arise occasionally between English- and French-speaking citizens, it is because Canada has not applied it with the necessary clinical detachment. Two of her provinces, Ontario and Quebec, holding more than seven out of a total of fourteen million inhabitants, have become so large in relation to the other eight that they might eventually wreck the Canadian union with their emerging intra-federal great-power complexes. Since the restoration of a smoothly operating balance amongst the unequal provinces can be accomplished only by applying the principle of division, proposals have already been advanced 'to settle Dominion-provincial differences by dividing Canada into 20 provinces'.[1] The particular danger in Canada is that, unlike Switzerland, one of the two nationalities lives in a single large state, the province of Quebec, thereby creating the basis of national *solidity* and consciousness which has been eliminated from the Swiss scene through the division of nationalities and the creation of *cantonal* consciousness instead.

The most significant illustration of the small-state principle as the mainspring of federal success is, however, not provided by contemporary examples but by one of the most unique political structures of the past, though it invariably produces nothing but jolly laughter amongst our sophisticated modern theorists when its name is mentioned. This is the Holy Roman Empire of which Lord Bryce has quite properly remarked that it was neither holy, nor Roman, nor an empire. It was a loose federation uniting in a single framework most German and Italian states, and lasting for the fantastic period of a thousand years. Still, our theorists, who are so infatuated with virile longevity and whose creations nevertheless rarely outlast even a decade, smile at it in inane tolerance. But with all its weaknesses it accomplished what Napoleon, Hitler, or Mussolini could not accomplish with all their strength. And with all its superstitious mysticism it achieved what our modern efficiency experts cannot achieve with all the enlightenment of science.

The reason for its singular success and its extraordinary duration was that it was easy to rule. And it was easy to rule because of its small component parts. Like every political organism, it was besieged by thousands of frictions and problems. But none of these ever outgrew the small power of its central government. Even its largest unit was so weak that an insignificant Swiss count, a Bavarian margrave, or a Luxembourg duke could hold it together with a handful of soldiers plus the symbol of the imperial crown. However, the latter added so little to their little power that Edward Gibbon could write of the great Charles IV, who ruled from 1347 to 1378 and hailed from the Duchy of Luxembourg, that 'such was the shameful poverty of the Roman Emperor that his person was arrested by a butcher in the streets of

---

[1] See editorial in *Ottawa Citizen* of 13 October 1948, discussing the proposal of Professor A. R. M. Lower of Queens University, Kingston, Canada.

Worms, and was detained in the public inn, as a pledge or hostage for the payment of his expenses'.[1] When the Empire eventually began to break down, it was not because it was ramshackle and weak. That was the reason for its success. It was because at last, after nearly a thousand years of romantic and ineffectual existence, strength began to develop in its corners, producing on its soil the unified great powers of Prussia and Austria. Regional union thus meant not the preservation but the destruction of this much-ridiculed though great and truly international realm. What had survived a millennium of small-state existence was finally smashed by the cancer of its own great powers.

Every successful international federation thus reveals the same administrative device: the small-unit pattern. As a result, the conclusion seems neither presumptuous nor forced that the one element common to all cannot be a phenomenon of coincidence. It must be the very cause of their success while, on the other hand, its absence from federal organizations must invariably lead to their failure, irrespective of the auspices under which they may have been established, the good will by which they may be animated, or the determination by which they may be carried out. This conclusion becomes all the more inevitable if we examine in addition to the successful unions a number of unsuccessful experiments such as the pre-Bismarck German federation, the League of Nations, the Western Union, the Indonesian Union, the European Council, or the United Nations. It may be disrespectfully macabre to write funeral orations while some of them are still alive. However, it would be still more macabre to rely on the assumption of their survival if the realization of their certain collapse can save us from both unpreparedness and unnecessary disillusionment.

3. Unsuccessful Federal Experiments

As there is a feature common to all successful federal experiments, there is a feature common also to all unsuccessful ones. None of them has applied the small-cell principle to its system of administration. All suffer from political cancer. All have tried what no healthy social organism can survive—the union of small with large states without first cutting the latter down to proportions which would permit their frictionless subordination under a federal government. The consequences of such attempts seem always the same. The end is destruction. Only the kinds of destruction differ. If a federation has *several* great-power participants, it will break apart. It will end in disintegration. If it has

[1] Edward Gibbon, op. cit., vol. 5, pp. 308–9.

only *one*, it will turn the smaller members into tools of the biggest. It will end in centralization.

Both variations of breakdown occurred in pre-Bismarck *Germany*. First the federation disintegrated as a result of the conflict for leadership between its two great powers, Austria and Prussia. This phase ended with the expulsion of Austria in 1866. Next came a new federation uniting the smaller German states with the victorious colossus of Prussia. This was bound to follow one of two courses. Either it, too, had to fall apart, as it nearly did, or its central organs had to solve the administrative problem of acquiring a power equal in magnitude to that of its largest unit—Prussia. But there was only one practical way of amassing a power large enough to enforce federal laws not only on small member states but on Prussia as well. This was to make use of the power of Prussia herself. The enforcement of laws on weaker states such as Bavaria or Saxony would have constituted no executive problem since the necessary power could at all times have been easily obtained through military contributions from half a dozen other states. But no combination of member states could have yielded the power to enforce federal laws on Prussia. This only Prussia could do. Thus, if the new German federation was to survive as a single political organism, it had no other alternative than to become the instrument of its largest member, against whose opposition it could enforce nothing and without whose co-operation it could not be maintained. In spite of the genuine particularism existing in the German states and supported by their monarchical institutions, the federal structure, once this course was decided upon, became a historic fiction, and what actually emerged was not a Greater Germany but a Greater Prussia. Thus, the German federal experiment ended in failure twice, first through partial dissolution brought about by the expulsion of Austria, the rival great power, and then through centralization accomplished by the remaining great power, Prussia.

A fascinating contemporary parallel, and another example of destruction through centralization if a federal union harbours a single disproportionately large power, has been furnished by the short-lived *United States of Indonesia*. When it was created in December 1949, it was composed of sixteen member states of which one was so large that its subordination without its own consent was impossible—the Jogjakarta republic. This meant the union was born with cancer. As was inevitable in such a condition, Jogjakarta promptly assumed the lordly role of unification and, in the words of the *New York Times* of 8 April 1950, 'systematically and progressively dynamited the federal idea'. The result was a counter-movement on the part of the victimized members who wanted to destroy the unworkable federation the other way, through secession. Being too small, however, they had no greater chance of escaping the imperial sway of Jogjakarta, with which they had carelessly and trustingly been joined in union, than the German states had in escaping Prussian domination after the exclusion of Austria. They were bullied and beaten in best great-power manner until, six months after their establishment, they found themselves degraded to the status of centralized provinces of a suffocatingly unitarian state. The federation had broken down not because of the absence of good will or the desire for autonomous freedom, but because of the absence of the only administrative device ensuring success—the small-unit pattern.

The same structural weakness, and nothing else, caused the collapse of the *League of Nations*. This idealistic enterprise functioned well only in relation to its small members. Naturally, for these were units of a size that could be controlled. But, like other badly organized unions, it was afflicted with the cancer of big powers. While little was needed to keep the small ones in line, the League would again on grounds of sheer arithmetic have required an executive power larger than that of its largest member if it was to be effective over *all* its component parts. This, only the largest member itself, Germany, could have furnished. As a result, the League could have functioned only as a tool of Germany even as the German federation could function only as a tool of Prussia. However, being a structure composed of more than just one great power, its destruction could not have been brought about through centralization but disintegration. And this was the course it took. When it proved itself helpless in the face of Japanese aggression in China, Italian aggression in Ethiopia, and Russian aggression in Finland, it fell to ashes. And why? Again because no political organism containing large subordinate units can produce the enforcement power capable of holding them together.

The cause that wrecked the League wrecked also the *Western Union*, that already forgotten attempt of one group of member states of the United Nations to enter into a separate *regional* union for the significant purpose of protecting itself against another group of members of the same United Nations—an organization ostensibly created to make such separate mutual-help associations unnecessary. Though composed of the closest of friends—Great Britain, France, the Netherlands, Belgium, and Luxembourg—the Western Union foundered after it had hardly been launched not because of any lack of devotion but because two of its members were too large to be absorbed. This meant that again a union was born with political cancer. And again, the results were the same. Not only were its founders unable to solve the problem of executive power; every manifestation of existence threatened to become a problem, and every problem threatened at once to assume elephantine proportions. In a small-state federation such as the United States, for example, no one would ever have been so touchy as to protest against the appointment of a Chief of Staff on the ground that he is a Virginian or Missourian, or that he is *not* a New Yorker. But in the Western Union, the appointment in 1949 of an Englishman as Chief of Staff and of a Frenchman as head of the naval forces provoked such a storm of national misgivings amongst the peoples supposed to live in harmony that both Great Britain and France felt compelled to assure their citizens that the French would still be commanded by a French general, and the British navy by a British admiral.[1] Which was tantamount to declaring that neither of the participating great powers even dreamt of accepting the implication of union unless it could make the union its tool. As a result, another federal experiment fell by the roadside a victim of untreated political cancer.

This leaves us with the *European Council* and the *United Nations*. But there is no reason to assume that they would have a greater chance of success than their respective predecessors. For they, too, represent examples of the pathetic attempt to live with cancer by incorporating within their structure several untreated great powers. As Milton Eisenhower suggested at the UNESCO conference of Beirut in December 1949 with regard to the United Nations, and as may with equal validity be suggested with regard to the European Council, to render them effective it would be necessary to place at their disposal a police force stronger than any nation's armed forces or those of 'any likely combination of states'.[2] However, here again, only the great powers amongst these two associations have collectively the means of furnishing such colossal forces. But what are great powers? States which by their very definition recognize no master. Understandably, they have no interest in the world to assist in the establishment of an international authority whose effectiveness would spell their own eclipse. No wonder that the Big Five appeared for once in brotherly unanimity when

[1] An identical difficulty arose in 1951 among the great-power members of the North Atlantic Treaty Organization when the appointment of an American as Supreme Naval Commander was considered such a staggering blow to British pride that, instead of creating union, it threatened to create division.

[2] *New York Times*, 8 December 1949.

they proposed through the Military Staff Committee of the United Nations the creation of a world force of such ridiculous proportions that it could handle 'only disputes among small and medium powers', since the United Nations would at any rate 'be unable to take action against any aggression by one of the five great powers'.[1] As if *little* states were the peace disturbers against whom a pompous world organization had to be on guard!

But let us assume the great powers were willing to endow an international organization such as the European Council or the United Nations with the forces necessary to render them effective also in the face of their largest participants. The result would be a military and economic burden on the world of such monstrous proportions that it could not be supported for any length of time since the great powers, in addition to their *federal* contributions, would of course continue their own stupendous armament expenditure in order not to forfeit their coveted diplomatic pre-eminence. And if it could be supported for any length of time, the result would be the establishment of so formidable a controlling organ that what the world might gain in unity, it would lose in liberty. For only an executive authority of the most tyrannical omnipotence could keep such uneasy, clumsy, and cancerous colossi from disintegrating in violent explosion.

This explains why none of our present large-scale union experiments is able to bear us consolation. Instead of freeing us from war and fear, they have made them our permanent companions, since we have long become aware in our subconsciousness that, the more they succeed in solidifying, the closer they come to the critical mass where fission sets in not only helplessly and hopelessly, but spontaneously. Before they came into existence, the world had at least occasionally a spell of unperturbed peace. Now it has become an arena in which the advocates of a united mankind try to keep us huddled together by painting, like many a minister in his Sunday sermon, not the blessings of paradise but the horrors of hell. True, they offer us unity and peace, but a peace by threat, and unity by terror.

As a result, if we are interested in creating international unions not only effectively but also economically, peacefully, and democratically, we must fall back on the organizational principle which alone contains the secret of success, the small-cell principle, and apply the curative principle of division to every federal structure containing big powers. Thus, if our present unifiers really want union, they must have disunion first. If Europe is to be united under the auspices of the European

---

[1] Thomas J. Hamilton in the *New York Times*, 20 April 1950.

Council, its participating great powers must first be dissolved to a degree that, as in Switzerland or the United States, none of its component units is left with a significant superiority in size and strength over the others. In their present shape, Germany, France, and Italy can never be successfully joined together. Nor could France and Great Britain, as was demonstrated in the case of the Western Union. But Alsace, Burgundy, Navarre, Bavaria, Saxony, Wales, Cornwall, Scotland, Lombardy, and Parma can. Not only have they the federable size; unlike the present great powers, their history is free from the mortgage of such far-flung perpetual hostility as disturbs the relations of France, England, and Germany in a measure that not even their union could blot it out. The same applies to the United Nations if anybody cares for their preservation. Their present two chief antagonists, the United States and Soviet Russia, must likewise be dismembered, lest their struggle for hegemony break the enterprise which both must either dominate or leave. However, great powers are as tenacious in their resistance to division treatment as is cancer, and dismemberment may not be feasible. But then, union is not feasible either.

4. The Principle of Government

One final point should be made with regard to the small unit as the only workable basis of social organization. It underlies not only all successful *federal* government, but *all* government, federal as well as centralized. In other words, it represents not only *a* principle of government, but *the* principle of government, and politics, however incredible this may appear to the politicians of failure, cannot disregard it any more than physics can disregard the principle of gravity.

For this reason, effective administrators, rulers, and conquerors, instead of ridiculing it, have made it the constant stratagem of their success. Since time immemorial they have tried to increase the power of their government while simultaneously decreasing their governmental problems not by the difficult method of increasing the size of governmental power, but by the simple method of reducing the size of the governed unit. The Medes and Persians built history's first great centralized empires by splitting their conquests into numerous small *satrapies* whose domination was as simple as that of the large undivided blocks would have been difficult. Alexander's empire, which failed to apply this device, needed an Alexander to keep it together and promptly collapsed after his death. But the Romans applied it again, dividing their vast and long-lasting empire into coutnless small controllable *provinces* in which no power could ever develop in competition to the relatively small power of the Roman proconsuls. They also gave the principle its classic formulation: *divide et impera*—divide and rule. And the Catholic Church applied it on a still larger scale by dividing the entire world into such a finely spun network of *dioceses* that it can assert its rule by moral authority alone.

As empires applied it, so did individual states. France, when she was reorganized by that efficient administrator Napoleon into a modern centralized power, dissolved her few unequally large and particularist duchies such as Burgundy into more than ninety small mathematically denationalized *departments*. These alone could be successfully ruled by Paris without the requirement of a disproportionately large force which, being recruited from previously hostile states, might in addition have been more of a danger than a helpful tool in the hands of the central government. *Politically*, France therefore no longer knows a Burgundy, a Picardy, or an Alsace. They have been dissolved not into one but several *departments* in order to prevent any future development of autochthonous regional power on the soil that formerly constituted sovereign duchies.

A similar operation was performed by Great Britain who united her unequally large and mutually hostile nations by destroying them as political entities and replacing them with small and easily controllable units of approximately equal size, the *counties*. *Politically*, there is today neither an England, nor a Scotland, nor a Wales. What little chance a union of British *nations* rather than of British *counties* would have had can be seen from the fact that the moment one of them, the Irish, succeeded in reorganizing itself as a national unit, it burst the frame of the United Kingdom and broke away. There are similar attempts at *national* reorganization in Scotland and Wales. Should they succeed also, it would mean the end of the United Kingdom altogether. It would break the small-county organization which now enables London to rule effectively in all corners of the British Isles. Once this gives way to *national* organization, London would confront accumulations of political power which could be kept under control only by military pressures of such magnitude that, as the case of Ireland has proved, not even a great power can impose them indefinitely.

A similar administrative device was applied in Germany when she was reorganized as a tightly centralized state under the nazis. To strengthen his hold, Hitler transformed her previous large-unit into a small-unit pattern. For the historic German states, with their unequal size and power, would have constituted an element of danger even to such formidable masters as the nazis. Thus, as France cut her states of ancient and dangerous glory into *departments*, and Great Britain hers into *counties*, Germany divided her old historic *Länder* into nondescript *Gaue*. In all three cases, the reasons were the same. The new artificial units had no history, no disruptive hatreds, no competing ambitions, and no power to obstruct the rule of a central government intent upon dominating a maximum of area with a minimum of means. The small-cell device permitted this. Prussia was thus divided by Hitler, not the Allies, as the Allies believed. If he did not touch historic names and titles, it was merely to hide the enormity of his innovation and to soothe the impact of his revolutionary measures. But where he applied them with a vengeance, as was the case in Austria which had caused so much of his early misery and had defied him for so long, he not only eliminated the state as an administrative unit, but even tried to strike the ancient name from the pages of history for ever.

Finally, to complete the picture, the small-unit device, which we have traced through federal as well as centralized political organizations, prevails also on the level of local government. The individual states dividing the American federation are themselves subdivided into a number of counties of approximately equal size. Moreover, whenever one of them shows a tendency to excessive growth, the administrators of their superior units, instinctively anxious to preserve the small-cell pattern, immediately draw their knives and cut them back to size, redrawing boundaries, or creating new counties altogether. The same is lastly true of cities which the principle of sound administration forces us to divide into boroughs. But even this is not the final step since boroughs are divided into wards, and wards into blocks. Below that, the social organism begins to dissolve into the sphere of individual existence, and only then does the process of division stop. We have arrived at home.

Thus, wherever we look in the political universe, we find that *successful* social organisms, be they empires, federations, states, counties, or cities, have in all their diversity of language, custom, tradition, and system, one, and only one, common feature—the small-cell pattern. Permeating everything, it is applied and reapplied in unending processes of division and subdivision. The fascinating secret of a well-functioning social organism seems thus to lie not in its overall unity but in its structure, maintained in health by the life-preserving mechanism of division operating through myriads of cell-splittings and rejuvenations taking place under the smooth skin of an apparently unchanging body. Wherever, because of age or bad design, this rejuvenating process of subdivision gives way to the calcifying process of cell unification, the cells, now growing behind the protection of their hardened frames beyond their divinely allotted limits, begin, as in cancer, to develop those hostile, arrogant great-power complexes which cannot be brought to an end until the infested organism is either devoured, or a forceful operation succeeds in restoring the small-cell pattern.

This is why such attempts at international union as the European Council or the United Nations are doomed to failure if they continue to insist on their present composition. Comprising within their framework a number of unabsorbably great powers, they suffer from the deadly disease of political cancer. To save them it would be necessary to follow Professor Simons who said of the overgrown nation-states that:

'These monsters of nationalism and mercantilism must be dismantled, both to preserve world order and to protect internal peace. Their powers to wage war and restrict world trade must be sacrificed to some supranational state or league of nations. Their other powers and functions must be diminished in favour of states, provinces, and, in Europe, small nations.'[1]

This is, indeed, the only way by which the problem of international government can be solved. The great powers, those monsters of nationalism, must be broken up and replaced by small states; for, as perhaps even our diplomats will eventually be able to understand, only *small* states are wise, modest and, above all, weak enough, to accept an authority higher than their own.

[1] Henry C. Simons, op. cit., p. 125.

Chapter Ten

THE ELIMINATION OF GREAT POWERS

Instability of present unions. Division of great powers essential. Question is not: Can it be done, but How can it be done? Division by war. Division by proportional representation. Assigning more votes to great powers on condition that federal representatives are elected not at national but district level. Federalization of great powers. Gradualness and imperceptibility of their dissolution. Districts correspond to ancient state units—division therefore not artificial. Native particularism ensuring popular approval. One cannot turn back the clock. Prevention of reunification of small states.

Can it be Done?

THE preceding chapter has demonstrated that no *satisfactory* local, national, or international organization can function except on the basis of a small-unit pattern. It is the only pattern that solves the problem of effective administration. As a result, it would seem that neither a United World nor a United Europe can last for any length of time on the basis of the existing arrangements uniting, as they do, an indigestible medley of small as well as large states. Organizations of this nature lack the vital *internal* balance that could give their federal structure more than a passing success. In their present form, the various attempted international unions of our day can therefore be held together only by means of an external force such as the threat of aggression. Once this is passed, they must either burst, collapse, or be transformed into single-power tyrannies. As free, democratic unions of nations they cannot survive.

While a federal balance could theoretically also be established on the basis of a large-unit pattern, leaving the great powers intact and uniting as a counter-measure the small states until they, too, were to form powerful blocks, a balance of this kind would produce so inelegant and clumsy an arrangement that every slightest tug or twitch would threaten its existence. For all practical purposes, therefore, international unions must seek, instead of the heavy stable balance of great-power organizations, the fluid mobile balance of multicellular small-state arrangements. The solution of their problems lies in the micro- not in the macro-political field. They must eliminate from their system not the small states but the great powers. This alone will furnish them with the internal mechanism for coping with the daily frictions of social life without the necessity of building up a governmental machine of such proportions that it could not be maintained even if it could be created.

The question now poses itself, even for those who have been convinced by the arguments of this book: can it be done? Can the great powers be divided? Will Soviet Russia and the United States accept their dissolution merely to save the United Nations? Will France, Italy, Great Britain, or Germany ever give their consent to their own liquidation merely because this would be wise? Can the clock be turned back?

One might answer this question very simply by saying that it is not the question in the first place. If regions such as Europe really desire union, the question to be answered is not: *can* the great powers be eliminated? but *how* can they be eliminated? If regions containing great powers *want* to unite, they *must* divide these powers. And what *must* be done, *can* be done. Even the clock can be turned back—to pick from the barrel of objections one of those stereotypes with which our theorists so often try to wreck a case without taking issue with it. Those who use this slogan as an insurmountable barrier to the break-up of large political powers are frequently the same who advocate in the economic field decartellization, the break-up of great economic empires, without realizing that this means turning the clock back, too. What they call reactionary politically, they call progressive economically. No engineer will dream of hiding behind this slogan when he discovers flaws in a nearly completed bridge. Instead of saying that he cannot turn back the clock, he will do precisely this, if he is to save his reputation. He will tear down the structure and begin building it all over again. No author, writing himself into a blind alley, will perpetuate his frustration by insisting that, having advanced so far in pursuit of his plot, he cannot turn back the clock. Maybe he cannot, but then his work will be a failure. But if he can, he may turn it into a masterpiece yet. Finally, even in the most literal sense, the famous clock slogan, which has caused so much intellectual havoc, is not only meaningless as an analogy, but silly in its own right, since there are few things that are easier than to turn back the clock. Just try it. In fact it is so easy that one does not even need to apply an outside force. Unaided and unbullied, the clock comes back to where it started every twenty-four hours simply by moving ahead on its slow and gentle course.

Thus, the clock *can*, of course, be turned back, and the great powers *can* be eliminated just as the great powers themselves, such as France or Hitler Germany, were able to eliminate their internal power blocks without listening to the particularists protesting that they could not do this. They could and did. The sole question to be answered then is: *how* can it be done?

One way of splitting the great powers would be through war. A man like Hitler could have done it and, maybe, would have done it. The victorious Allies have done it with regard to Germany which, for the first time in a hundred years, with Prussia subdivided into a number of smaller co-equal states, has a chance to federate successfully. By the same token, the Allies could have gone a step further and dissolved the last remaining framework still holding the German states together. However, no one can suggest so blunt and bloody a method for the destruction of other powers without being called a warmonger. It is mentioned here as a method only in reply to the argument that the division of great powers is impossible. If it cannot be brought about by other means, it can be by force of arms, and, since this is a method too, it seems that division *can* be effected.

But war is fortunately not the only means by which great powers can be divided. Engulfed in a swamp of infantile emotionalism, and attaching phenomenal value to the fact that they are big and mighty, they cannot be *persuaded* to execute their own dissolution. But, being infantile and emotional, they can be tricked into it. While they would reject their division, if it were presented to them as a demand, they might be quite willing to accept it, if offered to them in the guise of a gift. This gift would be: *proportional representation* in the bodies governing the federal union of which they form part. The acceptance of this offer would cause nothing less than their eventual disappearance.

1. *Division through Proportional Representation*

The *conventional* federal principle of government grants an equal number of votes to each participating sovereign unit of a federation irrespective of the size of its population. This is quite reasonable since international law does not distinguish amongst sovereigns, and does not make the degree of sovereignty dependent on quantitative considerations. France, with forty-five million inhabitants, is not more sovereign than Liechtenstein whose population numbers less than thirteen thousand. While she has more *might* than Liechtenstein, she has not more *right* than that miniature principality. Nor does she have more of a physical existence. For this reason, large member states of international organizations are always clamouring for proportional rather than state representation so that their numerical strength might be brought into play in a more realistic manner. But as long as the law of nations considers every sovereign state the co-equal of any other, the great powers have no chance of gratifying their passionate desire to be considered not only bulkier than small states, but greater, and endowed with more rights as well.

This unsatisfied desire is the key with which the great powers can be tricked into accepting gracefully their own liquidation. They shall be given what they so sorely want—but with a string attached. Let us illustrate this with the example of the *European Council* which is composed of four large powers, Great Britain, France, Germany, and Italy, and a number of small states such as Belgium, Luxembourg, Denmark, or the Netherlands. Its principal problem of survival is the division of in four self-centred and thus basically uncoöperative great powers. France—to illustrate the technique of division on a country clinging with particular tenacity to power and glory concepts—would never agree to be split up into her original historic regions. But she would certainly not object to the invitation to sit in the representative bodies of the European Council with, let us say, twenty voting delegates compared with, let us say, one delegate from Luxembourg, three delegates from Denmark, and five delegates each from Belgium and the Netherlands.

However, while France and the equally favoured Great Britain or Germany would naturally be agreeable to such a redistribution of votes, Luxembourg, Belgium, Denmark, or the Netherlands would not, for the simple reason that it would leave the great-power domination of the European Council unchanged. In addition, it would make an unpleasant actual condition legal as well. But the smaller countries would raise few objections if the twenty members of the French delegation were elected, not nationally, but regionally and were, consequently, to be entrusted only with *regional* responsibilities and *regional* representation. Such a shift in the source of delegation would alter the entire picture in an imperceptible, yet radical and fundamental manner. It is this that would bring about the eventual dissolution of France. Why?

France, as she effected her subdivision into more than ninety *departments* for reasons of internal administration, would now, in order to benefit from the increase in her voting strength, have to divide herself into twenty federal districts in the administrative interest of the European Council. Each of these districts would directly elect its representatives to the various federal bodies, and each would remain the exclusive formulator of the mandates and instructions given to its own delegate. Thus, the twenty members elected in the various districts of France would not appear in the federal assemblies as a unit, but as twenty individual members representing not one but twenty electorates, not one but twenty majorities, and not one common but twenty different regions. These members would serve only two political organisms, their district and the European Council, as the Swiss serves only two organized units, his canton and the overall federation. And, as already pointed out, just as Switzerland recognizes no half-way organization in the form of a subfederation of German or French cantons to act as a disruptive intermediary between the canton and the federation, so the *European Council* or, as it might eventually be called, the United States of Europe, would recognize no disruptive intermediary in the form of a subunion of French districts. From a federal point of view France, as also Great Britain, Germany, and Italy, would therefore cease to exist as a component part of a European union.

However, the mere division of France into European-Council districts would not be enough. France is a tightly centralized state and, like others, owes her development as a great power to this very fact. As long as centralization exists, great power exists, and any division under these circumstances would be but fiction. To make division effective, the great powers would have to undergo a fundamental internal change. As a preliminary step towards *successful* integration in a larger international organization they would have to transform their present centralized systems into decentralized federations. This would make their division real and thus actually usher in their gradual dissolution. It is a characteristic feature of true federations that the principal share of public power is entrusted to the small member unit, while progressively diminishing amounts of power are reserved to the higher governmental levels. In this way power is given where it can do no harm, and withheld where it might assume dangerous proportions and invite abuse. With the highest organs in a federation possessing but few powers in their own right, no obstructive power complex can develop at the top. As a result, it would be relatively easy to transfer the last weak remaining national powers to a larger international authority. In this manner, division could be effected by the inoffensive device of the internal federalization of the great powers brought about through the offer of proportional rather than national representation. Professor Henry Simons has expressed a similar idea when he wrote:

'A great virtue of extreme federalism or decentralization in great nations is that it facilitates their extension toward world organization or their easy absorption into still larger federations. If central governments were, as they should be, largely repositories of unexercised powers, held simply to prevent their exercise by constituent units or extragovernmental organizations, then supranational organization would be easy if not almost gratuitous. Indeed, such great-nation decentralization or deorganization is both end and means of international organization.'[1]

The question now is: could France or any great power be made to accept such self-division through federalization? The answer is yes, and for a variety of reasons. In the first place, as has just been pointed out, division would be presented in form of a gift. Instead of one voice in the European Council, the French (though not France) would be offered twenty. Since federalization would mean transition by steps and stages, with governmental powers not to be eliminated but merely redistributed, and with no official act terminating the state of France, no patriotic feelings would be hurt. The revolutionary change would be purely internal in character. It would be destruction by which nothing that counts is destroyed. It would be elimination without victims. There would be no foreign laws, no foreign occupation, no change in traffic or commerce or anything except in the fact that government and sovereignty would suddenly have come closer to the individual, endowing him within the smaller sphere of the new sovereign units with a dignity and importance not previously possessed. He would find this charming, not distasteful. His district would be infused with new vitality, his provincial capital would assume new glamour, and his prefect would be transformed from an appointed functionary into an elected head of state. A whole new range of intriguing activities would now take place close to his home instead of in distant Paris, new governments and parliaments would spring up and, instead of the ambitions of a few, the ambitions of many could be satisfied.

The actual political and international dissolution of France would thus go practically unnoticed. But it would be effective none the less. The provincial delegates from Normandy, Picardy, or Pau would no

[1] Henry C. Simons, op. cit., p. 21.

longer meet in Paris but in a new federal capital city that may develop in Strasbourg or elsewhere. Being the capital of a larger area than France, they would meet there the delegates from the other federally dissolved regions of the union. While there might still be a lingering of traditional unity amongst the groups of French, German, Italian, or English speaking delegates at the beginning, the groundswell of regional particularism and individualistic difference would soon break down the last vestiges of the present great-power blocks. In the absence of any unifying intermediary authority, we would soon find conservative Burgundians siding with conservative Bavarians against socialist Saxons and Normans for the same reasons that cause Swiss or American political representatives to take sides not on the basis of regional but intellectual or ideological groupings. In the end of the development Paris, like Olympia or Athens in ancient Greece, would be merely the *cultural centre* of the French-speaking world, while its *political* authority would not transcend the boundaries of its own little state of *Île de France*. With the transfer of the basic state powers from the nation to the district, the districts would automatically become the true sovereign members of the European federation. Then proportional representation could once more give way to state representation. Since the districts would all be of approximately equal size, the traditional federal principle of equal votes for equal sovereigns could again be restored.

2. Restoration of Europe's Old Nations

This leads to a second reason why France and other great powers could be induced to accept their division. I have called these new subdivisions *districts*. But they are not simply districts. As Chapter III has shown, they are France's and Europe's original *nations*. Their restoration would consequently not mean the creation of an artificial pattern but a return to Europe's natural political landscape. No new names would have to be invented. The old ones are still in existence, as are the regions and peoples which they define. It is the great powers which lack the real basis of existence and are without autochthonous, self-sustaining sources of strength. It is they that are the *artificial* structures, holding together a medley of more or less unwilling little tribes. There is no 'Great British' nation in Great Britain. What we find are the English, Scots, Irish, Cornish, Welsh, and the islanders of Man. In Italy, we find the Lombards, Tyroleans, Venetians, Sicilians, or Romans. In Germany we find Bavarians, Saxons, Hessians, Rhinelanders, or Brandenburgers. And in France, we find Normans, Catalans, Alsatians, Basques, or Burgundians. These little nations came into existence by themselves, while the great powers had to be created by force and a series of bloodily unifying wars. Not a single component part joined them voluntarily. They all had to be forced into them, and could be retained by them only by means of their division into *counties*, *Gaue*, or *departments*.

It may be objected by our modern unifiers that, though this be true, centuries of joint living have fused them into inseparable units and created changes which it would be reactionary to undo. One cannot— *hélas*, again—turn back the clock. But nothing has changed. So little fusion has taken place that, whenever the grip of a big power seems to loosen, its component parts, far from coming to its rescue, try everything to liberate themselves. When Hitler crumbled, the Bavarians wanted to secede from Germany and restore their ancient kingdom. Similarly, the Sicilians tried to set up an independent state after the defeat of Mussolini. The Scots of today are as Scottish as they were three hundred years ago. Living together with the English has only increased their desire for living apart. In 1950, they petitioned the King for the establishment of a separate parliament in Edinburgh, and a few months later dramatized the fact of their continued national existence by 'liberating' the *Stone of Scone* from the 'foreign' soil of Westminster Abbey. In Cornwall guide books greet the English tourist by telling him, gently and humorously, but still telling him that, as long as he is on Cornish ground, he must consider himself a foreigner. And in France, even in relatively calm and settled times, there is a constant undercurrent of separatist movements and sentiments not only amongst the Alsatians, but amongst Catalans, Basques, Bretons, and Normans as well.

Thus, in spite of having been submerged in great unitarian states for long periods and having been subjected to an unceasing battering of unifying propaganda, particularist sentiments still exist in undiminished strength, and few of Europe's numerous little nations, now held together within the framework of great powers, could be left alone for a single week without at once getting busy with the establishment of their own capitals, parliaments, and sovereignties. There are, of course, people such as elementary-school teachers, national politicians, military men, collectivists, mankind maniacs, and others glorying in unitarian developments, who will oppose the concept of small democratic states with fanaticism and the outcry of reaction—as if the pattern of nature could ever be reactionary. But the bulk of the inhabitants of the regions in which these states would be restored have shown time and again that they think differently. They do not seem to want life in vast meaningless realms. They want to live in their provinces, in their mountains, in their valleys. They want to live at home. This is why they have clung so tenaciously to their local colour and provincialism even when they were submerged in great empires. In the end, however, it was always the small state, not the empire, that survived. That is why small states do not have to be created artificially. They need only be freed.

3. Preservation of Small-state Pattern

One final question to be answered is whether the small states would not immediately begin to form new alliances and great-power combinations. Eventually they would, since nothing ever lasts indefinitely. But it might take them as many centuries as it took the present great powers to form. It must not be forgotten that the creation of a divided small-state pattern may mean unification in a larger international federation. This entails that there would now be an *effective* federal government whose task would be not only to keep the member states united but also to keep them apart. There is no reason to believe that under a small-state arrangement, created for the very purpose of rendering federal government effective, the prevention of interstate alliances would pose greater difficulties than the same problem poses to the governments of the United States, Canada, Mexico, or Switzerland. With the federal government having an easy margin of strength over the small individual states or even a combination of them, the danger of a successful regrouping of great powers would be a remote possibility.

From all this we see that the technical obstacle to the division of great powers and the preservation of a small-state pattern is anything but insurmountable. By using the device of proportional representation together with an appeal to the powerful particularist sentiments always present in human groups, the condition of a small-state world, so essential a prerequisite of successful international union, could be established without force or violence. It would mean nothing but the abandonment of a few silly, though cherished, slogans of the turn-the-clock-back category, a bit of diplomacy, and a bit of technique.

It can be done! And if unions are to survive, it *must* be done!

Chapter Eleven

BUT WILL IT BE DONE?

N^{o!}

Chapter Twelve

THE AMERICAN EMPIRE

'There are, at the present time, two great nations in the world which seem to tend toward the same end, although they started from different points: I allude to the Russians and the Americans. . . . Their starting-point is different, and their courses are not the same; yet each of them seems to be marked out by the will of Heaven to sway the destinies of half the globe.'

TOCQUEVILLE

The mood of the time. Dwindling number of great powers. Tocqueville's prediction. 'We shape our buildings, and our buildings shape us.' America's anti-empire. Our new colonies. Imperialism by headlines. Assertion of American overlordship. Empire by sacrifice. Coca-colonization. Let us enjoy empire. The role of the United Nations as a tool of imperialism. The two United Nations. The ultimate world state. And little states once more.

No! It will not be done!
This looks like a sad ending for a book whose principal purpose was to prove that there could so easily have been a better one. And sad endings are not at all in conformity with the *mood of the time* of which our opinion experts tell us that it is opposed to purely destructive analyses, ignoring the fact that its chief intellectual offspring, existentialism, is the most sensuous rave of destructiveness the world has enjoyed for centuries. Nobody would be so childish as to demand happy endings in Sartre! But if the pressure of an old-maidenish public for rosy outlooks is considered infantile in literature or philosophy, why should it not be the same in politics? And who is this new autocrat, the *mood of the time*, who even in democracies tries to prescribe the limits of debate, permitting criticism only on the understanding that our basic conceits are not touched? It is the same wily old tyrant whom we have already encountered under so many

other disguises, here as average man, majority, people, and there as fatherland, proletariat, party line. Now he shrouds himself in the mantle of time demanding, presumably, that I end this book on a less cynical note than a confession of my inability to believe in the applicability of my own conclusions.

Yet, although it should make no difference, this is neither cynical nor destructive. The purpose of an analysis is to analyse, to conclude, and to suggest. This I have done. To come forth with ringing appeals to humanity and declarations of faith in its wisdom, as is now so fashionable, is an entirely different proposition. In this particular case, most will even agree that, to believe in the willingness of the great powers to preside over their own liquidation for the purpose of creating a world free of the terrors which they alone are able to produce, would not be a sign of faith in the first place, but of lunacy, as it is the sign of lunacy, and not of faith, to believe that atom bombs can be produced but need not necessarily be detonated.

Nevertheless, I agree that this analysis cannot simply be ended with a declaration of lack of faith. There is still one question to be answered. If there is no chance of the restoration of a small-state world because of the unwillingness of the great powers to apply the principle of division to themselves, what then?

1. The Road of Bigness

Obviously, the only alternative to littleness is bigness, and the only thing the world can do if it refuses to go back is to go ahead, treading the road of great power to its logical end. Where does this lead us?

It has been pointed out before that the road of bigness is characterized by the gradual shrinkage of the number of great powers. As some of them continue to grow, others must by necessity give way. This has not always been the case, since previously each could satisfy its appetite for expansion by feeding on little states. However, the supply of the latter became to all intents and purposes exhausted with the end of the nineteenth century when those still in existence at that time became unavailable for further absorption through entering, if not the actual territory, at least the power orbit of their large neighbours. As a result, ever since then the great powers have had to fall on each other. World War I thus saw for the first time in many centuries the disappearance not of small but of large countries, Turkey and Austria-Hungary. World War II eliminated three more, Japan, Italy, and Germany. And this was not all. When peace returned, two others were discovered along the road in a condition of complete exhaustion, China and France. Unable at first to arise, and, once arisen, to keep afoot by their own efforts, they still bear the name of great powers but clearly no longer fit the definition.

Of the nine great powers entering the twentieth century with the customary belief in their own indestructibility, only three can therefore be said to have reached the mid-century mark, Russia, Great Britain, and the United States. And even amongst these the process of further shrinkage has already begun to manifest itself so that before long there will be actually only two survivors, Russia and America. Though these two joined the circle of the mighty last, they were destined through the interplay of their overwhelming population potentials and the vast expanse of their territories to outlive all the rest from the very beginning. Indeed, so inevitable was their course that as early as 1840 Alexis de Tocqueville was able to foresee every step of their development in such minute detail that what he wrote would be one of history's great prophecies were it not simply a masterpiece of deductive reasoning spun from premises that permitted no other conclusion. These are his words:

'The time will therefore come when one hundred and fifty millions of men will be living in North America, equal in condition, the progeny of one race, owing their origin to the same cause, and preserving the same civilization, the same language, the same religion, the same habits, the same manners, and imbued with the same opinions, propagated under the same forms. The rest is uncertain, but this is certain; and it is a fact new to the world—a fact fraught with such portentous consequences as to baffle the efforts even of the imagination.

'There are, at the present time, two great nations in the world which seem to tend toward the same end, although they started from different points: I allude to the Russians and the Americans. Both of them have grown up unnoticed; and while the attention of mankind was directed elsewhere, they have suddenly assumed a most prominent place among the nations; and the world learned their existence and their greatness at almost the same time.

'All other nations seem to have nearly reached their natural limits, and only to be charged with the maintenance of their power; but these are still in the act of growth; all the others are stopped, or continue to advance with extreme difficulty; these are proceeding with ease and with celerity along a path to which the human eye can assign no term. The American struggles against the natural obstacles which oppose him; the adversaries of the Russian are men; the former combats the wilderness and savage life; the latter, civilization with all its weapons and its arts: the conquests of the one are therefore gained by the plough-share; those of the other by the sword. The Anglo-American relies upon personal interest to accomplish his ends, and gives free scope to the unguided exertions and common sense of the citizens; the Russian centres all the authority of society in a single arm: the principal instru-ment of the former is freedom; of the latter servitude. Their starting-point is different, and their courses are not the same; yet each of them seems to be marked out by the will of Heaven to sway the destinies of half the globe.'[1]

In the meantime, the condition so lucidly foretold has become a political reality. The unpreventable consequence of the road of bigness which the world has chosen in preference to life in small communities has arrived with such punctuality that there are only two real sovereign states left today, the United States, now indeed a nation of 'one hun-dred and fifty millions of men', and Soviet Russia. As a result, what we actually have is not a world whose one half is dominated by Russia enforcing the principle of servitude while the other is composed of a multitude of free nations joined for a common purpose. What we have is a world composed of two empires, each swaying the destinies of half the globe, and fulfilling nobody's purpose except that of their two central powers. And this answers the question of the alternative to a world of little states. It is a world of two great empires keeping each other in a terror-spreading uneasy state of balance.

2. The Anti-empire

We find, of course, no particular pleasure hearing this word applied to America and, if we accept its implications at all, shall do so only under protestations of innocence. For is not our whole history charac-terized by our consistent fight not for but against imperial domination? Even today our sole aim is to liberate the world, not to master it. And if we are so determined to unite at least one half under our leadership it is, in fact, not to create an empire but an anti-empire.

Which is quite true. But conditions breed their own mentality irres-pective of our personal preferences. This is once more a materialistic way of looking at history, but is it not once more the same thing

[1] Alexis de Tocqueville, *Democracy in America*. London: Oxford University Press, 1946, p. 286–7.

Winston Churchill implied when he said in defending the reconstruction of the British House of Commons in its original narrow and oblong form: 'We shape our buildings, and our buildings shape us'? Just as the essence of British democracy with its cultivation of brilliant debate and its rejection of platitudinous oratory was thus presented by one of its staunchest defenders as a result not of a flattering national character but of the intimacy forced on its politicians by the physical narrowness of their meeting place (and, one may add, on its citizens by the narrowness of the English pub), so a country's imperial predestination is the result not of its historic ambitions but of the physical character of the home it has decided to build for itself.

Empire may be contrary to everything we have planned and cherished. But if we did not want it, we ought to have organized ourselves in a manner that would have precluded it. We ought to have built a different house as did the New Zealanders who were satisfied to live within the confines of a relatively small island world. Instead, we set out at the very beginning of our history to eliminate all restrictive boundaries and to create a country of such spread and wealth that, once its population had reached a certain density, it was doomed not only to become a great power but a power that could in the end have only one rival. We were an empire at birth.

Though it is true that we never wanted world dominion, it has been thrust upon us none the less. But what difference does it make to the foreign subjects of our new imperialism, how we got that way. As Tocqueville has said, our starting point was different from that of Russia. We believed in liberty and they in servitude; we in the ploughshare and they in the sword. And the courses we followed were not the same. We acquired involuntarily and almost without our consent what the Russians acquired eagerly and with force. The nations of our side came by their own volition while those joining Moscow did so under duress. Yet, the results are identical. We find ourselves just as much in possession of one-half of the world as Russia is of the other. Our plan was to build an anti-empire. But anti-empire is empire, too, as we can see from the fact that the capital of this side of the Iron Curtain is not the seat of the United Nations but Washington. This is where the statesmen of the free world go to pay their respects.

3. Empire by Implication

If we still have illusions about the imperialistic implications of our power, few others have. Though joining us freely, they have long since discovered that, in spite of the huge material profits accruing to them, their partnership is not one of equality, and that there is only one nation which is truly free in this new arrangement, the imperial nation, the American.[1] This is why they give us the same mixture of hatred, abuse, and humility which subject peoples have at all times rendered their masters. They are humble because they cannot maintain their standards without our assistance. They hate us because they cannot have our assistance without taking our directions. And they abuse us because, in spite of the unchallenging facts of our empire, we have committed ourselves to retaining the fiction of their freedom and equality, not so much to respect *their* feelings as *ours*. For it is we who cannot believe that we have acquired an empire, not they. And it is we who were trained through our traditions to find no charm in the idea of an empire, not they who, overpowered by the proximity of imperialistic Russia, realized before us that their only alternative to absorption by the East was to place themselves under our protection. But what does protection mean except that the countries seeking it have become our protectorates?

By their own admission, once proud states such as France, Italy, Greece, or Yugoslavia exist only by our strength and grace. Unlike Great Britain, they have shown no disposition ever to try it the hard way again and do without our assistance which they demand not only for the present but for the future, and not only militarily, for their defence, but also economically, for the maintenance of their living standards. But what are countries so utterly and perpetually dependent on our support that they have practically written it into their constitution, other than our dependencies, our colonies?

Realizing this better than we do, they have lost no time in adjusting their policies. On the one hand, they treat us exactly as we want to be treated. They send us an unending stream of missions and personalities, calling us liberators and promising to be loyal to us, to consider our enemies as theirs, and to shun neutrality if war should come. When President Auriol of France visited Washington, the *New York Times*

[1] Illustrating this sentiment, the conservative Paris weekly *Le Monde* of 12 June 1951, writes for instance the following on the Atlantic Treaty structure: 'The fundamental inequality of the alliance is turning it more and more into a hidden protectorate in which protestations of national pride are not enough to compensate for a growing enslavement. The Roman Empire had its citizens, its allies, and its foreigners. The new empire has its allies of the first zone (the Americans), its allies of the second zone (the British), and its continental protégés: in spite of all their haughtiness, the latter are becoming to an ever increasing extent the Filipinos of the Atlantic.'

captioned its report: 'Head of Paris Regime Insists His Nation Will Shun Neutrality and Be Worthy U.S. Ally.'[1] But clearly, a country desiring to be worthy of any power other than itself can only do so if that power is its overlord. No French President could possibly commit his regime to a policy of worthiness of England without being accused of treason. Nor is it conceivable that an American President could promise that the United States would try its best to be worthy of France without being torn to shreds by our commentators and electorates. Worthiness of someone else indicates a purely one-way relationship of inferior to superior.

On the other hand, they pile upon us abuse in awareness, this time, less of their subjection than of the fact that we ourselves have not yet grasped the full impact of our domination. Whenever we make a step to withdraw from their political scene in accordance with our original illusion of having merely come to set them free, they tell us that we must be out of our minds. Instead of gratitude they show us insolence, and instead of releasing us from our contributions they threaten us in no uncertain terms that they will turn communist unless assistance is not only continued, but intensified, increased, speeded up, enjoying our malaise with the subtle sadism typical of those caught in hopeless subjection. They are almost clinical about it, as if it made no difference to themselves whether they are in our camp or in Moscow's, knowing that their continued adherence to the West is infinitely more important to us than to them. And they are right, in a way. While practically 100 per cent of Americans are interested in seeing Italy, for example, on this side of the great divide, only 60 per cent of Italians are.

But why should we, in Washington, feel it a threat to our interests if an allegedly independent Italy should decide to turn communist unless she has actually become a part of our defence system from which we cannot let her go even if we wanted because the only alternative open to her would be to join the defence system of our rival empire? However, if Italy lies within our defence system, our own boundaries must lie in Italy. This means that, whatever we may declare, subconsciously and by implication we consider her as one of our dominions, free to choose her own road only within the limits of our pleasure. And the same is true of all other countries this side of the Iron Curtain. To realize this, we need only scan the headlines of our newspapers and magazines which, in their condensed form, give frequently a sharper picture of an article's true significance than the article they try to summarize. Thus the *New Leader*, a great liberal publication and certainly

1 *New York Times*, 30 March 1951.

the last to endorse imperialistic ambitions, carried the following titles indicative of the advent of our empire in a number of recent issues: 'The Proconsul of Japan'; 'Only America Can Save France'; 'Turkey, Mid-East Bastion'.[1] Whose bastion? Certainly not of Belgium or Italy, neither of whom would spend a penny on its fortification. It is the bastion of the organism whose nerve centre is Washington. Since a bastion must lie within and not outside one's orbit of power, Turkey is thus by implication considered as inside the American orbit. But an orbit larger than a nation's boundaries is not a national but an imperial orbit. Only empire can stretch beyond one's country.

4. Empire by Attitude

However, even within our own ranks the awareness of empire is no longer just a subconscious apprehension creeping into headlines without registering on our minds. Those of our officials who, by virtue of their position, have come into direct contact with it, show already all the symptoms of *conscious* overlordship, leading to such critical pronouncements as General Eisenhower's remark regarding the civilian leaders of Western European countries: 'I don't think, sometimes, the politicians do too good a job',[2] or to such last-ditch counter-attacks as the protest of Canada's Secretary of External Affairs, Mr. Lester B. Pearson, who proclaimed the 'easy and automatic relations' with the United States a 'thing of the past', and emphasized that Canadians were 'not willing to be merely an echo of somebody else'.[3] Maybe they are not willing, but they will hardly be able to change the relentless logic of historic development.

Many other incidents illustrate this trend. In fact, whenever in recent years a foreign country has gone too far in insisting on the exercise of sovereign power it once had but now no longer possesses, our statesmen have shown no hesitation in setting the record straight and, as a rule, have done this in even blunter terms than was evident in General Eisenhower's gentle rapping of politicians whose supposed task is to please their domestic electorates, not an American general.

Thus, when Israel bombed a few border settlements in a reprisal raid against Syria in April 1951, neither the United Nations, nor Paris, nor London took any particular notice. But Washington sent her immediately a stern 'rebuke' without bothering for an instant about the

[1] *New Leader*, 19 March 1951, 25 December 1950, 5 March 1951.
[2] *New York Times*, 20 September 1951.
[3] *New York Times*, 11 April 1951.

minor legal technicality that it had no authority over actions of nations living five thousand miles away on the distant eastern shores of the Mediterranean.[1] A similar rebuke, though for different reasons, was sent to Italy after she had announced with a flush of pride that she had succeeded in balancing her budget of 1950. Although she hoped thereby to have given evidence of her wise use of American aid, she did not realize that the idea of a balanced budget had long ago ceased to be a sign of a flourishing public household in the United States. So, instead of receiving the expected compliments, she was surprised to see a minor ECA official arrive in Rome and deliver a stern lecture on the Keynesian principles of deficit spending together with a warning that, another balanced budget, and she would find herself struck off the list of American aid recipients. There was nothing left for the half-stunned and half-delighted Italian government but to accept the master's rebuke and promptly run up the required deficit.

An even sterner lesson was given Greece when her government had quite sensibly decided to buy a yacht for the king in order to relieve the drab misery of the people by investing at least their representative with a bit of the glamour and cheer they cannot have themselves. This is one of the great functions of a royal court, as the British have so well demonstrated during the long years of unbroken austerity. Yet our embassy officials, having been raised on a different diet, and never having experienced the emotional starvation that accompanies material misery, got so mad at this alleged provocation not of Greece's but, as they so characteristically asserted, America's public opinion that the embarrassed government of Athens had no alternative than to repent, vow chastity, and cancel a purchase in which not a single American dollar was involved.[2]

But the outstanding enforcement of our imperial will on foreign countries was directed at Great Britain who, after all, is still an almost-great power in her own right. Yet, when she decided to withhold support from the American-sponsored United Nations resolution declaring communist China an aggressor because this was in line with her own public opinion rather than ours, and reflected the judgment of the leaders chosen by the English rather than us, she was immediately put under such massive pressure that she, too, had to go the road of submission. And what was our weapon? An atom bomb? No! The simple threat of *catastrophic* consequences on the public opinion of the American people who is master of many but is mastered by none. We let everybody go his own way except in the case of conflicting interests.

[1] *New York Times*, 10 April 1951.   [2] *New York Times*, 8 June 1951.

Then it is *our* choice and interpretation that counts, not anybody else's, not even that of an international authority, as was shown by the blustering Senator of a charming cartoon. Pleading fervently for American adherence to an International Court of Justice, he proclaims in zestful imperial style: 'As we have never lost a war, so shall we never lose a case.' We never shall.

5. *Empire by Sacrifice*

But the American Empire manifests itself not only by our implied or deliberate behaviour as unchallengeable rulers. It shows itself also in the burden it carries. As it is an empire of domination, it is also an empire of sacrifice. And it is here, at least, where it seems to be different from the empire of the Russians. Unlike the latter, we meet the principal cost of defending our sphere of influence not through our satellites but by our own efforts. While Russia fought the Korean war by not participating officially in it at all and letting the Chinese do most of the dying, we were in it up to our necks. Though we called it a United Nations war, the armies involved, even those of other countries, were equipped with material not from the United Nations but the United States, and the soldiers dying were in the main American soldiers, not those of the agency in whose name their battles were fought, as the following breakdown of casualty figures issued in April 1951 indicated:

United States	57,120
Turkey	1,169
United Kingdom	892
France	396
Australia	265
The Netherlands	112
Siam	108
Greece	89
Canada	68
The Philippines	55
New Zealand	9
Union of South Africa	6
Belgium	0
Luxembourg	0

By April 1951 the United States, with a population of 150 million, had thus suffered 57,120 casualties, while all other participants on our side, with a combined population of 220 million (not counting Korea,[1] a non-member, nor the non-participating members of the United Nations) had suffered only 3,169. No American public opinion would have put up with such a stupendously unequal distribution of sacrifice were it not for the fact that it really reflected quite faithfully the distribution of interests involved.

As we carry the principal share of the cost of our imperial consolidation militarily, we do so also economically. While the Russians snatch from the larders of their satellites whatever passes their hungry vision, we fill those of ours with an unending stream of commodities drawn from our own store houses. While the empire of the Soviets is depressing the potentially higher living standards of its subject nations to the low level of its master race, we are raising the low and declining standards of our dependencies to the relatively still high level to which we ourselves are accustomed. Wherever we arrive, we come laden with the products of our ploughshare rather than the might of our sword.

And it is, indeed, this particular circumstance that illustrates the main difference in the manner in which Russians and Americans organize their respective empires. We proceed with seduction where the others use force. We assimilate the world through our goods, the others through their ideology. While the unity of the East is brought about by every Czech, Russian, or Chinese becoming a communist, the unity of the West is created by every Frenchman, Dutchman, or Italian becoming an American. This is preferable, I presume, but it spells national extinction for the peoples concerned all the same. We may say that, as Americans, they will at least be free, but so will all Czechs or Chinese once they have become convinced communists. Assimilation does not destroy freedom. It makes it meaningless.

It is thus in *our* sign, not in Europe's, that Europeans are assimilated and united. If their armies already look like a common instrument, it is not because they have developed common *European* features, and placed themselves under common *European* commanders. It is because they are all beginning to use *American* material and to follow *American* commanders. Similarly, if the differences in their habits and tastes are already visibly withering away, it is not because of their common appreciation of everything European but because of the common interest in everything American. Their new unity is a product of the U.S.A. It is not Italian Chianti, French Burgundy, Danish Akvavit,

[1] The casualties suffered by South Korea during the same period according to *Time* of 9 April 1951, amounted to 168,652.

or German beer which bring them together. In fact, these keep them distinguishable and apart. What brings them together is that they are all developing a fatal taste for Coca-Cola. Though this is the most harmless symbol of American life, it is so significant of our soft-drink approach to empire building in contrast to the strong-arm method of Russia that the irate Frenchmen have come to consider their liberty more endangered by this than anything else, and have given it the appropriate name of *coca-colonization*. They have long realized that a bottle of coke, or any other commodity so lavishly bestowed upon them at the slightest gesture of supplication, is as formidable a weapon of assimilation as a sword, and even more dangerous. For, while everybody resents a sword and the pain it inflicts, most everyone will eventually succumb to the gentle drug effect of a coke. We just need to put it on their table and, in time, they will reach for it by themselves. But whoever begins to drink of it will, at the last stage of the process, cease to be an Italian, Frenchman, or German, and become, spiritually at least, an American.

And this is what Europeans and many others at this moment are doing anyway. American products, ideas, tastes, advisers, and generals have become their only common denominator, and the only union they will have will be a union under the flag of American merchandise and the United States. This is why a country such as Syria, still trying to escape the whirlpool of coca-colonization, defiantly announced, though nobody had invited her to it, that she would not apply for Point Four aid for fear that Western imperialist penetration might be imposed on her in the form of gift parcels. How right she was could be seen from the slightly hurt manner in which *Time* drew the following 'lesson for the U.S.':

'It is not enough to offer aid to backward peoples; the U.S. *must* also *persuade* their rulers to use the assistance for their countries' *true* benefit or *find men who will co-operate* with the U.S. That is a very difficult job, at which the U.S. so far has been notably unsuccessful; but unless it is done, and *done well*, U.S. plans for help to backward lands will be doomed to failure.'[1]

The italics are mine. But the concentrated dose of a behind-the-Iron-Curtain sort of vocabulary advocating everything from forceful persuasion to the finding of men willing to co-operate and understanding correctly the true benefits in store for them is that of *Time*, an American magazine of singular influence. Even the languages of

[1] *Time*, 18 June 1951.

American and Russian imperialism are beginning to sound alike in their pontifical interpretation of what is and what is not a *true* benefit.

6. *The Two United Nations*

Thus, wherever we look we see the unmistakable evidence that the globe has not only been split into two political halves, but that the two halves are beginning to develop, for different purposes and with different methods, almost identical features. Both are consolidating around two heartlands, and both take the form of empires composed of giant central powers and a defensive ring of satellites. The two ultimate blocks will therefore not be Russia and the United Nations, but Russia and the United States.

One needs to be no Tocqueville to see this coming since the conditions described have already arrived. This is why I cannot see why we should continue to resist a destiny which is ours even though we did not want it, and to reject the implications of an empire engulfing us on all sides simply because, as one of my students put it with the most desolately sour face I have seen, 'empire is such an ugly word'. This may be so but, unless we take a more outspoken and positive attitude towards it, we shall either become a nation of hypocrites or of neurotics, and still not gain the approval for which we seem so pathetically to crave. Many peoples have had empire and, instead of flagellating themselves, enjoyed it thoroughly. Why should not we? Whether we enjoy it or not, we shall still have it and, what is worse, be accused of aspiring to it even if we had it not. This does not mean that I *advocate* empire. I advocate a world of little states. But we *have* empire, and what I advocate is consequently not the possession of what we do not have, but the enjoyment of what we possess. If we have measles, we can just as well enjoy them. For if we do not, we shall still have measles.

But what about the United Nations? Are not at least *they* a sign that our half of the globe will be different from that of the Russians, and develop into a world of free associates after all? Why should we otherwise adhere to them with such increasing faith and enthusiasm? Indeed, why should we? Obviously because we are discovering them increasingly as what they are, the cloak and tool of our imperial domination. This is why our first truly popular enthusiasm for their existence coincided with the outbreak of the Korean war into which they were led not by their but our determination. Up to that time we were more inclined to consider them as a tool of Russian obstruction, which they probably would still be had not Russia unwisely just then obstructed a bit too emphatically by not attending meetings. That gave us the first chance of turning them into an instrument of our own policy, and our instrument they have remained ever since. As *Washington Banktrends*, a realistic and unsentimental business news feature service, put it:

'This nation is, apparently, cast for a heroic role in world affairs. To lead and police the world will be costly, bringing many changes. For example, a permanent munitions industry will be developed ... It is a new kind of economy into which this nation is turning. It is the economy of world power, with world defence commitments of a permanent nature. With permanent arms and munitions will come, too, large standing armies and navies and air forces. Some form of the draft on a permanent basis is inevitable to support this heroic role in world politics. The subterfuge of a United Nations organization may serve to ease the transition period for those who find it hard to face the realities, but the burden of all accomplishment will be on the United States.'[1]

There is no reason to shed any tears about this apparent collapse of a great ideal because the United Nations never were such a great ideal in the first place. Though originally not meant to be the instrument of our imperial consolidation, they were not meant to be an instrument of the free nations either. Had this been their intent, they ought to have refrained from adopting the undemocratic veto principle or from turning the Security Council into a preserve of the great powers whose claim to their position of privilege rests not on wisdom but might. The best one could thus ever say of this great ideal was that it was a tool not of the free but of the big, and that, while not meant to foster the empire of one, it was designed under the 'subterfuge' of democratic verbiage to secure in perpetuity the empire of five.

The important thing, however, is that, even if the original intentions of the founders of the United Nations had been as idealistic as they appeared to be, the subsequent development would still have been the same. We have seen in analysing similar experiments that no international organization has ever succeeded in remaining an institution of free and equal associates if it had amongst its participants a few disproportionately large powers. If this was the case, the result was political cancer. And the consequences were always the same. Wherever it was attempted, the struggle for leadership amongst its principal members began almost with the instant the organization was set up, ending only after one of the two finalists had either been subdued or expelled.

[1] *Washington Banktrends*. Washington News Features, Washington 5, D.C., 5 January 1953.

If the rivals were of such overwhelming and almost equal power as Prussia and Austria were in the pre-Bismarck German federation, or as the United States and Russia are now in the United Nations, the subjection of one was, of course, impossible The only alternative to an internal collapse of the organism itself was then expulsion, with the rump organization gradually but inevitably becoming the instrument of the surviving great power within its frame.

As shown before, the latter variety of federal destruction occurred in the confederation of German states which, after the expulsion of Austria in 1866, became the instrument of Prussia. But it is so clearly shaping up also in the case of the United Nations that we have begun to consider them as the principal agent of the non-Russian or American half of the world though Russia is actually still one of their members. The only thing left for the latter is to ratify her already spiritual expulsion by withdrawing also materially. Russia has threatened this already, and it depends only on her timing when she will ring down the Iron Curtain for good.

But what then? Even her participation on the losing side has given Russia such an understanding of the advantage of a multinational sounding-board that she will hardly be content with a simple act of withdrawal. Rather, she will in all likelihood couple her official secession with the simultaneous announcement of the establishment of a United Nations of her own, an organization, this time, of *truly* free and democratic peoples, feeling *correctly* about every issue, and choosing as their new headquarters Leningrad which happens to be within as convenient a radius from Moscow as the headquarters of the Western United Nations is from Washington. As a result, we shall probably have two United Nations instead of one and, instead of looking different and decent with ours, we shall have just one more thing in common with the empire of the East.

This, then, is the prospective shape of the world in the near future. As the consolidation process advances, the two empires of East and West will dress themselves up as two liberal United Nations organizations. But their sole function will be limited in either case to serving their imperial masters as a convenient stage on which the mighty can perform in their favourite role as the humble. In contrast to the present United Nations, neither Russia nor the United States will claim any privilege in the succeeding arrangements in the form of a now meaningless veto power or a permanent big-power membership in the various councils. On the contrary! Instead of occupying seats of honour, they will be conspicuously satisfied with the places assigned to them by order of the alphabet. Insisting on the equality of all, they will permit the delegates of even the smallest country to orate volubly or slap them chummily on their backs. Their presidency will rotate, and their Assemblies will be like the Senate of ancient Rome where Caesar could prove how he was just another modest member of that exalted body, begging his colleagues to go along with him on this or that, provided of course that this suited the majesty of their will to which he was at all times ready to bow. Yet, as nobody in Roman times was fooled by the display of Caesar's gorgeous humility, no one in our time will be fooled by the role assigned to the various United Nations. Like the Roman Senate, they will be but bodies sitting in some famous piece of architecture with the privilege of hearing and accepting with proper laudatory remarks the decisions handed down to them from their true masters in Moscow or Washington, as the case may be.

There will be other similarities with ancient Rome, that great pioneer in elaborating devices of imperial domination. Russia has already begun to experiment with them by extending the chief right of her hemisphere —membership in the great councils of communism—to prominent personalities from satellite countries. Similarly, we shall soon begin conferring on deserving foreigners the chief right of our part of the world —American citizenship. Our first choice will be foreign heads of state, members of government, politicians, and soldiers willing to fight in our armies. As a next step, along with our citizenship, we shall grant not only the personal privilege but the *ex-officio* right to outstanding foreign representatives to address during their visits to the United Nations headquarters in New York also the true centre of power, the American Congress. Trends to that effect are already clearly discernible. Eventually, to the most deserving of them all, we shall grant membership in our Senate until they will some day realize that they are ruling their respective countries no longer by virtue of their domestic election but on account of their confirmation as senators of the United States. When this stage is reached, we may even decide to do away with the label United Nations for our own imperial system and simply call it the United States.

Thus, as Rome turned the world Roman by extending in ever-broadening waves of imperial generosity her citizenship to increasingly distant peoples, so we shall turn our part of the world American by an identical process.[1] Only Americans will have the full privileges

[1] Gibbon has given us an excellent description of the imperceptible Romanization of the ancient world through the same device by which both the United States and Russia are assimilating their respective dominions at the present time

of freedom, but this will not mean much as practically everybody will be an American citizen. A similar condition will be brought about on the Russian side with the single peculiarity that its common denominator will be an ideology rather than a nationality. But even this will not make us look very different if we realize that communism is not only the *natural* system of huge organisms but the *only* system by which they can maintain themselves. Hugeness, as we have seen, needs conscious direction, supervision, control, obedience, conformity, efficiency, standardization, discipline, alikeness in habit and thought, unity, centralism—all concepts which in their sum constitute the essence and operating basis of socialism. Our empire being as huge as Russia's, and requiring the same continuous state of preparedness, will need as much centralization and direction and, though we may call our brand anti-communism or, perhaps, the mood of the age, it will be communism just the same. Thus, a time will come when the two halves of the world, organized along such different roads, will be identical in everything but their name. And the reason for it will be the same which is responsible for the fact that the only thing looking exactly like the North Pole is its very opposite—the South Pole. And this will be the end of the process of consolidation.

7. *War, World State, and a World of Little States*

But it will not be the end of the story. The result of the coexistence of the two ultimate power blocks of Russia and the United States will be war. Not because one party would now want to conquer the other. On the contrary. The two survivors of the elimination process of great power will be the most pathetically genuine addicts to the peace of the world which history will have known up till then. They will feel that

—by the colonization of previous allies sweetened by the simultaneous extension of citizenship. 'Those princes', he writes, 'whom the ostentation of gratitude or generosity permitted for a while to hold a precarious sceptre were dismissed from their thrones, as soon as they had performed their appointed task of fashioning to the yoke the vanquished nations. The free states and cities which had embraced the cause of Rome were rewarded with a nominal alliance, and insensibly sunk into real servitude. The public authority was everywhere exercised by the ministers of the senate and of the emperors, and that authority was absolute and without control. But the same salutary maxims of government, which had secured the peace and obedience of Italy, were extended to the most distant conquests. A nation of Romans was gradually formed in the provinces by the double expedient of introducing colonies, and of admitting the most faithful and deserving of the provincials to the freedom of Rome.' (Edward Gibbon, op. cit., vol. I, chapter 2, p. 35.)

only madness could plunge them into the final catastrophe whose shadow will paralyse their thoughts with a perpetual fog of fear. True, only madness could under these circumstances lead to war. But the constant fear and terror of the other's potential if not of his intentions will drive the sanest mad. In alignments of such proportions, no human force can control the power the two ultimate antagonists will possess, and never surrender because neither will ever be able to trust the other.

So, unless the two empires will by some miraculous reason disintegrate as a result of the gigantic dimensions of their own efforts, the inevitable will occur. The mass of power accumulated on either side at a near critical volume will, somewhere, some time, touch the other, and detonate with the dreaded spontaneity of an atomic explosion.

The ensuing war may last a week, a month, or a century. Whatever its length, it will have only one survivor. This survivor will at last establish that monstrous ideal of our desolate planners, purchased to no purpose at such monstrous a price—the world state, the empire of total unity, conformity, and peace. Being an American, I have the hopeful presentiment that it will be American though this will mean no more to its eventual citizens than it meant to the latter-day Romans that many of their ancestors were defeated Carthaginians who once hoped to unite the world under their own sign. Man has the tendency to take to every nationality or ideology imposed upon him with sufficient determination and, as the multitude of flourishing political systems show, can be happy under almost any of them—which, though not to his credit, is his salvation.

We shall then, at long last, have the One World which has been prophesied with such enthusiasm. However, no authority could be powerful enough to keep it together for any length of time if the component great nations such as the German, English, Italian, or French were left intact, even if placed under the rule of the most reliably loyal proconsuls. Too soon, old powers would regain strength and challenge the central authority, however great it may be. As a result, the surviving empire, confronted with the task of administering the entire globe from a single control tower and without the balancing and containing effect of a great rival, will have to do what every other world power has done from the Persians, the Romans, and the Catholic Church, to Charlemagne, Napoleon, and Hitler. It will have to apply the principle of division to its great remaining national blocks, and cut them into units small enough to be governed without the necessity of a ruinously expensive executive instrument. In other words, the world state of total unity, if it wants to survive longer than the decade of its bloody act of birth, will have to recreate the very thing it may have imagined it had destroyed for ever—a world of small units, a world of little states.

Consequently, the conclusions of this study will, I hope, after all not be considered as so frivolous, destructive, and negative as they may have appeared when I suggested in Chapter XI, in the only word which it contains, that the principles of division and the small unit, which I had elaborated in the ten preceding chapters, would not be applied. They will be applied, though unfortunately not before but after another great-power war, and not for the sake of freedom but of rule. But they will be applied by the ultimate world state irrespective whether this be Russia or the United States.

However, since nothing is ultimate in this ever-changing creation, one may safely carry Tocqueville's predictions or, rather, deductions a step or two further and state that, whatever comes, the ultimate world state will go the road of all other ultimate world states of history. After a period of dazzling vitality, it will spend itself. There will be no war to bring about its end. It will not explode. Like the ageing colossi of the stellar universe, it will gradually collapse internally, leaving as its principal contribution to posterity its fragments, the little states—until the consolidation process of big-power development starts all over again. This is not pleasant to anticipate. What is pleasant, however, is the realization that, in the intervening period between the intellectual ice ages of great-power domination, history will in all likelihood repeat itself and the world, little and free once more, will experience another of those spells of cultural greatness which characterized the small-state worlds of the Middle Ages and Ancient Greece.

Appendices

THE PRINCIPLE OF FEDERATION
PRESENTED IN MAPS

Successful federation. With 48 states, roughly equal in size and potential strength, no authority in the United States except the federal can rule over all of them. Such a small-state organization makes the development of an oversized member impossible. Federal power, even if small, outweighs any other 47 to 1, is therefore always effective.

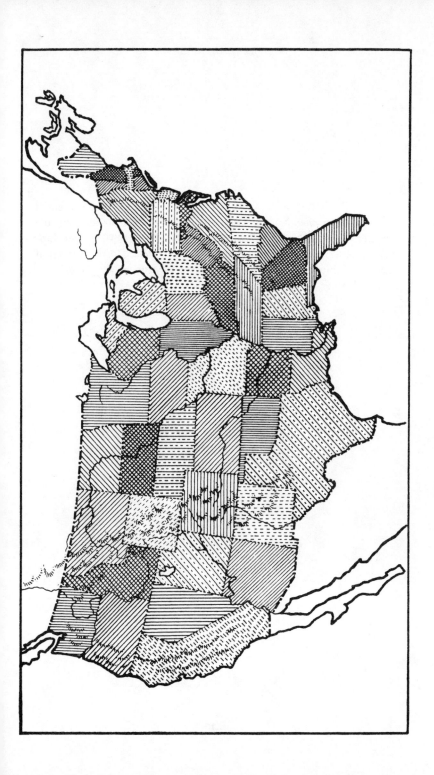

Successful federation. Switzerland, oldest federal experiment, is organized on the basis of 22 states (cantons), not of its four unequal nationalities. State division, without regard to nationalities, has destroyed the unbalanced blocks, has created the great idea of Swiss balance and village democracy instead.

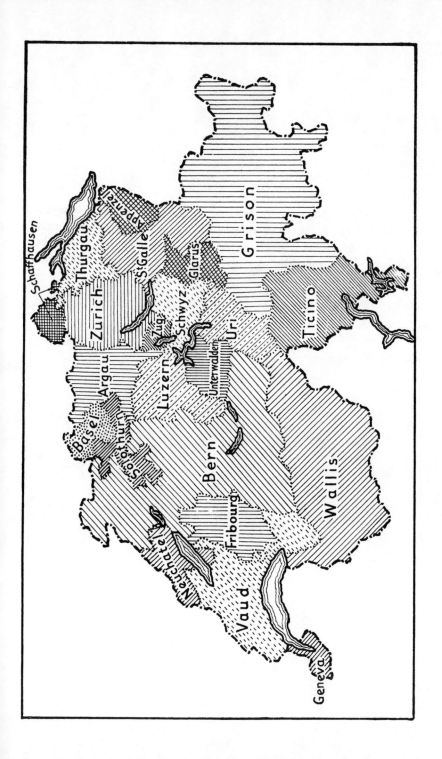

Unsuccessful federation. Germany's smaller nations were federated with the Great Power of Prussia which—with a population of 40 million—became naturally the dominant power in the federation. Germany was thus ruled by Prussia, not by a federal authority which could not have enforced its laws on Prussia without her consent.

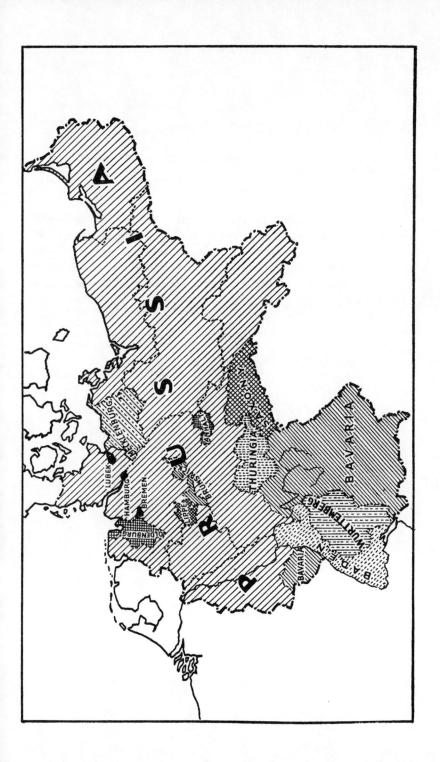

Unsuccessful federation. European federation, based on its great national blocks, unequal in size and strength, would in the end become a federation in the interest of Germany, because Germany alone would be large enough to enforce a federal law, and no law could be enforced without Germany's consent. Germany would be arbiter and master.

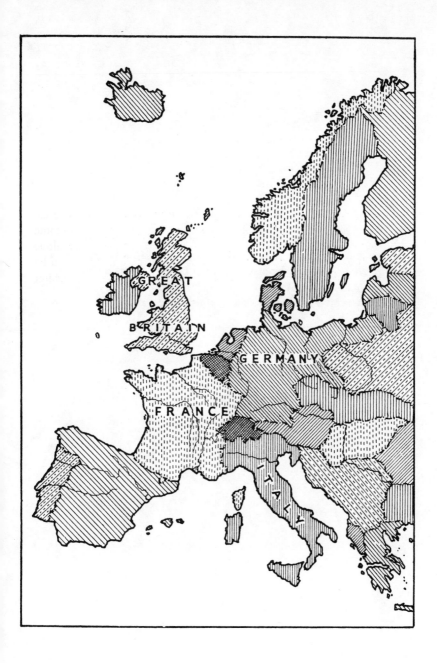

Unsuccessful federation. Were Switzerland organized on national lines as shown on this map, German Switzerland would outweigh the others 2 to 1. French, Italian, Romansch would be minorities. By cutting the unequal national blocks into numerous small states, every nationality has its own or several states, and is thus never a minority.

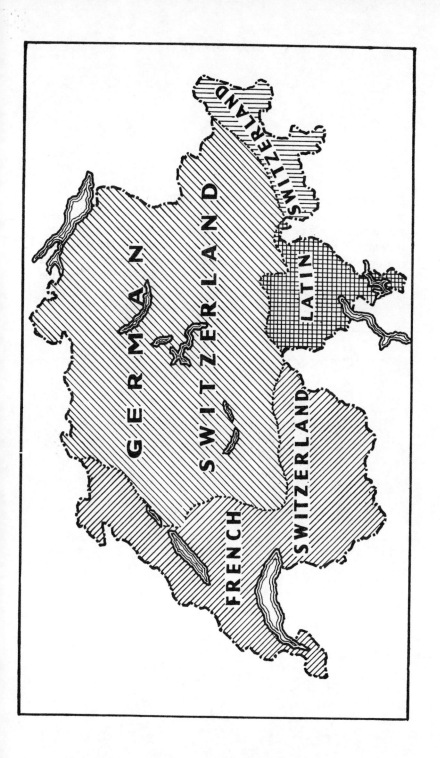

Unsuccessful federation. Were America organized as opposite, on the pattern of Europe's simplified, but unequally large blocks, Washington would be a purely decorative centre as Geneva was for the League of Nations. To enforce its authority it would have to ask the support of one or more of the powerful members. Wars would be as frequent as in Europe.

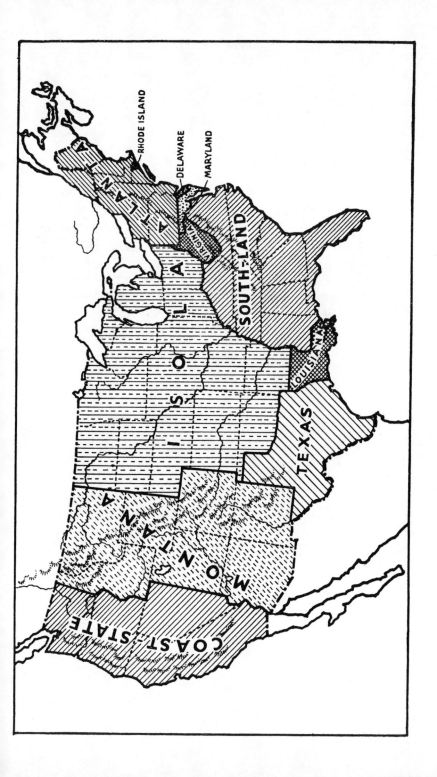

As on the preceding map America is shown 'simplified' in *European* style, the harmony and balance of its 48 states destroyed, this map shows Europe divided in *American* style. The arrogant, uncooperative, proud, self-glorifying nations (great powers) have given way to small states which could as easily be ruled by Geneva as the U.S. is ruled by Washington. A successful power maniac would be as harmless for the rest as Huey Long.

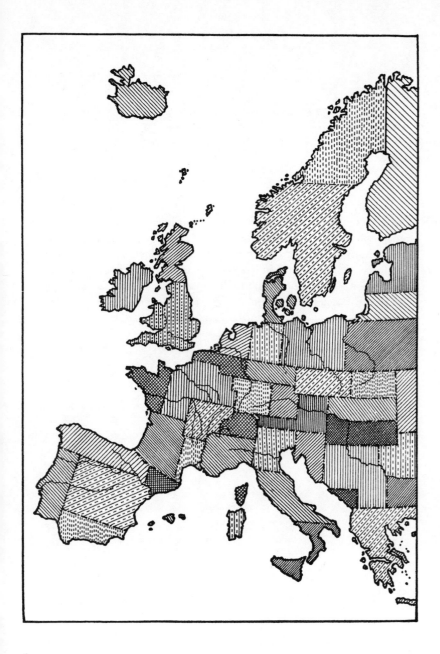

The purely geometrical division of America would, however, have to be modified in Europe along the traditional tribal frontiers. This map shows approximately the *genuine* component parts of Europe, historically subdividing the great powers, products not of nature but of force. Being all equal in size they are ideally fit to form a successful federation. Thus Europe's problem—as that of any federation—is one of division, not of union.

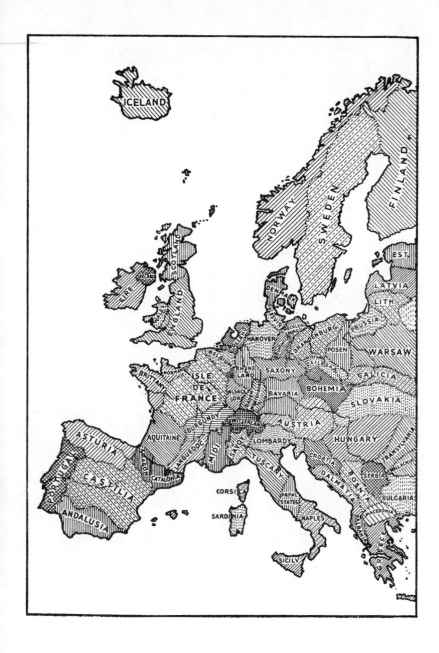

BIBLIOGRAPHY

List of Works Cited

Alexis, Stephen, *Black Liberator*. New York: Macmillan, 1949.

Aristotle, *Politics*. London: Oxford University Press, 1942.

Augustine, St., *The City of God*. London: Dent, 1931.

Bacon, Francis, *Essays and New Atlantis*. New York: Walter J. Black, 1942.

Baird, Henry M., *History of the Rise of the Huguenots*. London: Hodder and Stoughton.

Beauvoir, Simone De, 'Sexual Initiation of Women', *Anvil*. New York, Winter 1950.

Bible, George P., *The Acadians*. Philadelphia: Ferris and Leach, 1906.

Brandeis, Louis D., *The Curse of Bigness*. New York: The Viking Press, 1935.

Brown, Peter Hume, *The History of Scotland*. London: Cambridge University Press, 1911.

Carnegie Endowment for International Peace, Memoranda Series No. 1. Washington D.C., 1 February 1940.

Celler, Emanuel, 'Can a Congressman Serve 900,000 People?', *New York Times Magazine*, 11 March 1951.

Cicero, *Laws*.

Coulton, G. G., *Medieval Panorama*. London: Cambridge University Press, 1938.

Coyle, David Cushman, *Day of Judgement*. New York: Harper and Brothers, 1945.

Cuthrie, Ramon, 'The Labor Novel that Sinclair Lewis Never Wrote', *New York Herald Tribune Book Review*, 10 February 1952.

De Tocqueville, Alexis, *Democracy in America*. London: Oxford University Press, 1946.

Dumas, Alexander, *Celebrated Crimes*. New York: P. F. Collier and Son, 1910.

Figgis, John Neville, *The Political Aspects of S. Augustine's 'City of God'*. London: Longmans, Green and Co., 1921.

Freeman, Kathleen, *Greek City-States*. New York: W. W. Norton and Co., 1950.

Gibbon, Edward, *The History of the Decline and Fall of the Roman Empire*. 7 vols., London: Methuen, 1900.

Gosse, Edmund, *Father and Son*. London: Penguin Books, 1949.

Hoyle, Fred, *The Nature of the Universe*. Oxford: Basil Blackwell, 1950.

Huxley, Julian, 'Biological Improvement', *The Listener*, 1 November 1951.

Hyett, F. A., *Florence*. 1903.

Lucretius, *On the Nature of Things*. New York: Walter J. Black, 1946.

Malthus, Thomas, *Essay on the Principle of Population*.

Marcus Aurelius, *Meditations*. New York: Walter J. Black, 1945.

Municipal Yearbook. 1951.

Murad, Anatol, *The Paradox of a Metal Standard*. Washington: Graphic Arts Press, 1939.

Ortega y Gasset, *The Revolt of the Masses*. New York: The American Library, 1950.

Quinn, T. K., 'Too Big', *The Nation*, 7 March 1953.

Ranshofen-Wertheimer, Egon, *Victory Is Not Enough*. New York: W. W. Norton, 1942.

Reel, A. Frank, *The Case of General Yamashita*. Chicago: The University of Chicago Press, 1949.

Ross, W. D., *The Student's Oxford Aristotle*. London: Oxford University Press, 1942.

Russell, Bertrand, *Unpopular Essays*. New York: Simon and Schuster, 1951.

—— *Authority and the Individual*.

Schrödinger, Erwin, *What Is Life?* London: Cambridge University Press, 1951.

—— *Science and Humanism*. London: Cambridge University Press, 1951.

Schwartz, Harry, *Russia's Soviet Economy*. New York: Prentice-Hall, 1950.

Shakespeare, *Richard III*. New York: Grosset and Dunlap, 1909.

Shaw, George Bernard, *Geneva* . . . New York: Dodd, Mead and Co., 1947.

Simons, Henry C., *Economic Policy for a Free Society*. Chicago: University of Chicago Press, 1948.

Sorokin, P. A., *Social and Cultural Dynamics*. New York: American Book Co., 1937.

Statistical Abstract of the United States. 1951.

Sully, *Memoirs of the Duke of Sully*. London: Henry G. Bohn, 1856.

Swift, Jonathan, *Gulliver's Travels*. New York: Crown Publishers, 1947.

Symonds, John A., *Renaissance in Italy*. New York: The Modern Library, 1935.

Temporary National Economic Committee, *Competition and Monopoly in American Industry*, Monograph No. 21. Washington: Government Printing Office, 1940.

—— *Relative Efficiency of Large, Medium-sized, and Small Business*, Monograph No. 13. Washington: Government Printing Office, 1941.

Thompson, D'Arcy W., *On Growth and Form*, London: Cambridge University Press, 1942.

Thomson, Sir George, 'The Hydrogen Bomb', *The Listener*, 23 March 1950.

Villari, Pasquale, *Life and Times of Savonarola*. New York: Charles Scribner's Sons, 1896.

Whitbread, Jane, and Gadden, Vivian, *The Intelligent Man's Guide to Women*. New York: Schuman, 1951.

Young, Arthur, *Travels in France and Italy*. Everyman's Library, No. 720.

Young, G. F., *The Medici*. New York: The Modern Library, 1933.

Newspapers and Periodicals Cited

Anvil

Associated Press

Atlantic Monthly

Bank Trends

Barron's

Canadian Forum

Listener

Manchester Guardian

Le Monde

Nation

New Leader

Newsweek

New Yorker

New York Times

Ottawa Citizen

Quarterly Bulletin of the British Psychological Society

Richmond Times-Dispatch

Time

Washington Post

INDEX

Acadia (Nova Scotia), 13
Accumulation, capitalist, law of, 155
Acton, Lord, 1, 30
Aggression, biology of, 16
  flashpoint of, 35
  spontaneity of, 36
Alexis, Stephen, 12
Algeria, 13
American Civil War, 58, 175
Amritsar, 14
Andorra, 106
Animals, heraldic, 17
Annihilation, disadvantages of, 95
Anti-empire, 201–2
Appenzell, 60
Argentina, 177
Aristotle, xi, 67, 100, 107, 112–13,
  119, 159
Armies, relative strengths, 21
Assimilation, 208
Attlee, C. R., 18–19
Augustine, St., xi, 64, 68, 69, 70, 119
Auriol, President Vincent, 203
Australia, 177
Austria, 180
'Average man', 100–1

Bacon, Francis, 19, 108n.
Bagehot, Walter, 121
Baird, H. M., 11
Balance, bad, symptoms of, 90
  in nature, 87
  mobile and stable, 85–6, 88–90
Bank officers, defalcations of, 41
Barriers, vs. boundaries, 167

Basel, 60
Bavaria, Hitler and, 74
Begging, as profession, 144
Beirut conference, 182
Benda, Julien, 17
Bigness, a universal problem, ix
Blindness, as temptation, 41
Border territories, 58–9
Boswell, James, 77
Botzheim, J. W. von, 11n.
Boundaries, function of, 167
Brandeis, L. D., xi, 160, 162
Brazil, 177
Britain, subdivision of, 185
Bryce, Lord, 178
Bulk, as source of brutality, 27
  collective, 18
Burning, 30–1

Campanella, Tommaso, 108n.
Canada, 177
Capitalism, 4, 50–1, 155
Causes, primary and secondary, 1–2
Celler, Emanuel, 105n.
Chain reactions, 75n.
Chaplin, Charlie, 32
Charles IV, Emperor, 178
Cheating, of public services, 40
Chicago, 28
China, 4, 5
  and Britain, 206
Churchill, Winston, 47, 202
Cicero, 16, 23
Citizenship, American, as reward for
  deserving foreigners, 213